Hollywood Soundscapes

Hollywood Soundscapes

**Film Sound Style, Craft and Production
in the Classical Era**

Helen Hanson

A BFI book published by Palgrave

First published in 2017 by
PALGRAVE

on behalf of the

BRITISH FILM INSTITUTE
21 Stephen Street, London W1T 1LN
www.bfi.org.uk

There's more to discover about film and television through the BFI. Our world-renowned archive, cinemas, festivals, films, publications and learning resources are here to inspire you.

Palgrave in the UK is an imprint of Macmillan Publishers Limited, registered in England, company number 785998, of 4 Crinan Street, London N1 9XW. Palgrave® and Macmillan® are registered trademarks in the United States, the United Kingdom, Europe and other countries.

Cover image: courtesy of The Bill Douglas Cinema Museum EXEBD 31481 from the cigarette card set 'How Films are Made' produced by B. Morris and Sons, 1933.
Cover design: Kerry Squires

Set by: Integra Software Services Pvt. Ltd.

British Library Cataloguing-in-Publication Data

ISBN 978–1–84457–504–6 (pb)
ISBN 978–1–84457–505–3 (hb)

For Phil, a great listener, with love, and thanks

Contents

Acknowledgements

The research and writing of this book has taken place over a long period of time, and during all the stages of the project, from the initial and nascent ideas, through archival research to finalising the shape and content of the book, I count myself so very lucky and privileged to have had the support and encouragement of a large number of people.

Thanks are due to the British Academy and Leverhulme Trust for a research grant that allowed me to travel to archives in the USA, and to present my work at a number of international conferences. I am also very grateful for a Humanities Research Fellowship at the Harry Ransom Center at the University of Texas, Austin, supported by the Dorot Foundation Postdoctoral Research Fellowship in Jewish Studies. This fellowship allowed me to spend a fantastic month of archival research into the David O. Selznick papers. I am most grateful to all the staff at the Harry Ransom Center who made me welcome and provided me with wonderful support for my research. Thanks to Bridget Gayle Ground, Clare Donnelly, Steve Wilson, Michael Gilmore, Roy Flukinger, Chelsea Withers and all the staff at the HRC Reading and Viewing Room who helped with my research process. I am also very grateful to Jim Buhler for making me welcome in Austin, and for fun times with Natalie Ferris during my trip.

I have been very lucky to meet with such brilliant and knowledgeable archivists during my research. At the Margaret Herrick Library I benefited hugely from the insights and knowledge of Barbara Hall, Jenny Romero, Louise Hilton and Faye Thompson in Special Collections, and all the staff in the Reading Room. Genevieve Maxwell and Jade Takahashi at the Academy of Motion Picture Arts and Sciences Oral History Programme also provided great support for my project. At the University of Southern California, Cinematic Arts Collection, the truly marvellous Ned Comstock gave me invaluable help and advice, and at the Warner Bros. Collection I had wonderful support and help from Sandra Joy Lee Aguilar, Jonathan Auxier, and Brett Service. At the UCLA Performing Arts Collection I had help from Julie Graham, and at the American Film Institute's Louis B. Mayer Library I had the advice of Caroline Sisneros and Patricia King Hanson. In the UK I used collections in the British Library, at the British Film Institute, and collections at the Bill Douglas Cinema Museum at the University of Exeter. Thanks to Sarah Currant and Emma Smart at the BFI, and to Mike Rickard, Gemma Poulton, Angela Mandrioli, Phil Wickham and Christine Faunch at the Bill Douglas Cinema Museum and Heritage Collections at the University of Exeter.

The Department of English and Film Studies, and the wider College of Humanities at the University of Exeter, have provided support in many forms. I have been able to attend international conferences, undertake research trips and have benefited from periods of study leave which gave me time to pursue archival research, and to work on the final manuscript of the book. I have been able to test out aspects of my approach to classical Hollywood sound in my teaching at postgraduate and undergraduate level, and I have benefited greatly from the chance to work through ideas with students. My colleagues in the Department of English and Film Studies have provided constant and steady encouragement, from initial ideas through the long research process for the project. I would particularly like to thank Pascale Aebischer, Karen Edwards, Gabriella Giannachi, Jo Gill, Jason Hall, and Jane Spencer for their interest and encouragement.

Thanks to my Exeter Film colleagues, past and present, who have enthused with me about the research: Ranita Chatterjee, Felicity Gee, Sally Faulkner, Fiona Handyside, Will Higbee, Danielle Hipkins, Joe Kember, Song Hwee Lim, James Lyons, Steve Neale, Dan North, Debra Ramsay and Lisa Stead. I am particularly grateful to Joe Kember, who kindly read the manuscript and gave me invaluable input, to Steve Neale for many discussions about the project from beginning to end, and for his precise insights, and to Lisa Stead, for discussions about methodology and for her encouragement and great friendship.

The project has been nurtured by the wider connections I have made at conferences and through academic networks over the years, I am very grateful to Jay Beck, Eric Dienstfrey, Kevin Donnelly, Ruth Farrar, Ian Gardiner, Julie Grossman, Nick Hall, Nessa Johnston, Ilario Meandri, Katie Quanz, Martin Shingler, Andrew Spicer, Sarah Street, and Neil Verma.

My friends and family have given me unending support and encouragement, and listened patiently to stories from the research trail. I want to thank my friends Gaby Johnson and Mark Conrad, Bryony Dixon, Lynne McDonagh and Jorg Hensgen, Ruth Gidley, Sarah O'Brien, Jenny Harris and Jess Hall for the warmth of their friendship, their steady faith in me, and for life away from my desk. Thanks to my dear family: Don, Ed, Sue and Liz Hanson, Eddie and Dan Sangha, Judith, David, Isabelle and Dan Hill, and Shirley and George Wickham. And finally, deep gratitude and love goes to Phil Wickham – husband, research mentor, writing coach, editor, and best friend – for his time, patience and many kindnesses that smoothed the road to the end of the book.

The author and publishers would like to thank the copyright holders for permission to reproduce the following copyright material:

Excerpts from the archival files of *I Am a Fugitive from a Chain Gang* and *Cheyenne* granted courtesy of Warner Bros. Entertainment Inc.

Excerpts from the archival files of the Selznick Collection courtesy of Steve L. Wilson and the Harry Ransom Center.

Excerpts from the archival files of the Margaret Herrick Library granted courtesy of Jenny Romero and the Margaret Herrick Library.

Figures 61 and 62 from C. Dreher, 'Sound Personnel and Organization', in Lester Cowan (ed.), *Recording Sound for Motion Pictures* (New York and London: McGraw-Hill, 1931). Reprinted with permission from McGraw-Hill Education.

Tables 4 and 5 from S. D. Smith, 'Beginnings of Local 695: Part 2', *Local 695 Quarterly*, vol. 3, no. 1, 2011. Reprinted with permission from Scott Smith and Local 695.

Table 6 from S. D. Smith, 'Beginnings of Local 695: Part 3', *Local 695 Quarterly*, vol. 3, no. 2, 2011. Reprinted with permission from Scott Smith and Local 695.

List of Illustrations

List of Tables

Introduction: Sound and Silences: Writing the History of Sound Craft in Hollywood's Studio Era

> They can make or break a picture, yet they seldom rate more than a passing nod. They're the forgotten men of an industry that forgets easily. That's the technical mob, those worthies who struggle with gadgets and can turn up with anything that is humanly possible of contrivance. Remuneration for their work is manifested at the pay window and an occasional credit mention on the subtitle frame for a quick and unimportant flash of recognition which the public seldom reads, cares less and gets impatient to get over with.
>
> 'Hollywood's Unsung Heroes', *Variety Anniversary Edition*, Wednesday 6 January 1937, p. 46

The technical crafts of sound in the classical Hollywood cinema have, until recently, been largely 'unsung' in the histories of the studio era. Since the transition to sound by Hollywood's major studios, broadly completed by 1929, film sound, in its entire array (voice, music, sound effects), has been a crucial aspect of film style, and key to engaging and holding audiences. In the classical Hollywood sound film, sounds emphasise visual action, underline character, enhance settings and develop mood and ambience in a myriad of inventive and affective ways. The recording, editing, mixing, balancing and precise placement of sounds was the responsibility of the 'forgotten men' referred to above, who mastered the technical roles of sound production: the Sound Recordists, Boom Operators, Sound Production Mixers, Sound Editors, Sound Mixers, Sound Effects Editors and Sound Directors who formed the sound departments of the Hollywood majors in the studio era.

'Sound design' is now widely accepted as an important area of creative labour in contemporary film production; the role of 'sound designer' emerged with technical innovators such as Walter Murch and Randy Thom, working in the production cultures of post-1970s cinema, cultures that contrasted with the classical Hollywood mode of production in terms of work regimes and organisation.[1] However, the long and complex history of this crucial, yet largely invisible work and the technicians who executed it still remain largely unknown in film history.

This book restores sound technicians to Hollywood's creative history. Exploring a range of films from the early sound period (1931) through to the late studio period (1948), and drawing on a wide range of archival sources, I reveal how Hollywood's sound craft worked, and why its practitioners worked in the ways they did. The book demonstrates how sound technicians developed conventions designed to tell stories through sound; it places them within the production cultures of studio era filmmaking, uncovering a history of collective and collaborative creativity. I trace the emergence of a body of highly skilled sound personnel, able to apply expert technical knowledge in the science of sound to the creation of cinematic soundscapes alive with mood and sensation.

The concept of a 'soundscape' has informed my study. Established in the work of acoustic ecologist R. Murray Schafer, a 'soundscape' connotes a 'sonic environment' and, as Schafer details, the term 'may refer to actual environments or to abstract constructions, such as musical compositions and tape montages', and, by extension, to the creation of the ambient narrative territories of cinema.[2] Schafer's definition of 'soundscape' draws on the field of cultural ecology; for him, the soundscape of a specific location is shaped by its environment – it has a morphology – and can be imbued with cultural, and place-specific, resonances. The term 'soundscape' has gained a presence and relevance in discussions and debates about film sound, and it has gradually acquired a critical currency in film sound studies, evident in work by sound practitioners, such as David Sonnenschein, and sound theorists and historians, such as Emily Thompson, Randolph Jordan and Jonathan Sterne.[3] As these writers acknowledge, 'soundscape' has come to connote both the acoustic environment created for a listener by the sounds that surround them, and the forms of knowledge (cultural, aesthetic, technological) that structure listening. As set out below, I draw on Schafer's idea of the structuring of a soundscape by different sounds, and I understand the soundscapes of the classical Hollywood cinema as shaped and conditioned by the forms of knowledge and practices of the body of sound technicians who produced them.

Schafer conceptualises the soundscape as a 'sonic environment' composed of distinct strata, or layers, of sound: 'keynote sounds', 'signal sounds' and 'soundmarks'.[4] The keynote of a soundscape is formed by the sounds so frequently heard that they comprise the 'background', the 'fundamental tone around which the composition may modulate'.[5] Keynote sounds form a 'ground' against which 'signal sounds' stand out. 'Signals sounds are foreground sounds', some of which constitute 'acoustic warning devices: bells, whistles, horns and sirens'.[6] The third stratum of Schafer's soundscape is formed by soundmarks, 'a community sound which is unique or possesses qualities which make it specially regarded or noticed by people in that community'.[7]

Research for this project began with my attention being captured by cinematic soundscapes: the layering and patterning of sound effects and silence in dark thrillers such as *Cat People* (Jacques Tourneur, 1942), *Phantom Lady* (Robert Siodmak, 1944) and *Dark City* (William Dieterle, 1950). The soundscapes of these films include sequences exhibiting expert and effective sound design – the beat and pacing of footsteps create suspense, whilst the sonic contrasts between silence and sound, and the layering of ambient keynote sounds, form the narrative territories of the cities in which they are set. I have analysed the sound conventions and style in those films elsewhere, but the initial question that surfaced, for me, on hearing those films was: 'Who did the sound?'[8] The question initially seemed simple – a matter of attributing credit by finding the names of technicians who worked on the sound for these films, but as I began to pursue the trail of technicians, it became clear that the question needed refining. It was not only a matter of researching 'who' undertook the tasks of sound recording, mixing, editing and re-recording in the sound departments of the Hollywood studios, but of understanding the material practices of the 'doing' of those tasks, and of grasping the forms of knowledge (technical, aesthetic, pragmatic or contextual, and economic) that underpinned that 'doing'. As I pursued my research further, it became evident that as a body of workers Hollywood's sound technicians were operating in a much wider field of activity than simply at the end of a microphone boom, or sitting at a mixing console; they were involved in cross-institutional technical research, the development of standards, the dissemination of practices and of conventions in sound aesthetics. In accounting for this wider field of activity, my research question moved from 'who did the sound' to a wider investigation of the framing contexts that shape sound technologies, style and practice. Hence, the concept of a soundscape can serve a dual purpose in thinking about the histories of Hollywood film sound; it can refer to the ways that sounds build the acoustic territory of the diegesis – a narrative soundscape – and it can refer to how a film's soundscape is shaped by the morphology comprising its technological and production contexts. The book analyses four distinct spheres of activity in which sound technicians exercised their influence on classical Hollywood soundscapes: through their shaping of technical research, in their formation of aesthetic discourse, through their work 'below-the-line' in classical Hollywood's production cultures, and in their participation in institutional networks and labour organisations.

The period the book covers extends from the early stages of sound production (1931) to the end of the major studio era (1948). Periodisations in film sound history have, understandably, focused upon major moments of change. The transition between silent and sound cinema seemingly offers one of the clearest marks of periodisation in film history. As Donald Crafton argues, 'few demarcations are so sharply drawn, so elegantly opposed, so pristinely binary'.[9] The transformations in technology, industry organisation and film style that the coming of sound brought to Hollywood have offered rich material for insightful film histories, and the changes in the transitional period have been very thoroughly mapped.[10] The temporal definitions assigned by historians to the transitional period have been part of a conceptualisation of change; period boundaries necessarily mark not only a distinctive break at their boundary points, but simultaneously construct an internal consistency within and between these boundaries. In the existing critical literature of film sound histories, the transitional period is constructed precisely *as* a period of change, and consequently, the period 'beyond', in which changes are less pronounced, has been constructed as one of comparative stability. David Bordwell, Janet Staiger and Kristin Thompson, and Donald Crafton, adopt 1931 as the date marking the end of major technological and stylistic changes.[11]

Recent historical work on film sound has begun to periodise change in new ways. Rick Altman's work on the multiple and intermedial practices of combining sound, song, voice and music with silent film exhibition demonstrates that audiovisual combinations in cinema have long established traditions, and that many practices in post-transitional sound cinema retain traces of earlier contexts.[12] In his work on the coming of sound, James Lastra pinpoints 1934 as marking a stabilisation in practices and models of representation in sound; and Lea Jacobs establishes that the early sound period was marked by widespread innovation in methods of creating pace in narrative movement, dialogue timing and underscoring. Her study traces changing practices up to the mid-1930s.[13] Michael Slowik analyses scoring practices from the beginning of the transition up to 1934, tracing varying practices with distinct musical styles, different film genres and levels of budget.[14] Katherine Spring presents the transition to sound anew by tracing the convergence between Hollywood and the popular music industry, and the role of the pop song in early sound cinema.[15]

The primary focus of this book is the agency – that is, the activity and influence – of Hollywood's sound technicians between 1931 and 1948; this period is 'beyond' the transition to sound, although of course the transition forms a crucial background context to my study. The major period of the Hollywood studio system of the 1930s and 1940s has often been conceived as characterised by relative stability and homogeneity in film style and production, but if the historical focus is recalibrated from a macro level to a closer tracking of the activity of the sound craft across the period, then it becomes evident that this period is alive with myriad changes and modifications to sound technologies, style and production practices. The book conceives of these changes as 'dynamic', rather than linear; conceptualising change as dynamic permits an understanding of change processes as uneven, and as varying according to the agents and contexts within which they occur. The term 'dynamics' has applicability in a range of fields – in physics it describes the motion of bodies dependent on the intensity of their mobilising forces; the term also incorporates the idea of the patterns of change, and of the role of interaction in change; and we can speak of 'personality dynamics' or 'group dynamics'. Dynamics shift with variations in force or intensity, and, depending on the intensity of movement, a dynamic can be arrested, and re-stabilised.

During the period examined in this book, the activities and influence of sound technicians evolved. From their position as Hollywood's newest workforce in the early 1930s, they deployed highly specialised technical knowledge to shape film sound technologies and standards, they developed and disseminated shared values in sound film style, they applied their craft in sound film production processes and they participated in and influenced industrial institutions and organisations. Through detailed archival and empirical research, I trace how the work and agency of sound technicians was engaged in influencing the processes, or dynamics, of change.

The book is organised to examine the dynamics of film sound in the broad areas of activity in which sound technicians participated: it analyses dynamics in technological innovation; the dynamics of sound film style; dynamics in the contexts of film production and the dynamics of labour relations and organisations. Changes occurred in these different, but concurrent and related, contexts at different rates, and on different scales. The book considers the issue of scale by choosing case studies illustrating the dynamics of film sound at different scalar levels through the period. I examine dynamics at a 'macro' level, analysing, for example, cross-industry projects on defining sound standards in the mid-1930s, projects which involved Hollywood's senior sound technicians. I also turn my attention to 'micro-level' contexts on specific film productions by analysing the fine-grained production decisions made by sound technicians that underpin the crafting of sound for a sequence. Between the macro and micro levels is a middle level, the level of studio and of craft, and the level at which organisational and shared craft conventions in sound practice were shaped by groups of technicians. The book examines these shared conventions, as well as some instances of how these conventions were oriented towards the 'practice preferences' of particular studios.

Concepts of scale and level have been important in studies of media industries, and in film history, and these concepts define the 'level of analysis' at which research takes place, the methodologies used, and how claims about causality, agency and power within work cultures are calibrated.[16] Amanda Lotz defines the most common levels used in the field as those of national/international, the focus on specific industrial contexts, analyses of particular organisations, and research into individual productions and studies of individual agents. Lotz notes that the level of organisations, productions and individual agents typically have a 'more micro level focus', within which researchers 'place much emphasis on understanding the complexities of practices and the varied agency of those who may work within vast media conglomerations'.[17] She observes that, traditionally, micro-level studies have diverged from macro-level studies, in that these studies 'often have not supported deterministic hypotheses proposed by theories produced at the macro level, or at least have suggested that the daily processes of production of media industries are far more complicated than the macro-level views might have the field understand'.[18] It is possible to connect micro- and macro-level studies by 'negotiating' between the methods of analysis, and by combining the concerns of political economy, grounded in empirical data, with an understanding of the often 'complex, ambivalent and contested' nature of the cultural industries.[19]

Scaling my study to draw on case studies at the distinct levels of micro-, mid- and macro-industry analysis has allowed me to capture an overall field of activity for Hollywood's sound technicians. Alongside their demarcated roles in the vertical hierarchies of studio sound departments, and the production hierarches on specific films, many of the technicians were involved in wider horizons of activity. This included institutional committee work for the Academy of Motion Picture Arts and Sciences (AMPAS), participation in professional networks, such as the Society of Motion Picture Engineers (SMPE) and connections with corporations in the research sector, such as Electrical Research Products Inc. (ERPI) and the Radio Corporation of America (RCA). Sound technicians, then, had occupational roles organised vertically – their place within departmental or studio hierarchies, and professional or institutional roles organised horizontally in communities of expertise. Their activity, influence and agency were framed in distinct ways in these different contexts, and I trace these different axes of activity. Each chapter of the book examines the work of sound technicians within a distinct sector of their overall field of activity. Attention to sound work at different levels, and along different axes of influence, makes it possible to offer a history of the complex and networked cultures of technical work in the classical Hollywood cinema. Hence, the book does not only offer a picture of below the line labour, though that is part of the study, but also attempts to analyse the dynamism of technical workers by tracing their influence at the nodes of networks that spanned different scales and levels of film production and the wider industry.

In order to understand the labour, occupational roles, practices and place of sound technicians within the Hollywood studio system, it is necessary to consider how technical work has been culturally defined more broadly within industries and organisations. The term 'technician' gained currency in the early twentieth century as the number of technical occupations developed in the fields of modern mass technologies of electricity, the telephone, radio, the communications industry and the forces.[20] Ethnographic research on technical labour, such as that by Stephen Barley, pinpoints the ways that technical roles present challenges for definition in work cultures.

Technicians cross the boundary between science and craft: technicians hold specialised knowledge, but frequently work in job roles requiring the practised action, the 'way of the hand' common to craft work.[21] They work at an 'empirical interface' and 'using sophisticated instruments, techniques and bodies of knowledge technicians [stand] with one foot in the material world and the other in a world of representations'.[22]

Technicians are often placed in organisations in supporting roles; in terms of vertical role hierarchies, their occupations sit below management and administration, but technicians frequently form wider communities of practice, communities which define the shared horizons of technical expertise.

Technicians' labour can violate the traditional boundary between white collar and blue collar roles; and organisations form strong dependence on technicians: within a production process, technicians are often 'tightly coupled' to the technological processes that are essential to process completion; their absence can bring production to a halt.[23]

As a group, Hollywood's sound technicians exemplify these cultural constructions of technical work. This book explores how these constructions of technical identity formed within the industry cultures of Hollywood. It analyses the formation of sound craft out of its technical background, a formation which was conditioned by the placement of sound technicians on film productions, in studio sound departments and within the wider industry and networks.

Chapter 2 of the book examines the emergence of a technical culture in Hollywood in the wake of the transition to sound production, and it traces the work of sound technicians at a cross-studio level. The new workforce was employed by the Hollywood majors, but sound technicians were at the nodes of wider technical networks. These networks included partnerships and relationships with the wider research sector, and were shaped by cross-industry institutions – namely, the Academy of Motion Picture Arts and Sciences, founded in 1927. The chapter traces the group activities that formed the projects of these networks. In the early sound period these projects were focused on pragmatic problem-solving: improving sound recording and reproduction quality, and fitting sound practices into production regimes. As these problems were overcome, the technical networks formed new agendas, established standardisation programmes for film sound, and investigated new possibilities, including early trials with stereophonic and multi-speaker sound. The chapter examines the changes in film technology up to the advent of magnetic sound and the point at which industrial organisation was reconfigured with the Paramount decrees at the end of the 1940s. Drawing on a wide range of sources in technical journals, institutional publications, trade press and archival sources, the chapter demonstrates the dynamics of technological innovation in classical Hollywood sound within its industry framework.

Chapter 3 examines the activity of sound technicians at the level of sound craft. It analyses the development of aesthetic discourse for sound work, tracing the formation of broad principles by sound technicians for deploying sound appropriately in different storytelling contexts, and the practices and techniques that underpinned them. These principles and practices were developed to appeal to the 'ear' of the audience. I trace how sound technicians formed these principles by developing a consciousness of how sound interlocked with, and had to be responsive to, other crafts. I offer audiovisual analyses of a range of film soundscapes by choosing sequences in which sound functions in diverse ways to build mood, establish setting, emphasise action or develop character. The chapter draws on a range of sources that offer insights into the aesthetic discourses on film sound style, analysing those of sound technicians, but also how other crafts, such as screenwriters and editors, conceived sound film style in order to situate sound style as a shared aspect of film style.

Chapter 4 examines sound work at a detailed level by using archival production sources to reconstruct, investigate and analyse the decisions that shaped the construction of selected film sequences. Analysis at this fine-grained level – the level of the single shot and sound take – offers insights into the textures of sound work, and the subtle variations and adaptations which shaped decisions; these are nuances which can escape our attention in wider discussions of the 'norms' of practice. The chapter examines case studies in different genres, and identifies some distinct forms of practice in particular studio cultures.

Chapter 5 examines the ways that sound work has been defined, and recognised, by organisations at different levels of the industry: that is, on productions, in studio sound departments, within labour organisations and by institutions. The chapter discusses the typical tasks and workflow of a studio sound department, and offers some brief career profiles of specific sound technicians. It examines the place of sound technicians in the turbulent history of labour relations in Hollywood in the 1930s, and the jurisdictional struggles over sound technicians by the IATSE and IBEW unions. The chapter offers insights into how the specialised work of sound technicians positioned them, as Barley argues, at 'the cut point' of industrial production, and how in labour struggles sound technicians could potentially halt the flow of production.[24] It analyses the gradual definition and demarcation of sound roles by labour organisations from the early sound period in 1930 to the role classifications for sound work established by the National Labor Relations Board in 1939. The chapter ends with a case study of two senior sound technicians working for different film companies: Nathan Levinson and his role as Warner Bros.' Head of Sound, and James G. Stewart and his relatively brief experience working for David O. Selznick's Vanguard Pictures. By examining the contracts and working conditions of these figures, the chapter offers insights into the position of technicians in contrasting production cultures.

Research for the project drew on a wide range of archival collections and primary sources. I have worked with the collections of particular filmmakers, such as the George Stevens Papers at the Margaret Herrick Library and the David O. Selznick Collection at the Harry Ransom Center at the University of Texas, Austin. I have consulted scripts, production papers, legal papers, technical drawings, patent and sound department files in the Warner Bros. Archive at the University of Southern California, and production files, budgets and production reports in the RKO Papers in the Performing Arts Collections at the University of California, Los Angeles. I consulted the MGM Scripts Collection, the Paramount Pictures Collections at the Margaret Herrick Library, and institutional collections, such as the Academy of Motion Picture Arts and Sciences Papers, also at the Herrick. I have worked with oral history memoirs, interviews and recollections by members of the sound craft, and in addition to these archival collections I have drawn on and synthesised a very large number of sources on sound technology, practice, style and labour from professional and technical journals, trade press, fan magazines and studio house magazines.

During my archival and primary research, the question 'who did the sound' became more refined, and instead of searching for 'who' as a single figure, the findings directed me to think more widely about the work of groups, and the importance of networks.

Tracing workers in roles that lie below-the-line in production hierarchies can be a challenge (the work of producers and directors is much more fully documented than the labour of sound workers), but by correlating archival sources with wide contextual research – in technical journals and publications, in oral histories, in trade press and craft-led journals – it is possible to get a vivid sense of the many technicians who exercised expertise and creative agency over classical Hollywood soundscapes.

My aim in the chapters that follow is to analyse the expertise and agency of sound technicians in the Hollywood studio era, showing, through the case studies I have chosen, how film sound technologies, style and labour were constantly shifting and changing, and revealing that this was a period alive with dynamic activity.

2

Art, Science and Showmanship: The Technical Cultures of Hollywood's Sound Engineers and the Shaping of Film Sound Technologies

INTRODUCTION

This chapter investigates the shifting dynamics between technology, economics and sound film production from the early sound period to the late 1940s. It analyses how technological changes were both facilitated and constrained by the contexts and cultures in which these sound technologies were used, discussed, researched and applied. 'Facilitation' and 'constraint' are twin concepts that structure studies of the production cultures of media industries, and have currency in work by writers such as Richard Peterson, Paul Hirsch, Vicki Mayer, Miranda J. Banks, John Caldwell, and John L. Sullivan.[1] The 'five constraints' on the production of culture, defined by Peterson as 'law, technology, the market, organization and occupational careers', have also been key issues in the strong tradition of industrial and stylistic histories of Hollywood cinema. Studies in this area are numerous, but key perspectives are offered in David Bordwell, Janet Staiger and Kristin Thompson's *The Classical Hollywood Cinema*, Janet Staiger's collection *The Studio System*, and work by Donald Crafton, Thomas Schatz, Tino Balio and Douglas Gomery.[2]

The chapter begins by examining the formation of a 'technical culture' of Hollywood sound engineers in the wake of the transition to sound. It analyses how, from 1929, the agendas for technological change were defined, pursued and managed. The placement, and participation, of technicians with institutions also influenced sound research, and the chapter traces the role of institutions such as the Academy of Motion Picture Arts and Sciences (AMPAS), its committees and Technical Branches, and the role of professional organisations such as the Society of Motion Picture Engineers (SMPE). These organisations represent examples of what Janet Staiger has termed 'industrial interest groups' and were involved in managing the balance between innovation and standardisation, and hence between stability and change, in the Hollywood film industry.[3]

Changes in film sound technology during the studio period occurred at different scales and on different levels of the industry, and at different rates. In this chapter I contrast incremental improvements during the period with changes tackled by technicians on a large scale, such as the Academy's cross-studio standardisation programme for sound quality during 1937 and 1938. I also trace the dynamics of innovation and standardisation, examining how 'alternatives' to standard Hollywood sound were offered to the industry during the period 1938–1940 through experiments with multi-speaker sound and early forms of stereophonic reproduction. These innovations were led by companies in the research sector – Bell Labs, and their motion picture arm Electrical Research Products Incorporated (ERPI), and the Radio Corporation of America's (RCA) Photophone Division – but the changes involved Hollywood's technical culture in translating the inventions to the wider industry.

The period examined in this chapter, and the study as a whole, ends around 1948. This date marks changes in the Hollywood studios' organisation, in sound technologies and in the institutions managing change. The year is a familiar signpost in film history as the date of the Paramount Decrees, a ruling that marked the end of vertical integration. It signals a technological shift: the transition from optical to magnetic sound recording by most of the majors (between 1948 and 1950) modified production practices, and brought the era of optically recorded, and predominantly monophonic, film sound to an end.[4] The date also marked a change in the organisation of Hollywood's technical cultures. In October 1947 the Academy reorganised its research operations; the Academy Research Council, which had co-ordinated technical research projects since 1932, was replaced by the Motion Picture Research Council (MPRC). This separated the Research Council from Academy governance and funding, and the MPRC was run under the auspices of the Association of Motion Picture Producers (AMPP). This change in organisation allowed for an expansion of the technical research programme, and for the research to be funded, and potentially commercialised, by external companies.[5]

THE DYNAMICS OF HOLLYWOOD'S TECHNICAL CULTURES

Technological changes in film sound in this period did not happen according to a simple 'narrative of progress', but are better understood as part of a shifting dynamic of stasis and change. The dynamics of technological change were strongly influenced by the networks of sound technicians, who either joined the Hollywood studios during the transition to sound production, or who influenced Hollywood film sound from their position in the allied research sector. Specific figures will be tracked further in Chapter 5 of the book. With common research backgrounds in fields such as electrical engineering and acoustics, or experience in allied communication and media industries such as the telephone, radio or phonographic industries, these men formed a 'technical culture' connecting the studios with the research sector.[6]

Connections between technicians were both informal, based upon acquaintance, and formalised through the technicians' participation in activities for industrial interest groups. Technicians' networks were fostered by their committee work for organisations such as the SMPE and AMPAS, and their connections were structured by the legal agreements, licences and patents shared between the studios and companies such as ERPI and RCA Photophone. The technicians formed nodes of exchange between the research sector and the sound departments of the Hollywood studios, and many technicians had multiple, rather than single, affiliations and involvements. Technical networks formed communities of expertise, and over time constituted shifting 'bodies of knowledge', and network activities facilitated the ways that specialised knowledge was developed, shared and disseminated.[7] Far from being static, the technical culture of Hollywood's film sound technicians was one of perpetual innovation: solutions to existing problems in film sound technology, and new ideas for apparatus and practices, were generated constantly.

The extent of the technicians' influence on processes of technological change was managed by Hollywood's studios, through institutions like the Academy and through industrial interest groups such as the SMPE and AMPP. Discourses on technological change in film sound can be traced in publications of organisations like the Academy and the SMPE, as well as craft or occupation focused publications, such as *American Cinematographer* and *International Projectionist*, and trade press for a wider audience, such as *Variety*, *Hollywood Reporter* and *Film Daily*. Reviewing these sources, it is evident that there are recurrent clusters of coverage around specific topics, these clusters constitute discursive themes and tensions, and these points of tension occurred most often where technical cultures met, and sometimes clashed with, the entertainment industry over how forms of technology, and their uses, were described and conceptualised. Discursive tensions about new sound technologies were structured by oppositions, such as that between 'co-operation' and 'innovation' in the processes of industry change. These tensions over technological change lay in the background of industry relationships, such as that between the vertically integrated majors and their shared exhibition sector. Recurrent discursive tensions are also evident in sources such as technical publications and the trade press. In these sources it is clear that there were differing concepts of what film sound could be; in other words, there were differing models of representation held by technical experts in sound to those held by production-oriented filmmakers. This could be summarised as a conceptual opposition between 'realism' and 'entertainment values'. Further recurrent tensions in the trade and technical press include those between the 'art' and the 'science' of film sound, and between 'ideal' and 'expedient' innovation.

In tracing case studies of innovation in film sound technologies at different scales or levels of the industry, the chapter demonstrates how discursive tensions recur, and how these tensions were negotiated in the interaction between technical cultures and production cultures. My analysis of these discursive negotiations is guided by the notion of technologies as 'social shaped' or socially constructed.[8] The social construction of technology (or 'SCOT' approach) is strongly associated with the foundational work of Trevor Pinch and Wiebe Bijker, and it has been developed widely by social scientists and cultural theorists of technology.[9] It has been productively applied to the histories of film sound by Rick Altman in his *Silent Film Sound* and by Jay Beck in his work on American film sound in the period 1967–1979.[10]

Pinch and Bijker argue against a macro-economic framework that understands any technological development as solely driven by wide economic forces, suggesting that attention must be paid to how different forms of technology develop out of bodies of technical knowledge, and are influenced by social structures and groups.[11] They challenge conceptions of the innovation process as simple, linear, orderly and rational. They argue that attention should be paid to the uneven development, the hiatus and failure that are often part of research and innovation processes.[12] They suggest that new technologies emerge in a 'multi-directional' manner, and that designs vary subject to influences by 'relevant user groups', organisations and other constraints.[13] They argue that 'the "successful"' stages in the development are not the only possible ones'.[14] This approach to understanding technology shaped by users and institutions, and attention to failed, as well as successful, innovations offers a framework to understanding the dynamics of change in film sound in the 1930s and 1940s. In the wake of the transition to sound, technicians and institutions worked to solve problems in film sound, and innovated in trialling new forms of style and presentation. The period is marked by the social shaping of sound that these groups undertook through organising networks, agendas and projects, and by the negotiation of discursive tensions that mark the gradual integration of technical and production cultures. In order to frame the period in which this integration occurred, it is necessary to establish how the technical networks of sound formed in the transitional period.

DEFINING PROBLEMS, FINDING SOLUTIONS: THE ACADEMY'S SCHOOLS OF SOUND

The transition to sound in Hollywood required rapid adjustments in the technologies, techniques and production regimes of filmmaking. The studios recruited personnel to take on new roles in sound and music recording, editing and post-production, and staff to install and service the new and unfamiliar equipment, to head up the new sound departments and to take a lead on supervising sound practices, policies and research. One of these department heads, Carl Dreher – RKO Radio Pictures' first Director of Sound – estimated that by 1931 there were sound jobs for around a thousand sound workers in Hollywood.[15] Dreher came to RKO from RCA Photophone, Inc., a company organised in 1928 as an RCA subsidiary designed to exploit RCA's sound-on-film system. Dreher was RCA Photophone's Chief Engineer, and moved to RKO when the studio was formed in 1929.[16] His career trajectory, moving from a predominantly technical and development role in an allied sector to one within the studio system, is typical of Hollywood's sound workforce.

Hollywood's new sound experts had considerable pedigree in technical aspects of sound recording and playback, but were less familiar with the studios' production regimes and the conventions of cinematic storytelling. The transition to sound production required the application of technical knowledge to solve a range of stylistic problems before the entertainment values of the sound film as a new form could be realised.

The problems and limitations of sound technologies in the period 1927–1929 have been widely covered in existing histories of Hollywood and sound technology, most fully in the work of Donald Crafton and James Lastra.[17] Sound in the transitional era was difficult to manage and control for a number of reasons. The first generation of microphones were omni-directional and unselective, picking up unwanted noises on the set. They had a limited range, could not be moved and had to be placed close to the action, which became more static in its staging. They were heavy and cumbersome and had limited pickup at each end of the frequency range. Cameras and arc lights were noisy. Edward Bernds, who came from working as a radio engineer to take up a role as a sound production mixer at United Artists in 1928, and who later worked at Columbia

Pictures, paints a vivid picture of the transitional era.[18] He recalls his first impressions of the United Artists' lot:

> What I saw was stunning; a huge set, a street of old Paris, filled with people, lighted by hundreds of arc lights. The big ones were called sun arcs, but the light they produced seemed whiter and bluer than sunlight. It was a noisy, crowded set; there seemed to be a dozen things happening at the same time. I tried to discern whether there was some sort of order in this chaos ... I found myself wondering how we, the sound people, could fit into that turbulent new world and what changes we would bring. For one thing, the sun arcs would have to go ... each arc ... was fed by carbon rods; these had to be rotated – driven by electric motors – to ensure even burning. The stage was filled with the grinding noise of the motors and the high-pitched whine of the flames.
>
> Edward Bernds, *Mr Bernds Goes to Hollywood: My Early Life and Career in Sound Recording at Columbia with Frank Capra and Others* (Lanham, MD, and London: Scarecrow Press, 1999), p. 62

In the earliest days of sound, a range of production practices evolved to try to master the technical difficulties of recording the soundtrack, the kinds of issues highlighted by Bernds in his memoir. As detailed by Bordwell and Thompson, 'getting a clear, complete soundtrack had the highest priority' and consequently the shooting of the picture track, staging of the action and performance adapted to the demands of sound.[19] In the transitional period, scenes were frequently shot with multiple cameras filming simultaneously, and placed at different angles to the action.[20] The footage from these different angles was cut to fit the soundtrack. The cameras were housed in soundproof booths, or 'ice houses', to quell the noise of the machinery. The thick glass through which the camera had to film affected the quality of the image obtained, and limited the flexibility of the cameras to capture tight framings.[21] In contrast to the fluid camera movements and spatial depth of the late silent period, the early talkies seemed static and 'stagey'. The sound technologies of the earliest sound films made it difficult to isolate and separate the different sound elements of dialogue, music and sound effects, because early sound editing processes were complex, time consuming and hence expensive.

In order to address these practical and stylistic problems, the newly founded Academy initiated a forum where sound experts, studio personnel and manufacturers could work in tandem to identify common problems. The Academy was founded in 1927 'as an organization uniting all main facets of motion picture production'.[22] On its foundation the Academy was organised into five branches: Actors, Directors, Writers, Producers and Technicians. The branches were able to adopt an independent role, and met regularly to deal with issues pertaining to their areas of work. The branches were governed by the Academy constitution, and had representation on the Board of Directors.[23] The Academy began to undertake activities on technical issues that it believed would benefit the industry as a whole. The activities began under special committees focusing on specific areas of concern, such as the Screen Illumination Committee, but with the growth of technical activities accompanying the transition to sound, projects were centralised under the Producers-Technicians Joint Committee formed in November 1929.[24]

The need for such a committee to co-ordinate industry activities became evident early in 1929. In January a meeting was called between the Academy's Technicians Branch and the Pacific Coast section of the Society of Motion Picture Engineers. It brought together key figures representing the existing filmmaking community and sound engineers newer to the industry. Archival sources documenting the meeting suggest that significant tensions had emerged between the new group of film personnel with technical knowledge of sound processes and the existing studio personnel struggling to adapt to the new form. Some of the problems identified at the meeting serve as a prelude to the agenda of technical activities subsequently identified and progressed by the Producers-Technicians Joint Committee.

In the minutes the chair's opening statement defined the meeting as an opportunity for producers and technicians to 'get together on common ground' so that filmmaking personnel could put their concerns to the engineers, who 'will be able to take them back to their research laboratories'.[25] Issues covered included the limitations of the existing apparatus for sound recording and playback, and discussion of practices, such as the placement of microphones relative to the action and their use in multiple camera shooting. But alongside the technical discussions, several of the attendees identified the potential of the new sound medium. Douglas Shearer (of MGM) underlined the desirability of recording a greater volume range 'to allow the director to get more of the color that he wishes in scenes',[26] and Academy President, William C. de Mille, expressed the hope that the sound film would become a 'new art' that would have 'all the visual values of the silent motion picture, while having the ear values of the theatre'.[27]

Following the January 1929 meeting, the Academy undertook a wide-ranging industry survey to determine the extent and scope of sound production problems, and to identify and share aspects of best practice.[28] The Academy proposed to standardise 'fundamentals' in sound processes, but without impinging on the 'exclusive processes being developed by the various studios'.[29] In other words, the Academy were attempting to negotiate a tension between the desire for proprietorial control of new technologies and the necessity for non-competitive co-operation on key areas of sound technology and production practice that permitted the studios to offer a standardised sound film to the exhibition sector.

This project was the beginning of the Academy's involvement in sound standardisation programmes. During 1929 the Academy co-ordinated activities designed to foster 'a better understanding between the art and the scientific or technical side of the industry' on sound matters, with a particular focus on fostering a common language for writers, directors and technicians.[30] It organised the activity by forming the Producers-Technicians Joint Committee, bringing together technical experts and producers – the key decision-makers in the studio system.[31] In early 1930 the Joint Committee was retitled the Academy Technical Bureau (absorbing the Technical Bureau of the Association of Motion Picture Producers), and in 1932 it became the Academy Research Council. A bulletin from the Technical Bureau in July 1930 captures the tenor of the discourse from this group – that of co-operation:

> Motion pictures may be called an art existing by grace of mechanics, but it is the art and not the mechanics that is sold to the public. Studios all need good cameras for instance, but the

only use of the camera is to photograph a scene. It is the value of the scene which will be in competition with the product of other studios. If every camera could be made twice as efficient, the competition would remain the same, but the industry as a whole would benefit and every studio in proportion.[32]

The Academy surveyed sound quality and practices at the major studios, and presented a report to the heads of studio sound departments.[33] A conference in July 1929 identified three areas of priority for development: acoustic control of recording (principles governing microphone placement and production mixing), dubbing (used in the period to describe the editing of sound effects in post-production) and volume control in movie theatres.[34] These three areas – sound production, post-production and exhibition, defined as key issues in the wake of the transition – remained on the Academy's research agenda, in one form or another, for the next twenty years.

The conference also agreed on an education programme – the Academy School in Sound Fundamentals – comprising a series of lectures and demonstrations to provide an understanding of the apparatus and basic physics involved in sound recording and reproduction. Beginning in September 1929, the Academy Technicians Branch, the sound departments of the major studios and the departments of physics at the University of Southern California (USC) and the University of California at Los Angeles (UCLA) collaborated to run ten-week courses on aspects of sound recording and reproduction.[35] The content was designed to 'present the basic principles in language understandable to those in *other* than the technical departments'.[36] The course was open to all studio employees in production roles, and the major studios had agreed to release employees to partake in classes that were scheduled during studio hours.[37] The ten-week course could accommodate a cohort of around a hundred students at once, and the Academy promised to run it as long as demand required.[38]

The Schools of Sound – as they became known – were well attended; it was estimated that by mid-1930 around nine hundred studio personnel had attended the course.[39] They also demonstrated a core Academy principle: fostering industry co-operation on common problems rather than competition. 'Co operation' was the theme of Irving Thalberg's report on the Schools of Sound for the *Journal of the Society of Motion Picture Engineers* (*JSMPE*). The influential MGM producer was the Chair of the Producers-Technicians Joint Committee (and later the Technical Bureau). He enthused that while 'the traditional policy of the production industry, particularly in technical matters, has always been strongly competitive ... [the Schools of Sound project] has advanced the general welfare of the industry. It has "sold" the whole industry on the vital principle of cooperative industrial education,'[40] and that 'the technical leaders of the industry, too, have been drawn together, by cooperation in administering the course'.[41]

It is understandable that Thalberg, representing the Academy and the rank of producer, would want to publicly underline the success, and value, of the problem-solving Schools of Sound, but relations between different crafts working together on the new sound film were not always as harmonious, as James Lastra has illustrated in his examination of tensions between cinematographers and sound personnel in the transitional period.[42] Nevertheless, the considerable activity in 1929 set a precedent for the research agenda to address problems in production, and had put in place the networks to achieve this.

From 1930 the Academy's Producers-Technicians Joint Committee set up subcommittees on specific issues pertaining to sound. Research was also taken forward by committees of the SMPE, with interchange between AMPAS and the SMPE via technicians who held memberships in both bodies and formed the connecting nodes across these groups. Research was disseminated through a range of publications. The Academy published *Technical Bulletins* on specific projects. It also collected together key papers from the Schools of Sound course in its 1931 publication *Recording Sound for Motion Pictures*.[43] The monthly *Journal of the Society of Motion Picture Engineers* regularly published articles on new apparatus, improvements in sound processes and guidance on standards.

By 1931 significant improvements had been made in the quality of sound, along with a step change in sound production practices. The key gain was a greater control of all aspects of the sound process. Writing in 1931, Academy President, William de Mille, captured a sense of the sound film moving forward out of the transition and into a new phase:

> It soon became evident that the arts of the dramatist, the director, and the actor could not produce a satisfactory result as long as they had to meet the severe physical restrictions imposed upon them by the scientific machinery of two years ago. Science then began to adapt itself to the requirements of art, and instead of the engineer telling the director what he must do, the director began to tell the engineer what he wanted to do and the engineer began to make it possible for him to do it.
>
> William de Mille, 'Preface', in *Recording Sound for Motion Pictures*, ed. Lester Cowan (New York and London: McGraw-Hill, 1931), p. v

Sound production routines were aided by a range of improvements. Unwanted noise on the set was addressed; cameras were 'blimped' in smaller soundproofed cases and released from their bulky booths, and noisy arc lights were replaced with incandescent lighting.[44] Omni-directional microphones were superseded by more responsive directional ones. Some, like RCA's 'ribbon' microphone introduced in 1931, were bidirectional, and could be positioned between actors to capture dialogue exchange, whilst its bidirectional field meant that equipment noise perpendicular to it did not register on the recording.[45] Mobile sound recording practice was made easier and more flexible by the introduction of microphone booms. An early boom was developed by the Mole-Richardson company, after collaboration with MGM's Sound Department.[46] By mid-1930 all the major studios had transferred to recording sound-on-film rather than on disk for most production tasks, although disk recording (and playback) was still widely used for certain processes, particularly the recording of music, and 'pre-scoring' (the playback of music and/or songs to which the action was co-ordinated). Greater control over production routines and the quality of the soundtrack was facilitated as the studios moved to recording image and sound separately, the so-called 'double system'.[47] The recording of sound footage on film stock with edge numbers allowed image and sound takes to be accurately re-synchronised in the editing phase. By 1933 advances in editing apparatus (such as improved moviolas) and practices, along with the use of double-system recording, allowed the soundtrack to be 'stratified' into its components of dialogue, music and sound effects, and permitted these components to be mixed, balanced and more precisely controlled.[48]

As Donald Crafton notes, by 1930–1931 the soundtrack was 'well tempered' and 'newly modulated'.[49] The uses to which sounds were put had shifted stylistically from the early part of the transition period; Crafton defines this as a shift from the 'foregrounding' of vocal performance and synchronous sound effects that 'accentuat[ed] the unique or novel properties of a [new] medium'[50] towards an approach in which sound was more fully 'contained', an approach characterised by the 'integration' or 'orchestration' of effects to augment a soundtrack organised around dialogue.[51]

THE ONGOING EVOLUTION IN FILM SOUND IN THE POST-TRANSITION ERA

With sound centrally on the research agendas of institutions (AMPAS), industrial interest groups (such as the SMPE) and their allied and affiliated research companies, like ERPI, Bell Labs and RCA, improvements in sound quality continued to be made. Beyond the transitional period, and throughout the 1930s and into the 1940s, research into, and refinements of, sound technologies led to advancements in all aspects of sound recording, editing, playback and reproduction through advances in microphone technology, moviolas for sound editing, multi-track mixing apparatus and refinements in the quality of film stocks, photographic emulsions and sensitometry.[52] One commentator, Barrett Kiesling of MGM, writing in 1937, estimated that since the introduction of sound around five hundred improvements in sound recording and reproduction had been made at that studio alone, and that 'for the entire industry such variations would run into thousands'.[53] The Academy took stock of the numerous improvements in sound technologies, and in the spring of 1936 its Research Council, which, from August 1932, replaced the Technical Bureau in co-ordinating the Academy's technical activities, ran a new sound training course, updating the Schools of Sound, publishing the lectures as *Motion Picture Sound Engineering* in 1938.[54]

While the post-transitional era is best characterised as one of evolution rather than revolution, it was one in which the soundscapes of Hollywood's films gradually changed through an interplay of technology and style. These innovations frequently took place in group contexts, and a group might be constituted by sound department, studio, or professional and industry association. The interactions between technical cultures and Hollywood's production cultures for the sound film can be traced through the sources and discourses disseminated from the different groups indicated. As noted earlier, identifying discursive positions and tensions in conceptualisation is productive in allowing us to pinpoint interactions, and sometimes contestations, in the languages that signal the cultures of these different groups. Above I have illustrated how negotiations of the tensions between 'art' and 'science' featured in discourses of 'co-operation' published by the Academy's Technical Bureau and in the discourses of senior Academy figures, such as President William de Mille.

The discursive tensions between 'art' and 'science' were also implicit in the differing 'models of representation' held by sound technicians in the early sound period.[55] James Lastra has established that the technical background of Hollywood's sound technicians had an influence on how they defined the tasks of sound recording. The emergence of sound experts from audio industries (radio, telephone and phonograph) and from the sound research sector shaped concepts of what constituted 'good sound'.

In technical cultures 'good sound' was conceived of as sound with clarity at all levels of the frequency and volume range, sound that reproduced speaking voices intelligibly and with 'presence', and sound which had a fidelity to its recorded source. Broadly, early work on standards by the SMPE and Academy sought to guarantee 'good sound' in this sense. However, the production cultures for the new sound film shared a different sense of 'good sound': desiring sound with 'entertainment values' and 'dramatic values'. Lastra traces two models of representation for sound that emerged in engineers' discourses in the technical cultures of early sound: a 'phonographic' model for sound technologies and recording that gave the listener 'perceptual fidelity', such as that experienced in a concert hall, and a 'telephonic' model for sound, one prioritising 'intelligibility' for the listener.[56] As is clear from his terminology, these models arise from the industrial backgrounds of sound engineers in the phonograph and telephone industries. He demonstrates that, during the early 1930s, these models of representation gradually become modified to a more pragmatic and production-oriented model, in which sound was conceived of as constructed in component parts, and was recombined according to the 'hierarchies of "dramatic" relationships'.[57] Lastra's outline of the tendencies in technical discourse is valuable, though his study ends around 1934, and it is clear that differing conceptualisations remain in tension in technical discourses throughout the 1930s and into the 1940s. The negotiation between competing conceptualisations of 'good sound' is evidence of the dynamic interactions between technical and production cultures, and between technology and film style. These interactions are evident at different levels of the industry and in the different spheres of technicians' activities. Three case studies serve to pinpoint these negotiations. At a 'micro' level I discuss a production case study, analysing how the negotiation and adaptation of sound recording practices for *One Night of Love* (Victor Schertzinger, 1934) illustrate how technological and style problems were solved within a studio context and for the needs of a specific film. I also trace the dynamic interactions between technical and production cultures at a 'macro' level, offering case studies of the industry-wide projects on sound, namely the Academy's project on standards. And, the final case study of the chapter examines how the research sector developed and trialled alternative options for sound, through experiments in stereophonic and multi-speaker sound. Analysing case studies at these different levels allows us not only to gain a picture of the technological history of film sound beyond the transitional period, but offers a much broader picture about how change and innovation were conceived, promoted and managed, giving us insights into how Hollywood's technical, production and institutional cultures interacted and functioned.

RECORDING PRESTIGE: *ONE NIGHT OF LOVE* AND GRACE MOORE'S VOICE

In 1934 Columbia Pictures, one of the 'little three' of the Hollywood majors and a studio which tightly controlled its budgets, had a hit with a musical with prestige elements and quality entertainment values. *One Night of Love*, directed by composer Victor Schertzinger, featured opera star Grace Moore as an aspiring young singer, Mary. The film's narrative traces her rise to success from a radio audition to the stage of the Metropolitan Opera in New York, via an apprenticeship in Europe under the strict tutelage of the renowned opera maestro Giulio Monteverdi (Tullio Carminati). The subplot of the film concerns the romantic attraction, and tribulations, between pupil and tutor, which resolves happily in Mary's magnificent final performance of Puccini's *Madame Butterfly* on stage at the Met as Giulio looks on from the prompter's box.

One Night of Love provided a return to the screen for opera star Grace Moore, and is credited as initiating a commercially successful cycle of musical films that exploited opera in the mid- to late 1930s.[58] Moore had a successful career in musical theatre on Broadway during the 1920s, and also performed at the Metropolitan Opera in New York and Paris in that period. She had appeared on screen in two musicals for MGM in the early 1930s: *A Lady's Morals* (Sidney Franklin, 1930) and with Metropolitan opera singer Lawrence Tibbett in a screen version of the operetta *New Moon* (Jack Conway, 1930). These two films were not strong box-office, or critical, hits. They were produced during the 1930–1931 season, when, as Tino Balio puts it, 'the musical … became box-office poison'.[59] This lull in popularity followed the glut of musicals of all types produced between 1928 and 1930 as the major studios rushed to capitalise on new ways of working with sound.

An additional reason for the hiatus in production of operettas on screen was the technological challenge of recording their key and central selling point: the vocal performance of their stars. Evidently, there had been some problems in recording and fully rendering Grace Moore's soprano voice during the production (and exhibition) of *A Lady's Morals*, as was reported by Mordaunt Hall of the *New York Times* in his review of the film.[60] Joseph Maxfield, a senior sound engineer at Bell Labs, and one of the key sound experts in Hollywood's technical culture, reiterated the challenges of recording frequency characteristics in the higher range to a meeting of the Academy's Technical Branch:

> With reference to the frequency range, one very interesting engineering factor of emotional value to the public is met with. If the higher harmonics are reproduced satisfactorily (commonly called 'cleanly'), they constitute a distinct asset to the reproduction. If, on the other hand, they are reproduced improperly, or if the harmonics are obtained by non-linear distortion of lower frequencies, the public strenuously dislike them and would much prefer them missing altogether. Throughout all of our tests during the last few years this factor has been constantly encountered and has been one of the real difficulties which had to be overcome before an extended range of frequencies was usable commercially.[61]

What was difficult to achieve in 1930 became more possible by 1934. Ongoing improvements in recording technologies and apparatus in the early 1930s meant that the frequency and volume range that typify the excitement, emotional drama and virtuosity of the soprano operatic voice could be more fully accommodated by film sound technologies.

The 'rise to success' narrative of *One Night of Love* allows the film to weave in operatic arias which fully exhibit Moore's star values, but it tempers these with popular songs to offer a blend of musical, and cultural, tones and genres. The theme song of the film, 'One Night of Love', by Victor Schertzinger and Gus Kahn, plays in an instrumental version over the film's title cards, which include Moore's name above the title. Then Moore's voice picks up the lyrics, delivering the song over the introduction of the main cast and providing a bridge into the opening shot: Mary Barrett singing into a radio microphone as she competes in the finals of the American Radio Auditions. Mary is accompanied by the radio house band, and the full duration of the music and song play across reaction shots of the audience within the radio station, and of the panel of judges, and then her song forms a sound bridge across a cut to a more remote listener as the action takes in Giulio and his lover Rosa Lally (Mona Barrie) on his yacht, listening in over the radio. The sequence serves to introduce a theme that recurs throughout the film – the ability of Mary's voice to enchant and connect a group of listeners, to create an audience.

After the radio competition, the action follows Mary to Milan, where she is determined to succeed in her singing career. A sequence, set at her apartment in Milan, re-emphasises her draw to an audience, and confirms her talent and star quality. The sequence begins with an establishing shot of the street below Mary's apartment. Windows and doors open onto the street, and, motivated by the sounds of musicians practising, a series of reframing tilts, pans and cuts takes in, and adds, different instruments to the music. The different viewpoints, matched by sonic clarity and foregrounding of each instrument as it is introduced, give a strong sense of the building parts, each adding and enriching the growing sound. The music begins with strings, led by a solo violin, which is joined by a group of children on violins conducted by their teacher. Lower tones are introduced with a cut to a double bass. Woodwind instruments and higher tones are added by a flautist, and then piano, a cello and finally a harp are included in the diverse mix. The musicians are united by the same tempo, and as they practise their scales there is a lightness and variety in the pitch of what is heard. The music builds and transitions into a more structured and purposeful movement as Mary, drawn out onto her balcony by the sounds, joins them, her voice providing the keynote sound around which the others are organised. Seamlessly, Mary's practised vocal trills and scales, and the instrumental music, move into a rendition of an aria, 'Sempre Libera', a section of 'Ah, Fors'e Lui' from Giuseppe Verdi's *La Traviata*. As Mary joins them, the musicians react happily, and some are drawn out into the street to play. A small crowd gathers as Mary performs on the balcony and, as the aria builds to a crescendo, rhythmic cutting around the performance space unites Mary, the musicians and the audience. The climax is met with rapturous applause, and the street audience improvise a bouquet, not of exotic blooms, but a more down-to-earth tribute: a head of celery, a bunch of onions and some herbs.

The whole feeling of the sequence is of an impromptu performance and, generically, it draws upon similar elements to backstage rehearsal sequences in musicals more widely. It signals Mary's nascent talent, popularity and the 'rightness' of her trajectory towards the opera stage. The sequence, though, also succeeds through its light touch with the complex operatic material – moving from practised scales into the aria bestows a sense of a naturally evolving musical moment in the backstreets of Milan, home of the Italian opera. In this sense the aria is integrated into the narrative, its thematic material – an expression of joy and freedom by *La Traviata*'s Violetta – expressive of the diegetic feelings of Mary, determining her own path as a singer.[62]

The performance of 'Sempre Libera' allows the narration to establish Mary as a 'natural' for opera, and it acts as a portent for her later performances. Mary meets Giulio while working in a Milanese café. She serves tables, and contributes to the house

Hollywood Soundscapes

entertainment by performing the Italian ballad 'Ciribiribin'.[63] Hearing her sing, Giulio takes her on as a pupil, on the condition that there will be no romance between them.

The middle part of the film details the rigours of Giulio's strict training regime and Mary's rise to success. An audiovisual montage sequence condenses Mary's successful tour of Italian cities, and moves the action to Vienna. Mary's growing fame has transformed her into 'La Barrett', and she is recognised as she and Giulio dine in a fashionable restaurant the night before her performance in *Carmen* at the Vienna Opera House. However, Giulio's strict regime causes Mary to rebel. Instead of resting for her big performance, she seeks out her friend Bill for a day of rebellious fun. At the Opera House Mary refuses to go on until, as the overture plays, Giulio declares that he loves her and always has. These backstage events give an appropriate dramatic frame of feeling to Mary's performance of 'La Habanera' from Georges Bizet's *Carmen*. Moore gives swagger and attitude to her performance of Carmen's entrance. The characterisation of Carmen and the confident tone of the aria allow a broad thematic concord to emerge between performed material and performing character, as did the earlier choice of 'Sempre Libera'. Contrasts to the Verdi aria, though, emerge through its staging and setting. The theatrical setting of 'La Habanera', and the build-up to Mary's performance, signals it as her entrée as a prima donna. The setting also firmly positions the aria as the film's presentation of opera proper.

In contrast to the Verdi aria, in which the reframing and editing linked the musicians, Mary and the improvising musicians, the structuring of the *Carmen* sequence observes conventions governing the presentation of an on-stage musical number. The sequence begins with an extreme long shot, from a camera position in the theatre stalls, which establishes the set and space, and location of the orchestra and the audience. After Mary's entrance, the shot scales, reframing and editing are motivated by her movement and performance, with the exception of some brief cutaway reaction shots to the wings, where her dresser, Angelina (Jessie Ralph), and rehearsal pianist, Giovanni (Luis Alberni), watch with rapturous attention, and to the prompter's box, where Giulio follows her delivery of the aria. The mixing and editing of the sound centres on Moore's voice as its key feature; it appears to be 'conventional', in the sense that Hollywood sound mixing has been described as 'vococentric'.[64] However, as I will go on to discuss, the recording and balancing of Moore's voice with the orchestral music, and the re-recording of the opera sequences within the frequency and volume range limitations of the sound apparatus available, give this sequence the status of sonic spectacle. It complies with the principles of 'good sound' from an engineering standpoint and simultaneously offers strong 'entertainment values'.

The film concludes with two arias from Giacomo Puccini's *Madame Butterfly*. As with the aria from *Carmen*, the narrative events that frame them lend extra drama to Mary's performance. The action has moved from Mary's success in *Carmen* to the New York Metropolitan Opera where Mary takes the starring role of Cio-Cio San. However, tensions have arisen between her and Giulio, as Mary wrongly suspects him of resuming his affair with his erstwhile lover. Mary has to prepare for the role without his coaching, and on the opening night she suffers from crippling stage fright, threatening not to go on. Her dresser Angelina coaxes her backstage in time for her entrance, and as she comes on stage she sees that Giulio is in the prompter's box. The final moments of the film combine the crescendo of Puccini's 'Un Bel Di' theme, a tearful but joyous exchange of looks between Mary and Giulio, and an ecstatic standing ovation for Mary's performance by the on-screen audience. The resolution of the romance between Mary and Giulio lends an extra expressivity to the aria that Moore delivers, and a broad thematic link to love.

Victor Schertzinger, director of One Night of Love (and of Love Me Forever, (1935) – Moore's second opera-based success for Columbia), attributed the film's success to the particular approach taken to opera. Writing in the JSMPE, he noted:

> Our aim was not to produce opera, as opera, but to use it as a motive, as a dramatic part of the story itself. The music was cast to the picture with an eye, and ear, to its dramatic effect and to its fitness to the situation. The aria from Madame Butterfly used at the finale of One Night of Love could not have fitted the situation more perfectly if we had had it written especially for us by the greatest musician in the world. It completely expressed the emotion of the star and paralleled her own situation perfectly in words ... we cast the music just as we would choose a player for a certain role, to perform a certain piece of business, to add to and build up a dramatic and emotional sequence.[65]

In his article Schertzinger considered both the technical and stylistic challenges of presenting opera on screen. He noted that 'today, thanks to the improvements made in sound recording equipment and technic and to the increasing skill of the technicians, the screen can do justice to a beautiful voice, or to the full strains of a symphony orchestra. The mechanical difficulties would not hinder us.'[66] He was more doubtful, though, of the practicality of 'putting full opera on the screen' from the 'producer's standpoint'.[67] The task that faced producers, Schertzinger argued, meant contending with and adapting 'moss-bound'[68] staging and performance traditions from opera, and finding 'acting-singing talent',[69] performers who could bridge both stage and screen.

The interplay between technologies and style in One Night of Love were, as Schertzinger's thoughts on adapting opera to the screen indicate, quite complex. This interplay was not simply a question of the mechanical capacity of sound apparatus to record the amplitudes of the orchestra or high frequencies of the soprano voice, although this played a part, but a rather more complicated interaction: the adaptation and mediation of performance to be convincing on the screen.

By the time One Night of Love was in production, there were well-established practices in managing the recording of musical and dance numbers through 'pre-scoring', mentioned above. This practice involved recording the orchestration of music and the visual performances of dance numbers separately. The music was usually recorded first (pre-scored), and played back on the set as a timing guide to the dance performance. This process afforded much-valued control over the different visual and sonic aspects involved in musical spectacle, and the production applications of pre-scoring were discussed at some length by R. H. Townsend, of Fox Film, in the JSMPE in 1935.[70] During the production of One Night of Love, Columbia's Sound Department did use a form of pre-scoring, but the specific stylistic demands of the film, namely the rendering of the opera numbers, required that the orchestra, the chorus and Grace Moore were all present and performing together.

Homer G. Tasker, a sound technician who worked in the motion picture research sector in the early 1930s, and later for Universal Studios, covered the technologies and techniques employed during the production of *One Night of Love* for the *JSMPE*.[71] He reported that Columbia's Sound Department devoted considerable time, planning and ingenuity to the recording of the musical scenes. Different types of microphones were used for the orchestra, the chorus and for Grace Moore's parts, recording them on separate tracks, along with at least a few sound takes with all elements recorded simultaneously, making this a complex recording set-up. Choices were made about the type of microphones used, and their placement was manipulated to ensure a differentiation between voice and music, but also to capture some elements of reverberation so that the recording did not sound too 'flat' or 'dry'.[72] Dynamic microphones were used for the orchestra pickup. They were able to handle the large sound amplitudes created by the orchestra without overloading, and were placed in two positions: the first close to the orchestra (30 feet), and a second further away (90 feet) to introduce 'reverberant quality'. As Columbia's acoustically treated sound stage deadened the sound, further reverberation was added with a filter on the second microphone. A unidirectional ribbon microphone was used to record Moore's performance, and a bilateral microphone recorded the chorus, grouped into male and female vocalists with the microphone placed between them.[73]

Columbia's Head of Sound, John Livadary, also commented on the specific production needs of the film in an article for *American Cinematographer*. Livadary highlighted that the recording of the opera numbers was governed by what he termed 'the singer's artistic caprices'.[74] He reported that 'Miss Moore desired an unusually close association with the orchestra',[75] so, rather than pre-scoring, the recording was arranged to allow her performance to be recorded at the same time as the orchestra. Livadary explained that this recording necessitated a particular design in the microphone set-up. Moore's microphone was placed in front of her, but at right angles to the orchestra, permitting a separation between her voice and the orchestral accompaniment. This close association in the performance was perhaps 'unusual' in terms of sound engineering, but was common practice for operatic performance.

The Columbia Sound Department recorded the musical numbers in two formats – optically, on film, and on 'hill-and-dale' disk. In post production the disk recordings were re-recorded onto film for release. Tasker explains the choice of disk recording as follows:

> The very wide volume-range of the hill-and-dale method enabled successful 'canning' of Miss Moore's none too predictable performance, which could thus be re-recorded with care and finesse so as just to reach, but never exceed, the upper volume limit of the release film.[76]

As well as accommodating the wide volume range appropriate to the musical numbers in *One Night of Love*, disk recording had other production advantages. It allowed sound quality to be checked without the delay inherent in sound-on-film optical recording, which had to be sent away from the set to the lab for processing before playback. Any variations in performance, as mentioned by Tasker, could be checked immediately and decisions made as to the necessity for additional takes. The ability to check the quality and character of sound was particularly desirable with complex recordings, where large numbers of musicians and vocalists were present, because recalling performers would incur significant extra costs. Both aspects here – Moore's close association with the orchestra, and the range in her performance – underline the fact that technological choices and applications in film production bear the traces of an array of social, cultural and economic demands and practices.

Columbia's innovations on *One Night of Love* were widely praised by other studio sound personnel, and the film won the Academy Award for Best Sound Recording in the 1934 (7th) ceremony. The Academy also gave the Columbia Sound Department a Class III (Scientific or Technical Award) 'for their application of the Vertical Cut Disc Method (hill and dale recording) to actual studio production' for the recording of *One Night of Love*.[77] The terms of these innovations are interesting within a technological history of sound, as, of course, sound-on-disk recording was an early sound format, and was discontinued as a release format by early 1930. However, clearly sound-on-disk had a continuing use-value for recording and pre-scoring in particular situations, such as the musical. The research sector continued to fund work on improvements to disk recording to eliminate pops and crackles, and studio sound personnel continued to experiment with a range of applications for disk recording.[78] This reveals that technological innovations often wove together existent and new technologies, governed by their use-value and appropriateness to specific situations and needs. As Tasker notes, aspects of Columbia's innovations were 'quite old in the art';[79] where they gained an edge was in their application of a mix of sound technologies to a specific production and performance situation, using disk recording to capture volume and frequency range, and to successfully master this onto sound-on-film for release. Applied to the exploitation of star characteristics and quality entertainment values, Columbia's technological innovations allowed the studio to demonstrate the feasibility of opera on screen, and gave the company a prestige hit.

STANDARDS, STUDIO PRACTICES AND STYLE: 'MANAGING' THE SOUNDTRACK AND THE QUEST FOR VOLUME RANGE

It is the business of a gyrostabiliser to keep the ship on an even keel when it is being buffeted by waves, not to stop the ship. Just so it is the business of a successful standard to help industry to maintain itself in 'dynamic equilibrium,' not in a 'static' condition.

J. W. NcNair, Technical Director, American Standards Association[80]

The standardization process must be thought of not as an inevitable progression toward dull, mediocre products ... but instead ... as an attempt to achieve a precision-tooled quality object.

Janet Staiger, in David Bordwell, Janet Staiger and Kristin Thompson, *The Classical Hollywood Cinema* (London and New York: Routledge, 1985), p. 98

The quest for volume range, and more plenitude on the soundtrack, was not confined to films featuring 'the ladies of the high Cs', it was a wider drive in sound research in the post-transition period.[81] This research objective was pursued at the same time as key moves towards defined industry standards for sound recording, for sound levels on release prints and for sound film projection and exhibition practices, thus the balance between standards and innovation was a dynamic one, as suggested in the quotations above.

Between 1936 and 1940, Warner Bros.' Head of the Sound, Nathan Levinson, and the studio's Chief Transmission Engineer, and researcher, William Mueller, experimented with several different innovations to try to expand sound film volume range. Writing for the *JSMPE* in 1936, Levinson defined limited volume range as 'one of the chief handicaps' in the dramatic presentation of sound, and described a method of gaining extra range by intercutting two different kinds of sound film – variable area and variable density.[82] As noted in Levinson's article, at this point the potential volume range of the Hollywood sound film was bracketed at the lower end by the ground noise inherent in the film medium on which sound was recorded and at the upper end by the limits of reproducing apparatus in movie theatres, which easily became 'overloaded' at high volumes. Levinson put this volume range at 40 decibels. In order to present films most effectively, while staying within the limits of the playback equipment, it was common practice for exhibitors and projectionists to 'manage' the volume levels during the projection of productions with the use of a 'fader' (volume) setting for the speakers in the auditorium. Studios routinely sent out fader 'cue sheets' advising projectionists on the fader settings most appropriate for specific sequences of particular productions.[83]

Levinson's method proposed to bypass the necessity for changing fader settings, and it offered the potential to exploit 'extra' volume range through its principle of intercutting. The intercutting used variable-density film for sequences where a normal range of volume modulation was required (such as spoken dialogue) and switched to variable-area film where higher modulation was required for 'the most dramatic and effective presentation', for action or spectacular sequences.[84] Levinson estimated that this method of intercutting extended the volume range by around 8dB.[85]

The new method that Levinson proposed was essentially a modification in practice that was easily achievable by the studios with little extra financial investment. As both variable-density and variable-area sound film were widely used across the major studios for release printing, the sound heads of projectors in movie theatres were designed to read both formats. The Academy recognised Levinson's efforts, and at the 1935 (8th) Awards Levinson was given an honourable mention by the Board of Judges and awarded a Class III (Scientific or Technical Award), cited as follows: 'for the method of intercutting variable density and variable area sound tracks to secure an increase in the effective volume range of sound recorded for motion pictures'.[86]

However, while Levinson's innovation captured more volume range from the studio-production standpoint, it was not so easy to realise this improvement in dramatic sound within the exhibition contexts of the mid-1930s. Levinson's article acknowledged this. He wrote: 'Before the full possibilities of the system can be realized, additional amplifier capacity must be provided in [many] theaters', but maintained, 'the system has shown itself to have great possibilities for enhancing the realism and naturalness of sound pictures'.[87]

Levinson's innovation initiated debate within the technical culture of the SMPE, and the discussions which took place reveal two potentially conflicting drives at play in sound research: the push for increased volume range, and the need to define standards to ensure reliable exhibition results. Evidently, other studios were seeking the drama of expanded volume; MGM had released two versions of their 1935 operetta *Naughty Marietta* (W. S. Van Dyke), one version of which was prepared for release and exhibition with expanded volume range.[88]

By 1935 the question of managing sound variations in exhibition was on the agenda for both the Academy and the SMPE. There were two strands to this activity: moves to try to improve sound reproduction in movie theatres, and efforts to manage cross-studio variations in the soundtrack of release prints, in terms of volume and frequency characteristics. It was the latter issue that was initially easier for the technical culture to tackle. The exhibition field was more variable and complex to influence than production practices; substantial changes in projection equipment depended on investment and required independent exhibitors, as well as the vertically integrated majors, to be convinced of the commercial logic. Hence, changes took place slowly and unevenly.

In spring 1935 the SMPE's Sound Committee outlined four distinct projects that would progress the industry towards more standardised sound.[89] The first project was to work towards more uniform sound recording across the studios. To achieve uniformity, the SMPE gathered comparative data on recording frequency characteristics at the studios. The second project aimed for a more uniform volume level balance as a standard for release across the studios to aid the exhibition sector.[90] Once this standard was agreed, it would be possible for the studios to specify if the release print of a particular production needed special treatment in exhibition. If, for instance, the production deviated from the 'normal' loudness standard, this information could be included on the 'film leader' (twenty-four frames of film identifying the film format and studio and including key information affecting the projection of the print).[91]

The third project was to establish uniform processing characteristics for sound film, and the Technical Branch of the Academy was concurrently working on this issue.[92] The fourth project was to measure the acoustics of studio review rooms and of movie theatres.[93]

SMPE Sound Committee member Otto Sandvik argued that finding a 'uniform frequency characteristic of the talking motion picture, as heard in the theaters, is the most important problem that is at hand ... it is a far-reaching problem, taking in all operations that have any relation to the sound, from the recording studio to the theatre.'[94] He predicted that once a standard had been established that played satisfactorily in 'the average theater', that some equalisation treatment of the frequency would be necessary.[95]

Defining a standard equalisation characteristic was a project that the Technical Branch of the Academy worked on between 1935 and 1937, and in the spring of 1937 they issued specifications for a standard equalisation of release prints.[96] This standard equalisation came to be known as the 'Academy Curve'. It was a solution designed to manage unpredictable sound quality, particularly in the areas of frequency response and volume range discussed above. The equalisation was applied in the final stages of post-production, after the picture and all the soundtrack elements were edited, synchronised and mixed. When applied to the soundtrack in re-recording, the Academy Curve attenuated high frequencies and slightly reduced the modulation of low frequencies. This managed the problems of low-frequency bass rumble and high-frequency

Hollywood Soundscapes

hiss, or the overload of systems, and worked to guarantee more reliable and predictable exhibition quality of the sound film.[97] The equalisation standard fitted the soundtrack to the exhibition context. In the Academy report, the committee stated that they had worked towards a standard 'which would present the recorded product of all studios to the public to the best advantage at this time, and which in addition would fit the acoustic characteristic of a majority of the theatres'.[98]

Variety reported the standardisation activities from the standpoint of the wider industry, and saw it as a distinct benefit to exhibitors:

> After several years of competition in which studios tried to outdo each other in turning out masterpieces of sound recording that were fine in projection rooms and a few key houses containing highly-tuned equipment, but duds when shown on average theatre apparatus, the sound engineers have now adopted the policy of providing the best quality of soundtrack for theatres to reproduce under normal conditions. In other words, instead of trying to achieve the best sound job possible on pictures, studios are now putting on the track a recording that will be reproduced at a uniform quality in the theatres and eliminate distorted sound where formerly more was put on the track than the average theatre reproducers could accommodate.[99]

The Academy's Committee on Standardising Release Prints was chaired by MGM's John K. Hilliard, an expert in sound engineering. Other MGM sound personnel also contributing to the Academy's technical activities on sound included Kenneth Lambert, the studio's Head of Re-Recording and an expert on equalisation. Service on these technical committees by MGM sound personnel evidences the considerable expertise of the department. The Academy's Subcommittee on Acoustic Characteristics were at pains to insist that this work was solely to guarantee quality, and should in no way impinge upon sonic variety or creativity. The Chair of the subcommittee, Jack Durst, wrote:

> Realizing that both art and science have played a most important part in sound motion pictures, there was no thought of introducing a degree of uniformity ... or lack of the effect of creative effort in sound as reproduced in the theater ... it was felt that this uniformity was necessary ... [to] obtain the utmost in naturalness and showmanship.[100]

It is clear that the Academy Curve was intended more as a defining framework within which sound work could take place than as a limiting characteristic, expressed in Durst's emphasis upon the dual values of 'naturalness' and 'showmanship'.[101]

NEGOTIATING NOVELTY: STEREOPHONIC SOUND, FANTASOUND, VITA-SOUND AND THE CONSTRUCTION OF THE 'INTELLIGENT COMPROMISE'

The dynamics of stabilisation and change in sound technologies in the studio era are vividly illustrated by the fact that during the very same period that Hollywood's technical culture was working to formulate widely agreed standards for sound recording and reproduction, within the same culture, technicians were trialling distinctly new models of sound recording and reproduction, and diversifying exhibition possibilities.

Between 1937 and 1940, a range of multi-channel and multi-speaker systems for reproducing sound, developed in the research sector, were demonstrated within the technical networks of the SMPE, and then shown to the wider industry. In 1937 ERPI demonstrated a two-channel multi-speaker stereophonic sound picture system.[102] Within the same period RCA collaborated with Disney on the 'Fantasound' process, and with Warner Bros. on the 'Vitasound' process. Fantasound was a multi-channel and multi-speaker system. It used three separate sound channels played back through multiple speakers, the volume of the speakers determined by a control track.[103] Disney-RCA demonstrated the possibilities with a roadshow release of the animated musical *Fantasia* (Joe Grant, 1940). Vitasound was a multi-speaker, rather than a multi-track, system. It used a single channel (i.e. monophonic) soundtrack, with a control track to 'turn on' additional speakers at the sides of the screen to 'augment' sound during chosen sequences of the exhibited film.[104] Warner Bros.-RCA featured their Vitasound in the Western *Santa Fe Trail* (Michael Curtiz, 1940), and added the process to selected film re-releases, which between 1939 and 1940 were given special presentation at chosen Warner movie theatres fitted for Vitasound exhibition. In very broad terms, Fantasound represented an 'ideal' presentation of multi-channel stereophonic sound, while Vitasound was a much simpler system, adding speakers to single-channel sound; hence, in comparison to Fantasound, it represented a more pragmatic and expedient design.

These two major research programmes for film sound in the mid-1930s – the standardisation of release prints and theatre presentation, and the diversification in new theatre reproduction systems – were concurrent but not fully synchronised, nor co-ordinated, so how might their relationship be characterised and more fully understood? On the face of it, the objectives of the standardisation and diversification programmes might seem directly opposed. The co-operative work of the Academy and SMPE committees on standards gave sound technicians across the industry a detailed working knowledge of the constraints of the exhibition sector. Having established broad consensus on the working standards necessary to fit those constraints, why would research technicians offer different and competitive models of exhibition that did not fit those constraints? It is by understanding technologies and standards not as static, but as dynamically evolving and responsive to contexts, that we can more fully understand the concurrence and points of interaction and interrelation between standards and innovation.

During 1936 and into 1937, the revenues of the Hollywood majors significantly improved as the industry began to pick up from the Depression years.[105] The new commercial climate made investing in new sound equipment for the production and exhibition sector more feasible and more attractive. Writing for *Variety*'s *Anniversary* edition in January 1937, technical correspondent Walter Greene identified a step change in the development of new sound technologies by the research and service sector. He claimed that: 'Greater activity and development in the sound field of pictures was generated during 1936 than any previous year since 1927.'[106] This climate was partly created by increased competition between the market leaders in sound equipment: ERPI and RCA. During 1936 ERPI changed the terms of its recording contracts with the Hollywood studios, and made them non-exclusive; this allowed the majors to use other equipment,

Hollywood Soundscapes

and opened up the field to ERPI's main competitor: RCA Photophone. ERPI and RCA Photophone competed to offer the Hollywood studios better terms on recording royalties, representing a cost saving for the majors of around 30 per cent.[107] Both RCA and ERPI introduced new lines in production sound equipment, and offered special deals on upgrading, servicing and maintenance. RCA introduced its 'high fidelity' apparatus, and incorporated improvements in optical recording processes.[108] ERPI introduced their 'Mirrophonic' recording and reproduction system.

With the growing conviction that good sound equated to good box office, the exhibition sector began modernising equipment that, in many movie theatres, had not been upgraded since before the Depression years. Greene noted that 'with greatly improved sound coming from the studios, theatres found patrons becoming conscious of quality of sound through comparison of two or more theatres they attended, and exhibitors started equipment replacements in large numbers'.[109] Greene reported that all the major exhibition circuits had started re-equipping their theatres, and concluded, 'the battle for business between the two electrics should continue to result in greater improvements in sound quality in both the studio and theatre ends of the business'.[110]

In early 1937 spokesmen for RCA and ERPI reviewed the situation on sound in the previous year for *International Projectionist*. Both noted significant improvements, and implicitly linked those to advances in apparatus or research at their companies. Edwin Hartley (RCA Photophone) described 'important advances in sound recording technique' tied to push-pull and ultraviolet recording; he advocated for the modernisation of exhibition, and noted, 'it has already been demonstrated that good sound makes for good box-office returns'.[111] C. W. Bunn (ERPI) described 'radical' improvements in sound production practice facilitated by advancements in re-recording apparatus and the 'pre-equalization' of sound in release prints, permitting better sound quality and frequency range.[112] Bunn also noted distinct stylistic uses of sound film style in the previous year:

> probably the most important and spectacular change brought about in 1936 has been the marked increase in the use of dramatic sound effects. Earthquake scenes, violent explosions, crashing buildings and similar massive sound values have all been made commercially possible this year by virtue of modifications in the speed of noise reduction units.[113]

With the exhibition sector seemingly more open to modernising its sound equipment, ERPI and RCA began to make more ambitious trials of multi-speaker and multi-channel sound systems, including demonstrations of stereophonic sound. These systems were conceptualised by the research sector and presented to the industry in a range of subtly different ways. Media historians, such as Susan Douglas, have demonstrated that new technology '[does] not simply appear ... in its fully realized form with all its components complete and its applications and significance apparent', but rather it needs to be 'elaborately constructed'.[114] She explains:

> Just as individuals and institutions worked, over time, to refine the invention, so did these inventors and institutions, as well as the press and the public, all interact to spin a fabric of meanings with which this technology would be wrapped.[115]

Tracing the ways these systems were defined within technical cultures, how these definitions emerged into the wider sphere of the industry, and how meanings were negotiated and modified in the trade press makes clear that conceptual and discursive tensions formed a 'fabric of meanings' around stereophonic sound. The varying constructions of multi-channel and multi-speaker sound represented ideas of new possibilities, and new models of representation, in film sound. But the new possibilities were framed by both pragmatic and imaginative constraints, constraints which give us insights into the dynamics between technical and production cultures.

The sound systems trialled in this period included an early form of stereophonic recording and reproduction put forward by Bell/ERPI, but while different systems emerged the technological developments in this period cannot be simply understood as pre- or proto-stereo forms, nor simply as milestones on a linear and predetermined path towards a clearly defined, 'ideal' goal of stereophonic recording and reproduction. The technological history behind the specific development of stereophonic film sound has been well established, for example by Jay Beck in *A Quiet Revolution*.[116] My focus here is rather upon what innovations emerged in Hollywood in the 1930s and early 1940s, and how they were shaped by their contextual cultures. In this period three differently conceived methods of presenting film sound emerged in parallel into the public sphere. Analysing this parallel emergence allows insights into Hollywood's technical cultures. These different methods of presenting film sound indicate competing systems and models of representation in classical Hollywood film sound. These competing systems share an experimental hinterland, where a range of possibilities in the presentation of sound, and not only stereophonic sound, were considered. These systems offered solutions to a range of sound problems, and were not designed solely to fulfil the 'single' goal of stereophonic reproduction, but offered solutions to previously defined technical problems. In fact, despite attracting a good deal of attention from different spheres and levels of the industry, none of the multi-channel or multi-speaker systems gained the economic or industrial traction for widespread adoption. This was due to a range of constraining factors in play, but in forming a historical picture of the character of invention and innovation in this period, it is important to consider the role of compromise in shaping and arresting technological change. Susan Douglas writes persuasively of the importance of understanding why things do *not* happen in technological history.[117] Douglas Gomery, and Trevor Pinch and Wiebe Bijker, demonstrate the value of understanding 'failure' as a feature of technological histories;[118] in Gomery's terms this provides a corrective to the notion that 'the history of American cinema belongs to the victors'.[119]

The term 'stereophonic' was coined in technical cultures, one of its first appearances being in the *Wireless World* journal in 1927.[120] 'Stereophonic sound' is now generally understood to be sound 'giving the impression of spatial distribution' in its reproduction, 'employing two or more sound channels of transmission and reproduction so that the sound may seem to reach the listener from any of a range of directions'.[121] However, as Beck points out, this popular understanding only stabilised from the late 1950s onwards, as two-channel recording systems became commonly available for home users to play back music recordings.[122] Up to that point the meanings and usages of 'stereophonic' were less precise. It was during the 1930s that the term 'stereophonic' began to disseminate outside the technical and research cultures of American audio engineering, and was used more widely in trade press and industry publications, as those technical cultures sought to capture the attention of the Hollywood film industry to new possibilities in the presentation of sound.

In the early 1930s Bell Labs established a programme of research into methods of stereophonic disk recording. The first experiments and demonstrations were all focused upon recording and reproducing music.[123] The experiments garnered several insights key to multi-channel sound. Bell engineers concluded that a satisfactory stereophonic spatial effect could be achieved with three, or even two, channels. They determined the microphone placements and recording levels that would best reproduce the orchestra and the spatial ambience of the concert hall.[124]

As well as presenting, and discussing, stereophonic sound within the professional networks of sound experts constituted by the SMPE, it is evident that Bell, and its associated motion picture research arm ERPI, were working in-house on stereophonic recording for film and wished to establish the exhibition possibilities of stereophonic sound in the minds of Hollywood producers.[125] In August 1936 Bell-ERPI organised a high-profile, large-scale event: the Hollywood Bowl was fitted with a stereophonic reproduction system, comprising multiple speakers to relay the performance of an orchestra. The installation was supervised by Bell Labs' Dr Harvey Fletcher, assisted by engineers from Paramount Studios.[126] Leopold Stokowski was engaged to conduct the musical programme. The first part of the event was a mixed programme arranged by Paramount's General Director of Music, Boris Morros, while the second part was conducted by Leopold Stokowski and included the performance of three arias from *Carmen* by Gladys Swarthout.[127] In its coverage of the event, *Variety* highlighted features of the technology: it would produce a 'faithful' reproduction of the orchestra; it would 'augment' the orchestra 'ten-fold' by its amplification power, which would 'make each of the 20,000 seats a first-row seat'; and it would offer '"auditory perspective" or stereophonic effect, by which a listener can identify the location of each instrument or voice'.[128]

The Hollywood Bowl presented a vast showcase for the demonstration, but ERPI also took the opportunity to try to win over Hollywood's sound craft: *Variety* reported that 'members of the Academy Technicians [sic] Branch will huddle following the Leopold Stokowski concert to learn the workings of Electrical Research Products' new stereophonic sound', and that invitations to all sound technicians had been sent out by Nathan Levinson (Chair of the Branch).[129] However, while *Variety* praised the 'showmanship' of the event, it reported that 'opinion was divided on the effect of ERPI's stereophonic sound reinforcing system'. Audience members who had recently attended operatic performances at the venue, 'favored the natural acoustics of the Bowl as against the new amplification'.[130]

Just days after the demonstration at the Hollywood Bowl, ERPI began widely advertising a new film sound exhibition system in the trade press: the 'Mirrophonic' Sound System produced by ERPI's licensed equipment manufacturers, Western Electric.[131] The key message of the advertisements was the 'fidelity' of recording that the system offered, the ads claiming that every sound would be reproduced 'as true as a mirrored reflection in a true mirror' (See Figures 1 and 2). The Mirrophonic system used a single sound channel, and thus was monophonic, but in their advertising and promotion Western Electric/ ERPI linked Mirrophonic to Bell Labs' research pedigree in invention and

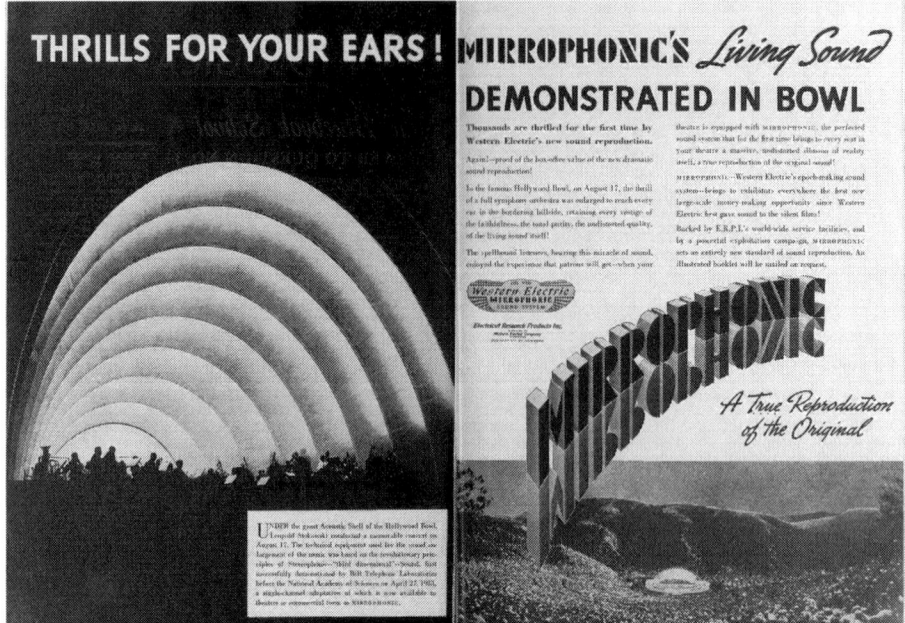

Figure 1 Advertisement for Western Electric/ERPI's 'Mirrophonic' Sound System, *Motion Picture Herald*, 5 September 1936, pp. 73–74 (Image Source: Media History Digital Library)

innovation, loosely tying the Mirrophonic system to Bell Labs' stereophonic experiments, and, in a double-page spread in *Motion Picture Herald* (reproduced in Figure 1), to the Hollywood Bowl demonstration.

The advertising design suggests that ERPI were keen to capitalise on the high-profile event, and their perception that the quality of 'fidelity' was a marketable quality to the motion picture industry. As discussed earlier, 'fidelity' was a key shared value of Bell Labs' technicians, and it was their research design that shaped the Mirrophonic system, and the stereo experiments.

Bell Labs' early stereo experiments emerged from the phonograph industry, and were designed to reproduce and mediate the richness and spatial qualities of the music as heard in a concert-hall setting. This model of representation was oriented to mediate a 'true' reproduction, and was not modelled on the possibilities that multi-channel sound might have to construct the narrative space of a film soundscape, nor to inflect sequences of cinematic action or dialogue.

The meanings of multi-channel sound, and the spectrum of its uses, were further moulded by the ongoing development work within the technical cultures of the SMPE. At the Fall 1937 meeting, one of ERPI's most senior sound experts, Joseph Maxfield, demonstrated stereophonic recording and reproduction for film.[132] Maxfield's demonstration comprised a short film with four different scenes; the accompanying sound had been recorded with two soundtracks and was reproduced through separate channels and via speakers at the left and right of the screen.

Maxfield underlined the potential of the stereophonic system to allow listeners to 'localize the sounds' and 'to correlate the apparent sources of the sound with the

Hollywood Soundscapes

Figure 2 Advertisement for Western Electric's 'Mirrophonic' Sound System, with a strong emphasis on its ability to produce a 'true reflection' of its sound sources, *Weekly Variety*, 26 August 1936, p. 44 (Image Source: Media History Digital Library)

images of the actors supposed to produce them'.[133] Maxfield presented a short film demonstrating sound tied to a point-source on screen, which illustrated Bell's command of stereophonic principles in sound engineering, but he did not advance, or imagine, narrative or stylistic applications for sound film production. Maxfield clearly conceived of this as outside the domain of the research: 'we believe that these possibilities are so well demonstrated that those who are skilled in the arts will see the dramatic possibilities also'.[134]

For stereophonic, and multi-speaker, sound to be adopted outside technical cultures, the invention needed to have an established meaning, or currency, in the wider context of the industry. The new sound systems had to be interpreted and translated into production contexts by sound personnel with production applications, and the pragmatics of production constraints, in mind. In other words, it was necessary to link the inventions to existing usages, practices and contexts of sound film production and style. The novelty that the new sound systems offered was a quality that had to be negotiated and managed to expediently fit the production and exhibition sectors.

It was during 1940 that stereophonic and multi-speaker sound was brought to the wider attention of the film industry. Tracing reactions in the trade press gives a picture of how Bell-ERPI and RCA placed the new formats in front of their industry audience. These two companies worked strategically and competitively to get attention for their devices, and to manage and channel the diverse reactions to the new formats in an attempt to bring the industry to a broad consensus on new systems for sound.

During 1939 and 1940, stereophonic sound was demonstrated at the New York World's Fair. The unifying theme of the fair was 'Building the World of Tomorrow', and ERPI featured their stereophonic sound system in an exhibition of technology titled 'Theatre of Tomorrow' in the AT&T building, which was located in the Communications Zone. With estimated visitor numbers of around 44 million over the two-year period, the New York World's Fair permitted ERPI to give huge exposure to stereophonic sound, directing public attention to new possibilities in sound reproduction. *Variety* reported that ERPI's system 'represents the perfect sound system several years hence', and that the development costs were $200,000, with installation costs of $30,000.[135] *Variety* noted that the 'enormous cost precludes marketing for some time to come', but that the system might be used for roadshowing of live music, such as an opera or concert.[136]

In the spring of 1940 ERPI had begun to elicit dialogue with Hollywood's senior sound experts about stereophonic sound by hosting many of the studios' heads of sound on a week-long trip to the East Coast. The trip included sessions on 'the recent and pending improvements' in equipment, and on 9 April the party attended a high-profile demonstration of stereophonic sound reproduction at New York's Carnegie Hall.[137]

The demonstration of stereophonic sound at Carnegie Hall, and RCA's development of Fantasound and Vitasound as alternative sound systems, caught the attention of *Motion Picture Herald*. The trade headlined themes of change, predicting a 'Sound Revolution' and forecasting competition between the leading manufacturers: 'Telephone Company and RCA in Race with New Sound, with Millions at Stake'.[138] Inside the magazine, a comment piece pronounced: 'After a decade without fundamental changes in sound for motion pictures, the industry is confronted with revolutionary sound devices, perfected by the Bell Telephone Laboratories and the Radio Corporation of America.'[139] But in their more detailed analysis, *Motion Picture Herald*'s opinion was more tempered: it covered the new features of the systems' 'three-dimensional effect' and 'tenfold sound increase' in volume range, whilst also noting the significant implications for changes in production and exhibition. *Motion Picture Herald*'s writer admitted that developments were at an early stage, and quoted ERPI President, T. K. Stevenson, who was careful to stress that change would be 'gradual'.[140]

Motion Picture Herald featured the reaction of senior industry commentator Martin Quigley to the Carnegie Hall demonstration. Quigley affirmed that 'the system appeared to do everything claimed for it. The illusion of a large symphony orchestra, choir or organ was perfectly created' and the system reproduced high volume without distortion.[141] But he questioned the 'entertainment value of sounds over a certain volume', and noted that in Bell's demonstration 'no endeavour was made to relate the demonstration to the motion picture screen', suggesting that 'the stereophonic qualities ... might be almost lost if the method were used in connection with a standard motion picture screen', and that if the new sound found public favour, the industry might trial widescreen pictures again.[142]

Other trades also reported the demonstration as one of possibilities rather than concrete applications; *Film Daily* saw the Carnegie Hall event as spectacular in terms of technology, but it also relayed the opinion of ERPI head, Stevenson, that 'it [was] now for the industry to determine how rapidly it is justified in applying the new technique', underlining the theme of 'gradual change' in sound.[143] Thus, the initial trade reactions to ERPI's unveiling of stereophonic sound might be described as interested, but cautious; the new sound possibilities were not immediately or easily fitted into the existing production practices and constraints of the industry.

In June 1940 ERPI organised a West Coast demonstration designed to capture the attention of Hollywood producers; it took place at the Pantages Movie Theatre, Hollywood, and was sponsored by the Academy. The arrangements committee comprised of Academy President Walter Wanger, Chairman Darryl Zanuck and the following directors of sound at key studios: John Aalberg (RKO), Bernard Brown (Universal), John Livadary (Columbia), Thomas Moulton (Twentieth Century-Fox), Elmer Raguse (Hal Roach Studios), Loren Ryder (Paramount) and Douglas Shearer (MGM).[144] The programme comprised a selection of musical recordings by the

Philadelphia Symphony Orchestra, and was directed by Bell-ERPI's frequent collaborator Leopold Stokowski.

ERPI's Hollywood demonstration elicited a range of reactions in the trade press, craft and technical journals. Most of the trades expressed a broadly positive reaction to the advances in technology presented, but were more measured in their predictions of how quickly changes might be adopted. *Variety* reported: 'Spectators Awed by Stereophonic Sound Demonstration', but just a few days later it ran: 'Pix Not Ready for New Sound, Execs Report'.[145] *Variety* pinpointed the reasons as 'technical and financial', and summarised the industry view that 'the too sudden unveiling of Stereophonic sound may bring ... an interim of confusion without proportionate benefits unless it is carefully handled', a challenge that 'film chieftains' compared to the coming of sound.[146] *Variety* quoted (unnamed) 'one of industry's top Sound Engineers', who, whilst acknowledging the 'superior' quality of ERPI's stereophonic sound to reproduce music, cautioned that when combined with 'the accompaniment of the visual element' it threatened to change an established model of representation, and sound–image relations:

> Effort now is concentrated upon centering audience attention on the middle of the screen, a task that might be made more difficult with the employment of stereophonic sound. When voices emanate from the right or left of the screen, auditory attention will be attracted to the side of the screen, and visual attention naturally will follow ... a revaluation in sound without an attendant change in visual technique merely substitutes a new set of illusions for those we now have and which the public through education accepts. Anything that threatens audience illusion requires the most cautious consideration.[147]

American Cinematographer focused on the quality of the entertainment presented by ERPI, praising the system for its capacity for presenting new volume range, but it noted that ERPI's demo had not trialled stereophonic sound with visuals: 'That show at Pantages the other night was with a blind screen – a lifeless stage ... the audience was interested in the quality of what was heard, only heard. It could see nothing.'[148]

All the major trades reported on the industry's cautious approach to the costs attendant on potential changes in sound systems, but there was some divergence in their judgments of how open the studios were to considering the changes in sound practice that the new technologies would bring. *Film Daily* reported that their sources indicated that 'stereophonic sound recording will get a try in 1940–41 product ... Producers, directors and technicians ... generally appraised stereophonic as a potent tool for expansion ... and plans are already underway to utilize the device.'[149] *Motion Picture Herald* reported that Universal Studios were planning on using 'a stereophonic effect' on musical numbers in their upcoming Deanna Durbin picture *Spring Parade* (Henry Koster, 1940). Universal's Head of Sound, Bernard Brown, was quoted as believing that once the new sound was adopted, it would grow fast, and that initially stereophonic films might be released, like *Fantasia*, on a roadshow basis with special presentation.[150]

Other industry figures identified obstacles with ERPI's system, particularly its requirement for three channels for sound, and for special projection and amplification equipment. John K. Hilliard (Chair of the Academy Research Council's Theatre Sound Standardisation Committee) noted that because the system required additional equipment, 'at best considerable time will elapse before any production could be generally released in this manner ... in special cases productions may be recorded for a very restricted release'.[151] And from his position of authority for advising and approving theatre equipment standards, Hilliard underlined that 'the new development will not make current equipment obsolete'.[152]

Co-operation on new sound was a theme propounded by Nathan Levinson (Head of Sound for Warner Bros.), and quoted by *Motion Picture Herald*:

> No one company would be apt to use the system without other companies doing the same. Through the basic committees, each studio has a minimum of six representatives on the [Research] Council. No single studio would be likely to act on such an important development without taking advantage of this representative cross-section of opinion.[153]

As the foregoing cited sources reveal, ERPI's demonstrations and their ongoing dialogue with studio sound directors following the event at Pantages Theatre in June 1940 functioned to put new forms of sound recording and exhibition centrally on the industry's agenda.[154] The high-profile presentations brought the question of change to the fore and compelled a discussion of stereophonic sound. This discussion fed back into, and was essential to, the ongoing development of new sound formats by the technical community. Before ERPI's demonstrations, 'stereophonic' sound was a term with meaning only within the technical community; putting stereophonic sound in front of the industry realised it as an object, and widened its currency. The conceptualisations of stereophonic sound by studio figures, and by the trades, allowed the research sector to gauge reaction and to pinpoint the qualities that might be most valued in the new systems. Similarly, the public identification and discussion of problems and obstacles to adopting a new system allowed them to redirect and refine research directions, and to shape their public discourses and their commercial interface with the studios and exhibitors to address and resolve the problems accordingly.

FANTASOUND AND VITASOUND: RCA'S NEW SOUND SYSTEMS

Stereophonic and multi-speaker sound were back in the industry's public sphere of discussion later in 1940, prompted this time by RCA's development work on new two sound systems: Fantasound and Vitasound. *Fantasia* was given a roadshow release in November 1940 using the Fantasound system, and *Santa Fe Trail*, utilising the Vitasound system in selected theatres, was released in December of the same year. By reviewing trade and technical publications, it is evident that RCA positioned its innovations differently to its rival. ERPI's demonstrations purposefully featured stereophonic capabilities rather than a concrete application of the device; ERPI's president was widely quoted as saying that applications of stereophonic sound were a matter for producers. In contrast, RCA formed collaborative relationships with two studios – Disney and Warner Bros. – and allowed their two different sound systems to be featured in specific productions.

Considerable anticipation about what Disney and RCA had achieved with Fantasound preceded the release of *Fantasia*; a month before the film's release, the editor of *International Projectionist* wrote: 'the why and wherefors relative to the technical aspects of this production have been agitating both the general and trade press'.[155] Fantasound was a multi-channel and multi-speaker system, and the article detailed the process that lay behind the recording, editing and projection of *Fantasia*. The studio had used special recording arrangements for the programme of music used in the film. The music was performed by the Philadelphia Symphony Orchestra, directed and conducted by Leopold Stokowski; the recording was done at the Philadelphia Academy of Music, using eight separate soundtracks for different sections of the orchestra and a ninth track for the whole orchestra. The soundtracks were edited at Disney's studio in Hollywood, where the multiple tracks were mixed down to three soundtracks and one control track. The control track determined the volume of the loudspeakers, and from which speaker specific parts of the orchestra were heard at particular times during the reproduction.[156] The multi-speaker arrangements for Fantasound were also described and it was acknowledged that these would be effective for big movie theatres with large screens. The editorial added:

> but it wouldn't mean a thing in the smaller theatre having, say, a 15-foot screen, which type of theatre goes to make up 80% of the total number of theatres … [*Fantasia*] is strictly a class, big-house, main-stem (sic) proposition that will have to be shown under roadshow conditions and at high prices.[157]

Reviewing the trades, it is clear that the prevailing discursive themes in discussions and reviews of Fantasound and *Fantasia* concerned the film's spectacle, its complex production (and exhibition), and its unusual mode of featuring image and sound in a series of vignettes. Ahead of the premiere, the *New York Times* covered the 'trailblazing' aspects of the film, but noted, 'there is no connecting story in "Fantasia": its parts are presented on the screen each with its own caprice in Disneyan choreography'.[158] The article also covered the sound recording processes, and the unusual production method, wherein the Disney team 'started with the music and fitted action to the music'.[159] Reviewing *Fantasia*, *Film Daily* declared that 'nothing more impressive has ever graced screen or stage'; the *New York Herald Tribune* called it 'a brave and beautiful work', stating that it 'marks a milestone in the development of a particular branch of the cinema'; and the *New York Times* proclaimed, 'motion picture history was made at the Broadway last night with the premiere of "Fantasia". It boldly reveals the scope of films for imaginative excursion. Thoroughly delightful and exciting its novelty is that one's senses are captivated.'[160] *Motion Picture Herald* suggested that '"screen poetry" perhaps best describes Walt Disney's "Fantasia"', stating that the film 'participates in the essence of beauty in sight and sound', but warning that 'the box office value of "screen poetry" is an unknown quantity'.[161] The reviewer described the Fantasound system as a '"trick effect"' available with the use of the control track, and stated that '"Fantasia" is itself a "trick picture"'.[162]

    Motion Picture Herald's *Better Theatres* supplement, which served the exhibition sector, devoted a lengthy article to discussing '"Fantasia" Sound: Its Processes and Their Portent'.[163] In contrast to some of the more hyperbolic coverage of *Fantasia*'s revolutionary qualities, the article was measured in tone. While it adopted a positive stance about the novel qualities of Fantasound, stating that 'the system brings the sound right out into the audience', the article identified the challenges that the system presented to exhibition practices and to the physical arrangement of speakers in auditoria and projection equipment in the projection room.[164] The power requirements to yield Fantasound's volume range, the space needed to accommodate the apparatus, and the 'complex acoustical work' in locating speakers appropriately so that no seats were in a 'dead' zone (the place where the opposing sound waves from Fantasound's directional reproduction met) were pinpointed as relevant for the exhibition trade. The article concluded by predicting that 'it is of course probable that the system would be somewhat simplified as a result of normal progress'.[165]

From the outset of its development as a prestige project, *Fantasia* had been scheduled for a limited, but highly prestigious roadshow release.[166] As noted above, discourses on *Fantasia*, and the Fantasound process, repeatedly underline its extraordinary, or non-standard, qualities. As a demonstration of the innovation of RCA's sound research engineers, the creativity of the Disney animators and the showmanship of Leopold Stokowski, *Fantasia* was a great success. It seems evident that RCA never anticipated, nor intended, the Fantasound process to move from the realm of 'special exhibition' to become more widespread and standard; certainly, the promotional discourses authored by RCA engineers in selected trades and technical journals position the system as 'special'.[167] This was because RCA was ready to launch an alternative innovation in sound, designed, or 'scaled', to be much closer to the industry's existing production and exhibition practices, and that format was Vitasound.

In the midst of press and public reaction to *Fantasia* and its Fantasound system, Warner Bros. and RCA launched Vitasound. The precise structure of the agreement between the studio and the research company is difficult to discern from available sources, but it is evident that it combined collaborative, commercial and competitive aspects. By analysing the content, the timing and the placement of articles and commentary from Warner Bros. and RCA in the trade press, it is possible to build a speculative picture of how these companies were trying to gauge the climate for change in the industry, and how they modified their innovation strategy accordingly – offering a 'spectacular sound system' in Fantasound, and a simplified version with Vitasound.

It is clear that the initial announcements about Vitasound were generated by Warner Bros., and it appears that the studio were prompted to 'introduce' the new sound format alongside *Fantasia*'s Fantasound, in order to present Vitasound as a comparative system, and thus as a serious alternative. In the press on Vitasound, Warner Bros., via commentary and quoted opinion from Nathan Levinson, reiterated that Vitasound was an expedient innovation, permitting producers and exhibitors to offer novel aspects of sound presentation with minor and affordable modifications to existing apparatus.

On the same day, and page, of its review of *Fantasia*, *Film Daily* announced that Vitasound would be introduced with Warner Bros.' prestige budget Western, *Santa Fe Trail*, starring two of the studio's biggest stars: Olivia de Havilland and Errol Flynn. *Santa Fe Trail* was due to premiere a month hence, in December 1940. Vitasound was described as a 'new control system developed by Warner Bros. in co-operation with RCA engineers', comprising 'a second sound track on release print' that 'regulates the sound control and is said to make possible startling improvements in theaters'.[168]

The costs for adopting Vitasound were estimated as $40 for an attachment to print the control track and around $1,500 for a theatre for additional amplifiers and speakers; the article concluded: 'the new method is advantageous in that it requires no additional equipment or changes in technique in the shooting of pictures'.[169]

Motion Picture Herald featured Fantasound and Vitasound alongside each other, and revealed something of Warner Bros.' appetite for press coverage for Vitasound:

> A few hours before the Broadway press gathered in New York ... for its first hearing of 'Fantasound,' Warner Brothers in Hollywood announced it had 'Vitasound' – described by Warners as 'a completely faithful reproduction of original sound without violent and expensive change in theatre and studio equipment.'[170]

The article reported that Warner Bros. were installing Vitasound reproduction equipment in their New York Strand theatre, and at their Hollywood theatre in Downtown Los Angeles; both venues were key locations for featuring the studio's prestige and special presentations, and *Motion Picture Herald* reported that 'other key Warner houses are to be equipped subsequently'.[171]

In the week following *Fantasia*'s premiere, Levinson organised a press demonstration of Vitasound at Warner Bros. The Vitasound system was used to present a selection of shorts and sequences, each offering a different showcase for the system's capabilities. These included: a musical short featuring jazz trumpeter Henry Busse; 'the gusher sequence' from *Flowing Gold* (Alfred E. Green, 1940), an adventure film set in the oilfields; a battle sequence from *The Fighting 69th* (William Keighley, 1940); a sequence from *Four Wives* (Michael Curtiz, 1939), a drama centred on the musical Lemp family; 'the earthquake sequence' from *The Sisters* (Anatole Litvak, 1938), a historical drama set during the 1906 San Francisco earthquake; a sequence of Beethoven's 'Egmont Overture' from *Four Mothers* (William Keighley, 1941), a sequel to *Four Wives*; and a patriotic short, *Service with the Colors* (B. Reeves Eason, 1940).[172]

Following the press preview, Warner Bros.-RCA secured an enthusiastic headline in *Variety* – 'WB-RCA Vitasound Termed Revolutionary' – but despite the animated tone at the head of the article that stated Vitasound had 'the power to make the screen a living breathing thing', the substantial point of the article was that Warner Bros., via Nathan Levinson, had been able to communicate the expedience of the design:

> While Vitasound may lack some of the refinements of the Disney-RCA Fantasound and the ERPI Stereophonic systems which are not yet economically within the reach of either producers or exhibs, it will stand comparison with its more costly running mates on many angles. It will, at least, provide something startlingly new and novel in pictures for which theatre operators have been pleading.[173]

Variety reported the effectiveness of the Vitasound system at the demonstration, and particular mention was given to the disaster sequence from *The Sisters*:

> with the control track attached, [it] gave the audience the impression that the projection room was actually falling upon them, so close and real were the sounds of crashing timbers and the screams of the dying and maimed emanating from the screen.[174]

The article also reported that 'Vitasound is now being readied for general usage throughout the picture realm', and that the Academy Research Council was setting up standards so that it could be made available to other studios.[175] There was further coverage, and similar comparisons made, in two articles in the *New York Times* in November and December of 1940.[176]

Warner Bros. widely publicised their intention to refit their prestige movie theatres with Vitasound equipment, and they revealed plans to refit all Warner houses as soon as equipment was available.[177] In adopting this public position, Warner Bros. offered an overt display of confidence in the new format they (and RCA) wished to commercialise, but their position was also, perhaps, an attempt to tip the balance of the industry towards taking a concrete step in modifying sound in exhibition. Warner Bros.-RCA capitalised on the fact that a range of formats had been demonstrated during the preceding months, and their overall strategy was to position Vitasound as the safe and pragmatic option for change. In trade articles on Vitasound, Levinson is repeatedly quoted as addressing the practical steps needed to get wide adoption of the innovation: seeking approval for standardisation by the Academy, the 'fit' of Vitasound with existing equipment (and hence its resistance to obsolescence) and the modest conversion costs for exhibitors. This stance prioritised an innovation fitted to context and it contrasts with the 'ideal' system presented by Bell-ERPI and the complex showmanship of Fantasound.

So, while *Variety* might have initially greeted Vitasound as 'revolutionary', other trades were more circumspect. Reviewing Vitasound in December 1940, *American Cinematographer* astutely described it as 'practicable perfection', and noted its expedient qualities,[178] it was Fantasound that it championed as 'really revolutionary'.[179] *American Cinematographer* asserted that '"Fantasound" succeeds in taking music and sound out of its customary accessory or incidental role in the theatre, and elevates it to the position of an important tool in the hands of the dramatist'.[180] The journal noted that the Fantasound system was 'at present limited to "Fantasia"', but predicted that 'it is expected nevertheless to form the basis for further research and development in the realm of sound on film, from which eventually will come new sound equipment which the average theatre can afford to install.'[181]

Terry Ramsaye, writing in *Motion Picture Herald* in early December 1940, identified a certain momentum for change prompted by the box-office success of *Fantasia*:

> To the motion picture industry and its showmen the main significance is that from the appearances of the initial run in New York the public is taking to 'Fantasia' in a big way. That, to be sure, also bears on the fact that, whether they admit it or not, the 'electricals' are not unmindful that this 'Fantasia' project is a sort of pressure, for some future day maybe, toward re-equipment of the screen theatre. There's gold in that whisper. And there is more than a nod at that aspect in the more recent announcement from Warner Brothers and Major Nathan Levinson of 'Vitasound'.[182]

It is clear that by early December 1940, the pressure for change in sound had been identified more widely. For the second time that year, *Motion Picture Herald* predicted 'New Sound Coming', but while their June coverage of ERPI's stereophonic system had been framed in terms of the potentially dramatic, and costly, changes to the industry,

Hollywood Soundscapes

by December they were reporting a much more widespread interest in change from the major studios. They revealed that six companies were developing new sound systems, designed 'so that speech and music in all theatres can be released from behind the screen and come from the whole stage or even from other parts of the theatre, to create more perfect illusions of reality'.[183] They listed the companies as: ERPI, RCA, Warner Bros., Paramount, MGM and Universal; they noted that Paramount, MGM and Universal were all working on systems with two soundtracks and a control track, systems that gave a 'stereophonic effect' by combining aspects of the Fantasound and Vitasound systems.[184]

In the same issue of the trade, *Motion Picture Herald's Better Theatres* section covered the technical aspects of Fantasound and Vitasound from the standpoint of exhibitors, and there was a confidence in the trade's prediction that 'the motion picture now appears to be about ready to take another long and resolute stride ahead as a medium of entertainment.'[185] Fantasound was described as 'a bit too specialized for consideration in the light of general industrial purposes', but Vitasound was seen as 'definitely ... representative of the current aim to give the motion picture more flexible, more dramatically convincing sound', and the trade underlined that exhibitors could more easily grasp the applications of a system like Vitasound.[186] The article clearly delineated Vitasound from stereophonic sound, and in this distinction it is evident that the new sound systems were conceived as offering variations on the 'standard' classical Hollywood soundscape and as eliciting different forms of listening. *Motion Picture Herald* described Vitasound's key features as follows:

this system cannot produce a stereophonic effect. It incorporates the advantages of increased volume range, freed from previous limitations of on-film recording. It spreads the source of sound across the whole proscenium opening, or narrows it to the center of the screen, as required, all by means of automatic control. ... The sound acquires a very marked increase in depth and 'presence.' The side speakers can be used to produce a background of off-screen sound, and to some extent to tie in the audible source of sound with the pictorial source in the action on the screen.[187]

The article also argued that any new system should be compatible with existing standards and equipment.

By early December 1940 there were signs that changes in sound exhibition had become realised as distinctly possible, and even imminent, in the minds of exhibitors. *International Projectionist's*

Figure 3 Advertisement for RCA Panoramic Sound, *International Projectionist*, May 1941, p. 3 (Image Source: Media History Digital Library)

'Monthly Chat' column reported it had fielded a lot of questions from its readers, projectionists and exhibitors, who were anxious about change, and the journal called for standards to be defined for control-track systems in order to stabilise the choice of the sound systems on offer.

By the turn of the year, from 1940 to 1941, other trade press were widely predicting a trend in installations of new sound equipment. *Motion Picture Herald* announced that 'The three-horn systems, control-track type of sound is to be made available soon to all theatres', and reported that the equipment manufacturers were ready to begin production as soon as standards were issued by the Academy.[188] However, by the time that *Santa Fe Trail* was on release, RCA had dropped references to 'Vitasound' entirely, and adopted instead the term 'Panoramic Sound' to describe their expedient sound system (see Figure 3).[189] Advertisements and exploitation for *Santa Fe Trail* once it was on release described its sound as 'Panoramic'.[190] And coverage of the Panoramic system in technical and trade press stated that 'RCA Panoramic Sound principles have been applied experimentally by Warner Bros. in "The Santa Fe Trail" now being released'.[191] The change in the branding of the system is intriguing, but from the archival sources that are available it is difficult to trace the background decisions informing it. Perhaps RCA moved away from 'Vitasound' because of the similarity to the term 'Vitaphone', and the association of these formats with Warner Bros.' innovations, whereas 'Panoramic Sound' might be free from a link to that particular studio. Or perhaps 'Panoramic Sound' was felt to more clearly communicate the features of the multi-speaker format. Whatever the ultimate explanation, this rebranding in the midst of the launch of the new format demonstrates a modification in how its representation was shaped to a wider public. RCA began to position 'Panoramic Sound' as the expedient adaptation of Fantasound. RCA's Edward Cahill, Manager of the Photophone Division, extolled the values of Panoramic Sound in exactly the same terms previously used to describe Vitasound. RCA also saw an opportunity to sell an innovation to small exhibition houses, suggesting that by adopting Panoramic Sound they would gain a 'considerable degree of the realism of RCA Fantasound' but at 'a small fraction of the cost'.[192] Cahill announced that RCA were awaiting the issue of Academy standards, after which equipment for their Panoramic Sound system would be placed on the market.[193]

In early 1941, just months before the bombing of Pearl Harbour brought the USA into World War II and shifted industries onto a wartime economy, several commentators expressed confidence about progress in improving the exhibition sector with new equipment. *Film Daily Equipment News* headlined '41 Film Equipment Outlook Brighter', and reported, 'Executives generally predict further progress despite National Defence Progam demands; exhibitors cautioned to place their equipment orders at once.'[194] Walter E. Green, President of the National Theater Supply Co., was quoted as saying, 'In 1941, more and more theatre owners will improve their theaters where their patrons can "see and hear the difference".'[195] Lead executives from both ERPI and RCA gave optimistic forecasts for the year ahead. T. K. Stevenson (President of ERPI) predicted that '1941 promises still further improvement. Especially this is true in the field of sound recording and reproduction,' and he asserted that stereophonic sound 'is rapidly making a niche for itself as a machine tool in the service of dramatic expression'.[196] Edward Cahill (RCA) announced that sales of RCA Photophone reproduction equipment had increased in late 1940, because 'thousands of exhibitors' understood the business sense of 'modernizing their houses'.[197] *Showmen's Trade Review* announced that:

> Plans for the complete revolution of theatre sound equipment, somewhat along the lines of the 'Fantasia' sound installation ... are rapidly maturing in Hollywood. Recording will be different, and will enable every theatre properly equipped to reproduce to a greater or less degree the new realism and special effects used in 'Fantasia'.[198]

But the trade predicted that the system finally adopted would be the one that was most expedient.[199] The same issue of *Showmen's Trade Review* also reported RCA Photophone's upswing in business in late 1940, and the magazine claimed an announcement on standards was expected 'in the near future'.[200] It reported that equipment manufacturers, such as the International Projector Corporation (makers of Simplex projectors) and RCA manufacturing, were ready to adapt equipment to the control-track type system once standards were issued. The Motiograph company, licensed by ERPI for the manufacture of Western Electric equipment, also reassured exhibitors that they were preparing to provide adaptations for control-track sound for the Western Electric 'Mirrophonic' system.[201]

In January 1941 the trades were full of summaries of the previous year's activities, and these constitute statements of the perceived industry status quo on sound. *Variety*'s Anniversary edition reviewed technical advances in 1940, featuring 'improved sound' as the 'highlight' of Hollywood's developments:

> The sound engineers, in both the research laboratories and studios, spotlighted the technical advancement division of the industry for 1940. They broke out with so-called multi-channel sound recording and reproduction apparatus that looms as the next major step in improvement of motion pictures for greater public reaction and, it is hoped, an upsurge in theatre grosses – especially in the larger houses.[202]

Variety coverage of the three systems in contention (ERPI's system, Fantasound and Vitasound) formed a 'narrative' of the industry's reception of the innovations. *Variety* characterised Bell-ERPI's Carnegie Hall event as demonstrating superior recording and reproduction, but that 'this type of recording was too expensive a proposition for the industry to tackle', particularly as its foreign markets were constricted by the conflict in Europe. 'Studios ignored the multi-channel method', *Variety* wrote, until the reception of *Fantasia* 'jogged the major companies into activity to see what could be done with adapting the stereophonic type of recording and reproduction'.[203] *Variety* covered Warner Bros.' work on Vitasound, calling it 'an inexpensive adoption of the idea', and predicted:

> At the turn of the year, indications point to some intensive work by sound engineers of all major studios to adapt the stereophonic system in some way for general use – with a good chance that a partial utilization of that method will be devised and used generally by nearly all major plants.[204]

As this chapter has demonstrated, between 1936 and 1941 forms of 'new sound' for Hollywood were widely debated. The term 'stereophonic' emerged out of the technical cultures of engineers and became more familiar to trade and industry press, and the demonstrations of Fantasound and Vitasound necessitated explanation in the public sphere of precisely how new sound production and exhibition might be achieved, as well as pinpointing the pragmatic and economic issues involved in adoption. Surveying the trade press has allowed me to identify discursive trends, and it is evident that as interest in the new sound systems became more widespread, that qualities of expedience were reiterated alongside qualities of novelty with increasing regularity. So how did this evident momentum for change and the increasing competition in formats become stabilised? Of course, the most obvious and intractable factor arresting the adoption of 'new sound' was the shift of American industry to the wartime economy. This shift affected the research sector, as manufacturing capacity was diverted to the war effort, and many motion picture technicians took up roles in defence research programmes.[205]

However, the war was not the only factor slowing the adoption of new sound systems across the industry. The discursive themes of the trades, synthesised above, show that there was a readiness for change, but that authoritative advice was being sought on what format of control-track sound should be adopted. The trades were seeking a 'closure' on the form of the new technology. As Pinch and Bijker observe, 'closing' the form of a new technology defines its shape and if this final form is successfully diffused, alternative versions have no further currency.[206]

It is evident that technical cultures had observed and noted reactions to 'new sound' in the trades, and wider industry. With expectations that an Academy Research Council decision on standards for a control-track system was imminent, RCA attempted bring the industry to consensus on the suitability of their control-track format. The spring 1941 Convention of the SMPE provided a forum where all the new sound systems were presented and discussed. Bell-ERPI and RCA presented their developments in separate sessions. The technical differences between the new sound systems were outlined by H. I. Reiskind (of RCA Manufacturing). Reiskind had been involved in the development work for RCA's control-track systems, including Vitasound, and he was named on an RCA patent for control-track apparatus.[207] He made a broad distinction between the two types of systems that had emerged: a 'stereophonic method' using two or three channels (illustrated by the Bell-ERPI system, and by Fantasound), and a simpler single-channel method (illustrated by Vitasound, and by RCA's 'Panoramic Sound'). The stereophonic method, he noted, aims 'to produce motion of the sound source' and 'allow the sound to follow the picture'; the Vitasound/Panoramic model does not aim for point-source sound but to 'broaden' sound 'beyond the screen area by the use of multipled groups of loudspeakers'.[208]

Reiskind argued strongly for the benefits of the Vitasound/Panoramic model. While it did not offer stereophonic reproduction, he recommended it because it proffered solutions to more modest, but widely shared, entertainment problems. He argued that Vitasound/Panoramic sound offered the increased volume range that producers sought, especially in rendering 'dramatic' sound, such as sound effects in action, disaster or thrilling sequences, which, Reiskind argued, would be 'augmented', intensified or 'reinforced' by the addition of extra volume coming from additional speakers at the side of the screen. Reiskind wrote, 'This arrangement would provide a spatial effect or "acoustic spread" for the music and effects reproduction and still maintain the intelligibility and "presence" of the dialog.'[209]

The Vitasound/Panoramic model added extra speakers outside the screen area. This can be seen in the outline technical drawing in Figure 6, and an indication of how the speakers might be arranged is shown in the advertisement for RCA Panoramic sound (Figure 3), showing a central speaker and two extra speakers to the left and right of the screen area.

The extra speakers in the Vitasound system were governed by a control track of varying frequency printed in the sprocket hole area of the release print. The control track was printed fourteen frames ahead of the sound that it amplified on the soundtrack (Figure 4). The addition of a photocell to a standard projector permitted the control track to be scanned and, as the frequency varied, to 'switch on' and control the circuits and amplification levels for the extra speakers.[210]

Reiskind saw the applications of the RCA Vitasound/ Panoramic system as much more oriented to delivering spectacular sound, with dramatic values, than to fidelity in reproduction (the quality reiterated by Bell-ERPI technicians for their stereophonic system). This difference in orientation is, therefore, indicative of a distinction in the models of representation held by the technicians: entertainment, or 'story values' as distinct from 'fidelity' values. The SMPE

Fig. 1. Composite print with sprocket-hole control-track.

Figure 4 Example of Vitasound control track on film release print. The control track is seen running through the sprocket holes on the left; as the control track narrows in width, the gain (power) to the added amplifiers increases, and consequently the sound volume does too). From N. Levinson and L.T. Goldsmith, 'Vitasound', *JSMPE*, August 1941, p. 148 (Image Source: Media History Digital Library)

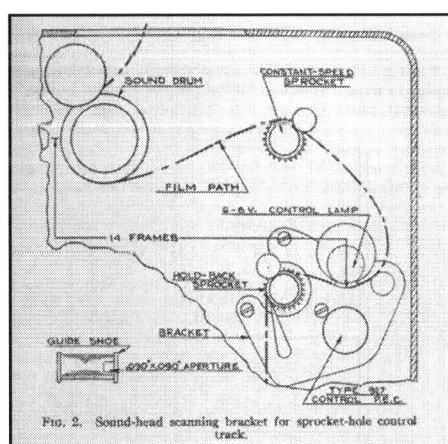

Fig. 2. Sound-head scanning bracket for sprocket-hole control track.

Figure 5 Equipment for use of control track in Vitasound system. From N. Levinson and L.T. Goldsmith, 'Vitasound', *JSMPE*, August 1941, p. 149 (Image Source: Media History Digital Library)

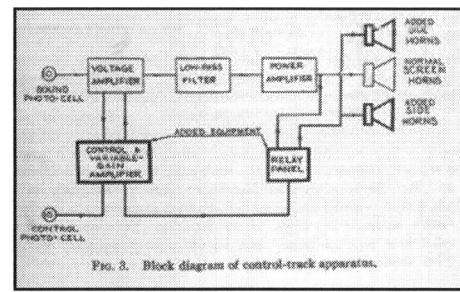

Fig. 3. Block diagram of control-track apparatus.

Figure 6 Diagram showing arrangement of control-track equipment and added speakers for Vitasound system. The three-speaker arrangement for Vitasound is similar to RCA's advert for the 'Panoramic Sound' system they were marketing in May 1941). From N. Levinson and L.T. Goldsmith, 'Vitasound', *JSMPE*, August 1941, p. 149 (Image Source: Media History Digital Library)

conference papers delivered by the RCA-Warner Bros. group (Reiskind, Levinson and Goldsmith) were strongly focused upon how a modest innovation in technology could meet production problems, enhancing the mood of genres, or sequences suited to spectacular presentation, but retaining overall familiarity in presentation for audiences.

Reiskind offered key and stringent principles that he believed the industry should use to evaluate the range of multi-channel and multi-speaker systems in the field, and these might be summarised as: contribution to drama, cost, fit to production and exhibition standards, and interchangeability.[211] Reiskind reiterated the choice on control-track systems that faced the industry:

> The various methods being tried out by the industry all have merit and the problem facing us is that of picking the method that offers the best engineering and commercial compromise. It is essential that we remember that the scheme adopted must not be very expensive, must be relatively simple to operate and maintain, and must not require special prints which can be played only on the new equipment. It seems to me that the single-sound track scheme using the sprocket-hole control-track that I discussed in my paper and which was described in detail by Messrs. Levinson and Goldsmith, offers the best compromise.[212]

Articulating these principles within the forum of the SMPE was, of course, strategic, and Reiskind's paper was less an objective review of the new sound systems than a rhetorical statement on the field with a view to closing the proliferation of experiments in sound with an RCA system, a system designed with expedience rather than an ideal at its centre.

However, despite Reiskind's strategic pitch, and the expedient compromise offered by Vitasound (and the 'Panoramic Sound' system that RCA were advertising in May 1941, illustrated in Figure 3), the 'closure' that might have modified Hollywood's soundscape and diversified sound reproduction was forestalled.

As noted above, this was partly because the defence agenda took over commitments of the research companies and their technicians, but even before this agenda was fully in place there were signs that, despite the trades' perception that an Academy ruling on standards was imminent, to make such a ruling could have been construed as a commercial decision. This would have been counter to the Academy's commitment to co-operative and cross-industry programmes, as defined in early statements by the Technical Bureau cited at the beginning of this chapter. In July 1941, *Showmen's Trade Review* perceptively commented on the inertia:

> Hollywood studios can't make up their collective mind as to what precise 'standardization' all will adopt for making use of the many new sound developments along 'third-dimensional' lines. The result is that many different systems of recording and reproducing so-called 'controlled track' [*sic*] sound are reposing – mostly in blue-print form – in pigeon holes at laboratories and work shops of projector and sound equipment manufacturing plants … The technical men, it is believed, could make their decision rather promptly, but it is the inter-studio indecision which holds up the parade to an elaborated type of sound for general release and presentation … According to reports, each of the studios has its own idea of which one of several methods of recording it likes best. Most of them are standing pat on their own

specifications, with the result that no recording of reproducing equipment that even a wizard could dream up could possibly be made.[213]

CONCLUSION

The case studies in technological change examined in this chapter illustrate that the 'post-transitional' period was one in which sound technicians both 'inside', and allied to, the Hollywood studios were networked in a technical culture, and were actively engaged in ongoing innovation in sound technologies. The scale and level at which changes were adopted by the wider industry were not only dependent on the merits of specific technologies, but on the complex and shifting dynamic equilibrium between standards and innovations, co-operation and commercial interest that formed the constraints on technological change in the Hollywood studio era. It would not be until industrial and institutional organisational structures changed, and the shift away from vertical integration put the studios on a more competitive footing in terms of exhibition, that Hollywood trialled 'new sound' again in the form of stereophonic sound in the 1950s. The work in technological innovation mapped in this chapter was just one of the spheres of activity for Hollywood sound technicians in the post-transitional era. Alongside technological change, sound technicians were establishing and refining the aesthetic conventions and stylistic practices for 'good sound', sound that engaged audiences in dramatic soundscapes and integrated sound as a key part of a film's story values. The evolution of the aesthetic role for sound technicians in the post-transitional era forms the focus of the next chapter.

3

'Ear Appeal': The 'Story Values' of the Classical Hollywood Sound Film

The introduction of sound meant that an entirely new cinema element must now be considered and dealt with – the *audible* effect of the film. In other words, where the writer formerly had to consider merely one element, the *visible* effect in the preparation of his script, he must now contend with two elements, and appeal to the *ear* as well as to the *eye*.

Tamar Lane, *The New Technique of Screenwriting* (1937)

This new medium of expression called for new techniques in writing, acting, photography, set design, stage construction, laboratory processing, and all the many phases of motion picture production. A new science, the science of the transmission and recording engineer, had wrought a change in an art and only by the complete and proper welding of this science and art could the motion picture realize its full capabilities.

George Groves, 'The Soundman', *Journal of the Society of Motion Picture Engineers* March 1947: 220.

INTRODUCTION: 'EAR APPEAL'

From the early 1930s, as the sound film became established as the major strand of the studios' production roster, the concept of 'ear appeal', one iteration of which is outlined by Tamar Lane in the quotation above, began to gain a currency in the film trade press. The term was a commonplace in the radio trades, connoting the 'showmanship' of compelling radio programming, but the application of the term widened to cinema as the trade reviewers began to discern the entertainment values of sound film. *Motion Picture News* observed that 'sound pictures' were making 'very considerable efforts to replace eye appeal with ear appeal'.[1] As Donald Crafton has illustrated, in the first seasons of Hollywood sound production audio elements were often strongly 'flaunt[ed]' or 'foregrounded'.[2] As the sound films found audiences, and sound elements were more fully narratively integrated and 'modulated', 'ear appeal' became expressed as a positive feature, connoting the strong entertainment values that sound and music might bring to the audience's experience. For example: Warner Bros.' *Flirtation Walk* (Frank Borzage, 1934), a musical featuring Ruby Keeler and Dick Powell, was described as 'run[ning] the gamut of eye and ear entertainment';[3] according to *Screenland*, Republic's *Follow Your Heart* (Aubrey Scotto, 1936) had 'plenty of eye and ear appeal';[4] and MGM ran adverts for *Broadway Serenade* (Robert Z. Leonard, 1939) promising that the film offered 'heart appeal, eye appeal and ear appeal'.[5] All of these examples are film musicals, but 'ear appeal' was not exclusive to the musical genre; commentators from Hollywood's crafts (such as screenwriting advisor Tamar Lane, quoted above) thought of 'ear appeal' as an essential consideration for screenwriters of the sound film.

This chapter will explore sound style in the Hollywood sound film. The focus is not a delineation or catalogue of sound film stylistic devices, rather it traces the processes and contexts that framed the emergence of sonic style. Recent studies, such as Patrick Keating's work on Hollywood cinematographers and Scott Higgins' research on Technicolor, have revealed the importance of contextual factors in shaping film style, establishing that technological change, industry agendas and the agency of technical crafts all mould film style within a specific period.[6] As indicated by George Groves, in the quotation above, a broad set of principles were developed by Hollywood's sound technicians for deploying sound to tell stories in different genres, moods and with diverse effects. These principles were formed in collaboration and interaction with other crafts, such as screenwriters, editors and cinematographers. In the period of Hollywood's transition to sound, these collaborations were not always harmonious, but with co-operative institutional programmes, such as the Academy Schools of Sound, and improvements in sound technologies discussed in Chapter 2, by 1930–1931 the production regimes of the sound film became less constrained.

The broad principles of storytelling with sound were, of course, integrated with the overall narrative needs of individual film productions, as well as being interlocked with other craft conventions. The principles formed by sound technicians emerged from the group work of Hollywood's production regimes. While the expertise of individual crafts were important to studio era films - at any particular moment one aspect or another might be highlighted within the larger film's story flow – most essential to the overall quality of Hollywood's product was the extent to which crafts and technicians recognised 'shared problems and linked solutions'.[7] In this sense, style can be understood as the meeting point between narrative needs, and the options or 'alternatives' that particular crafts were able to deploy to fulfil these needs.[8] In what follows I demonstrate how sound technicians, representing Hollywood's new craft, shared problems with other crafts, and developed and deployed a range of sound techniques and devices that came to underpin an array of 'flexible' conventions for storytelling with sound.

In his analysis of the craft of lighting, Keating productively develops the notion of 'multifunctional conventions'. He analyses how cinematographers evolved these conventions, which allowed them to deploy lighting devices that might serve several purposes simultaneously.[9] The sound craft also developed principles, or conventions, that served different functions, but there were notable differences between the craft of lighting and that of sound. As Keating outlines, cinematographers had an established tradition of techniques to call upon, whereas the sound craftsmen were trialling conventions newly developed in the transition to sound, and indeed were still developing and refining them during the 1930s. The established status of cinematographers gave them a widely accepted place within production regimes; while these changed for all production crafts with the shift to sound production, Hollywood's sound technicians were the most newly integrated craft in production. They gradually learned to be more responsive to bringing sound to production and post-production in ways that were 'flexible', and 'interlocking' with other crafts. The concepts of 'flexible' conventions and of 'interlocking' practices arise in technicians' discourses, discourses that I discuss more fully later in the chapter.[10] Understanding sound conventions as flexible allows us to comprehend how sound was calibrated with other crafts – that it was necessarily collaborative and responsive – and to recognise the practices underpinning classical Hollywood sound style as dynamic.

The principles held by the sound craft were that film sound functioned to narrate (through dialogue and sound effects); to situate (through setting evoked by ambient or background sound); to locate (through the evocation of space, or point-of-audition sound); and to characterise the agents of the film. These four broad principles defined how sound contributed to establishing the diegesis, its scape and scope. Alongside these four establishing functions were the story qualities that sound might contribute to: that of the temporal (the contribution of sound to the beat, pace and rhythm of narration); of subjectivity (the placement of sound in relation to character); of modality (the contribution of sound to the creation of mood, and in marking degrees or distance of narration); and of transitional sound (sound used to transition across temporal or spatial dissolves and particularly used in montage). The chapter explores these principles of sound craft by analysing a range of film examples from different genres, studios and moments during the 1930s and 1940s.

ESTABLISHING FILM SOUND'S 'STORY VALUES'

The relationship between the technical craft of sound and story shifted during the studio period, partly through the gradual integration of the sound craft into production regimes, but also through the development of an aesthetic discourse by Hollywood's sound men. The following examples of this aesthetic discourse serve to illustrate broad perspectives at different points in the period.

In 1931 Carl Dreher, at that point serving as RKO's Director of Sound and participant lecturer at the Academy's Schools of Sound, speculated on the parameters of the sound technician's role, and the extent to which sound men might engage with aesthetic concerns:

> opinions vary [on] the desirability of the sound man understanding something of story values, the technique of acting, and other elements of production somewhat remote from the transmission units and dynes per square centimetre which are naturally his first concern.[11]

Dreher maintained that it was 'essential' that senior sound technicians, such as the head of the Sound Department understood 'literary and dramatic aspects of picture making' in order to 'create the devices necessary to produce the desired emotional effect', and reflected that these qualities might be valuable lower down the production hierarchy, for roles like sound mixer, provided the sound man did not become 'a script meddler'.[12]

Writing just three years later, Harold Lewis, a sound recordist at Paramount, argued that Hollywood's sound technicians needed a nuanced and flexible understanding of how sound could be deployed to 'most fully benefit each scene and sequence'.[13] Lewis was a sound recordist on Paramount's *A Farewell to Arms* (Frank Borzage, 1932), a film which won an Academy Award for Best Sound Recording. Sound style in *A Farewell to Arms* is discussed in more detail later in the chapter. Lewis demonstrates subtle and developed thinking about how to vary techniques appropriate to different genres, and he displays insights into how sound might be used to create different moods and to channel audience reaction.

By 1938 Wesley C. Miller, of MGM Studios, described the sound man as 'the brain of the microphone', and wrote with confidence that the sound man understood the entertainment values of the motion picture:

> His real creative work involves complete understanding of the overall showmanship problem and of the interlocking requirements of the several crafts. ... the sound man's training has usually been such that he is able to assimilate the basic knowledge of the other fields and can meet them on their own ground.[14]

In 1947 George Groves, of Warner Bros., reviewed the first twenty years of sound, and noted a distinct change in the role and capacity of the sound technician. He described the 'evolution of the sound engineer from a man of mathematics, transmission circuits, recording equipment, and gadgets, with a foreign language of decibels and gammas, to the artist in whose hands rests the full dramatic impact which sound can impart to the motion picture of today'.[15] By 1948 Wesley Miller and G. R. Crane conceived of the re-recording mixer, undertaking the final re-recording on a film before release printing, as 'a controlling and creative force' upon whom all other personnel were dependent.[16]

These perspectives speak of the gradual evolution of the role of sound technicians, and their recognition of how their roles were integrated with other crafts in realising the sound film's 'story values'. In the early to mid-1930s, screenwriters, cinematographers and editors all expounded on the expressive possibilities that the sound film offered from their specific craft position. This period of conceptualisation, contestation and theorisation of sound film form by Hollywood's creative crafts can be traced through writings in a range of primary sources. In technical and professional journals, at Academy branch meetings and in advisory manuals, commentators debated, described and worked to conceptualise and define the sound film as, in the words of one commentator, 'the new cinema form'.[17]

The early sound period was one in which production regimes became more stringently organised, and production and post-production roles became more specialised.[18] Contemporaneous sources outlining the workflow of sound film production repeatedly emphasised that the sound film screenplay was a key document, both for the pragmatic planning of production and resources, and as the starting point for the execution of the creative project that the film comprised.

Screenwriting manuals advised on methods to integrate sound and story, and explored the new expressive possibilities that sound offered to the screenwriter. The manuals also outlined methods by which screenwriters could overcome some of the perceived problems with early sound film style. Many early sound films were criticised for being too static, because of the constraints of early sound technologies; too stagey, an effect of producers turning to the stage to find content for the new sound film; and too 'draggy', slowed by the necessity of presenting narrative through dialogue.[19] The objective was for the sound film to regain the story 'flow', pace and tempo of the late silent period.[20]

The relationship between tempo and sound in the early sound period has been discussed by a number of critics. Nancy Wood argues that '[i]t was as if the introduction of sound had caused an immediate "densening" or "thickening" of the more permeable spatio-temporal field of the silent film, thereby requiring more concrete and exacting definitions of the spatial and temporal dimensions,'[21] and David Bordwell suggests:

> Talking pictures created a concrete and inflexible tempo for the Hollywood film. Duration in a silent picture, even one accompanied by music, has a more abstract quality: crosscutting, inter-titles, ellipses, and even the varying rates of shooting and projection create a malleable and plastic duration. What one writer called 'the actual time-elapsed speed' of the talkie was more fixed, rooted in the pace of recorded speech.[22]

Recent work by Lea Jacobs has provided a rich and important account of the centrality of tempo in early sound film style and practices.[23] She traces the developments of techniques in the treatment of dialogue and music, and the ways in which these sound elements were organised and managed to preserve temporality and flow. I draw upon some of the same sources and resources as Jacobs' work, but my focus is oriented more towards sound craft with sound effects, and on the development of 'communities of knowledge' constituted by the shared practices and conventions of Hollywood's sound technicians.[24]

In their 1930 screenwriting manual, William Pitkin and William Marston highlighted the importance of the structure of the sound film screenplay. They emphasised the need to organise the screenplay in distinct sequences, comprising of related scenes in which the action had continuity.[25] They argued that a 'velocity' could be gained by sequences functioning as story units, each possessing internal rhythm which would contribute to an overall 'total picture tempo'.[26]

Other sources on the screenplay in the early sound period also advocated using sequences to structure screenplay.[27] Writing in 1937, Tamar Lane recommended 'the brief, speedy sequence', because it 'gives the film more movement, more sweep, and the illusion of more action'.[28] Lane also observed strong techniques for maintaining story interest within and across sequences:

> Today many of the better scenarists are 'ringing down,' so to speak, each episode with a strong 'curtain' or dramatic punch. Every sequence is treated with the theory that it is a new 'act' or phase of the story. It is built on a slowly rising interest in tempo and drama, then brought to a climax of some kind, and a quick fade-out or 'curtain' to be followed by other sequences in the same fashion.[29]

It is clear that structuring the screenplay in sequences allowed screenwriters to control the emotional dynamics of the drama, the temporality of the narration and the duration of events. In serving these functions, the sequence came to be a key unit of narrative. It also became a unit with a material basis in production regimes. The circulation of the script to all craft departments before shooting allowed planning for the specific requirements to achieve the story values of a sequence. In post-production, refining the sequence became a goal in the editorial stages for image, dialogue, sound effects and music. Editors of image and sound commonly worked on a sequence at a time, their practices were underpinned by shared conventions to structure the related events within a sequence and to imbue it with the appropriate rhythms and tempo.[30]

'AS PLASTIC AS LANGUAGE': SOUND EFFECTS IN THE SOUND FILM SCREENPLAY

Screenwriting advisors identified the treatment of dialogue as a priority for screenwriters for the early sound film, but they also considered how other sound elements could realise 'story values'. The potential functions, and the proper handling, of sound effects in the sound film screenplay were given attention. Pitkin and Marston wrote: 'the addition of sound to the motion picture both helps and complicates the story writer's problem. For sound is almost as plastic as language, and no one has yet sufficiently handled its art to recognize its infinite possibilities.'[31] For them, the crime film *Alibi* (Roland West, 1929) exemplified effective uses of sound to match the mood of the melodrama, they noted that 'the sound of prisoners marching in lockstep set the tone for the whole story'.[32] They also suggested how sonic contrasts, particularly silence, might be used: '[t]he most casual observer of talking pictures must have been increasingly impressed by this new quality of silence. Its use by contrast can achieve almost any desired effect, from the most terrific suspense to a poignant pathos. But silence, like sound, must be built into your story.'[33]

Tamar Lane encouraged screenwriters to 'be ever alert to the possibilities and enhancement values of sound' and considered sound effects as a key resource to suggest setting and mood; her evocative catalogue of effects is worth quoting at length:

> If concentrated upon, the setting, locale, or action itself will always suggest sound effects that might otherwise be overlooked. To enumerate only a few: the steaming of kettles on the stove, church bells tolling, typewriters clicking, rain pelting on the roof, traffic noises, the drone of airplane motors, the pop of champagne bottles, birds singing in spring, roosters crowing in the country, ambulance sirens, machinery in operation, the shrill blasts of boats along the waterfront, the even tread of a prison lockstep, pens scratching on paper, the whinny of a friendly horse, the thud of a blow as it lands on a man's jaw, the creaking wheels of an old carriage or wagon, tom-toms beating in the jungle, the wailing or crying of animals in the night, a telegraph instrument's dotting message, etc. Whatever the scene or location, whether it be the city or country, a factory, store, café, carnival, or commercial enterprise, there are always certain atmospheric noises that can be called into play. They need not be obtrusive, unless for a definite purpose. They can be utilized as background noises. In many cases it should be pointed out, they can come as *off-screen* noises. In other words, although they are *heard* their source need not be *shown*.[34]

Deploying sound effects expressively, in the ways that Lane suggested, was part of a wider strategy in refining the 'treatment' for the story; 'treatment' being: 'the technique, means and methods chosen, or created, to present the various incidents, situations, and characters in a story most effectively'.[35] Lane also advised that screenwriters should find the appropriate treatment for the type (or genre) of story. Noting that '[t]he matter of first setting the proper pace for the story is an important angle overlooked by a great many writers,' Lane recommended that 'melodramas, stories of adventure, thrills or action, gangster and Western yarns are ... best presented in fast-pace treatment'; 'mystery and detective tales, or weird yarns' could be presented at either fast or 'moderate' pace, depending on the 'feeling' desired; 'domestic dramas, sex dramas, modern love stories, and character portrayals [were] most effective in moderate pace', and finally 'the old-fashioned type of romance, the small town story, and the psychological tale' were best presented 'in a more leisurely technique'.[36]

It is evident that by the mid-1930s, these conventions for the appropriate treatment for different story types in the sound film were shared and applied across different areas of craft expertise. Paramount sound recordist Harold Lewis, mentioned earlier, argued that '[Like] the cinematographer, the recording engineer must vary the key of his recording to suit the dramatic needs of story and scene [and] ... how each scene fits into the pattern of the picture as a whole ... so that he can give it the best and most dramatically expressive aural treatment possible.'[37] Lewis outlined how sound practices should be 'keyed' for different genres: 'A Comedy ... is best recorded in a rather high key. The volume-level is usually higher than normal, and the tonal quality crisp, to add to the intelligibility of fast-paced dialogue and action.'[38] Lewis maintained that for audiences watching comedy, 'the dialogue must thus be brought to them; also a successful comedy is well punctuated with laughs, through which succeeding lines must penetrate.'[39] In contrast Lewis advocated recording dramas 'at a much lower key. Restraint – subtlety – are the keynotes of the modern conception of drama; a low-keyed recording matches this concept perfectly.'[40] This treatment was appropriate, he noted, because audiences at a drama were 'more alert – actively co-operating' and '[t]he theatre itself is quieter; there are fewer laughs and so on for the sound to penetrate.'[41] Finally, melodrama should be keyed as follows:

> A Melodrama requires strongly contrasted sound-treatment, even as it requires strongly contrasted photographic treatment. Many sequences will be recorded in a low key, suddenly punctuated by very highly-keyed scenes. Yet even in the low-keyed recordings for a Melodrama, one dare scarcely go as low as in a Drama, because of the very audible audience reactions.[42]

Examining a range of sequences from different films, and different points, within the studio era will demonstrate how these shared notions of sound's story values were realised through an array of devices. These sequences demonstrate that screenwriters did indeed exploit the 'enhancement values' of sound, and that the sound men who did the recording, mixing and editing of dialogue and sound effects developed a nuanced awareness of film sound's 'story values'.[43]

A FAREWELL TO ARMS (FRANK BORZAGE, PARAMOUNT, 1932)

Adapted from Ernest Hemingway's 1929 World War I novel, set in the context of the Italian campaign, A Farewell to Arms garnered critical praise for its prestige treatment of its story and was listed in Film Daily's 'Ten Best' films of the year.[44] The film displayed highly effective uses of sound, deploying spectacular sequences conveying the chaos of battle, but contrasting these with subtle, more restrained tones in which sound carried mood, feeling and pathos.

The narrative sets the romance of the central couple against the backdrop of the conflict in northern Italy. Lieutenant Frederic Henry (Gary Cooper) is an American who has joined the Italian side and is in the ambulance service. He meets and falls in love with Catherine Barkley (Helen Hayes), an English nurse. Their first meeting is inauspicious; Frederic is drunk and clumsily flirts with Catherine while they are crowded into an air-raid shelter during a bombing raid. They are reintroduced at a party by Frederic's close friend, Captain Rinaldi (Adolphe Menjou), who considers Catherine to be 'his', and jealously observes the growing attraction between her and Frederic. After Frederic and Catherine spend a night together, Frederic is ordered to the front at short notice. Unable to say goodbye before he leaves, and distressed at the notion that Catherine might think he treated her casually, he persuades his co-driver to turn back so that he can bid her a proper farewell. Their feelings for each other are observed by Rinaldi, who arranges for Catherine to be transferred to Milan.

The experience of Frederic's unit at the front is vividly portrayed through the setting of the action against the background conflict and danger. The fragility of the shelter in which the unit is stationed is underlined by the off-screen noise of soldiers marching past on their way to the front, and by the increasing volume and number of shells falling nearby. The personalities in the unit react in different ways to the pressure of their situation: one member of the group displays anger and cynicism, another is overtly fearful, but Frederic is characterised by his attitude of rather pragmatic acceptance. He calmly encourages the others to gather to eat, and dishes out the rations. He continues to eat even while the shells get so near that the group speculate on their type. Sound effects play a role in delineating the narrative space; diegetic space is organised into inside and outside through the building volume of the off-screen sounds approaching, and encroaching, on the group in their camp, and as the scene progresses the action of listening becomes particularly prominent. Visual cues, such as group's glances upwards and off screen, draw audience attention to the proximity of threat and the experience of being bombarded by the sounds. The divisions between inside and outside are rendered fragile by the building diegetic sounds, and the sound effects reach a crescendo at the end of the sequence as the unit takes a direct hit, and Frederic is seriously injured.

A distinct contrast to the cacophony of these sound effects is offered in the next sequence, in which Frederic is taken to Milan for treatment and recuperation, and where he is reunited with Catherine.

As he arrives in Milan, and is wheeled through the hospital into his room, the narration is restricted to Frederic's point-of-view and point-of-audition. As shown in Figures 7–10, the action is shot from a subjective camera position. The frame is mobile, and the dialogue of the hospital porter and nurse superintendent, and the sound effects of footsteps and the creaking of Frederic's stretcher, are heard in close proximity. The modality of sound and image places the audience proximally close to his experience. Gary Cooper adapts his dialogue performance to suit the character situation in the sequence. He delivers his lines from close to his body, rather than projecting them, and gives his vocal range full feeling. The low register of the dialogue, which hovers between speech, whisper and murmur, is recorded from a close miked position.

The dialogue takes on an intimate register with the arrival of Catherine. Closeness informs both image and sound: she is framed from Frederic's point-of-view, and, as she

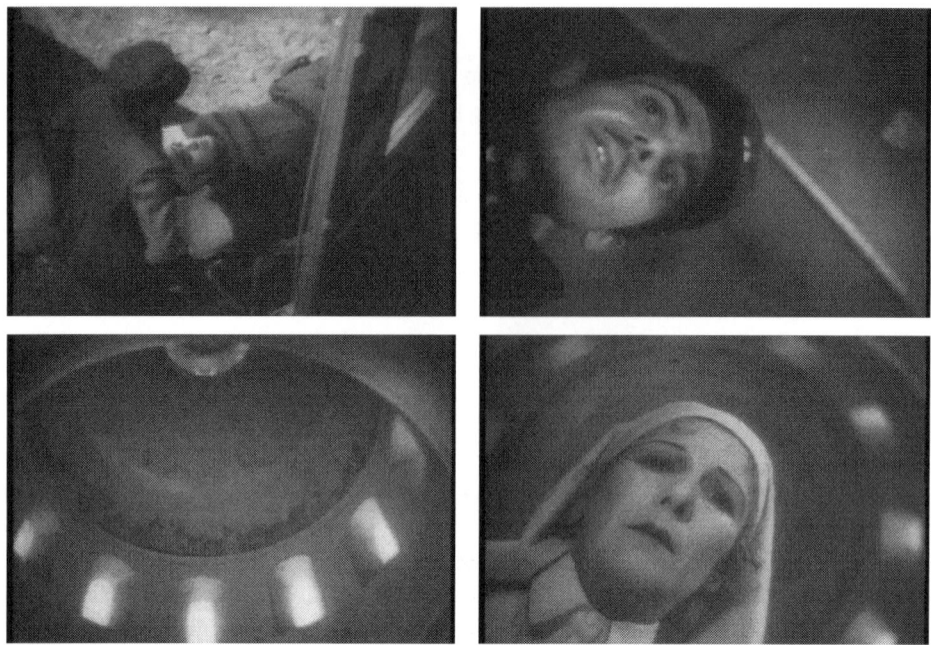

Figures 7–10 *Farewell to Arms.* Character experience is foregrounded through point-of-view and point-of-audition as Frederic arrives at the hospital in Milan

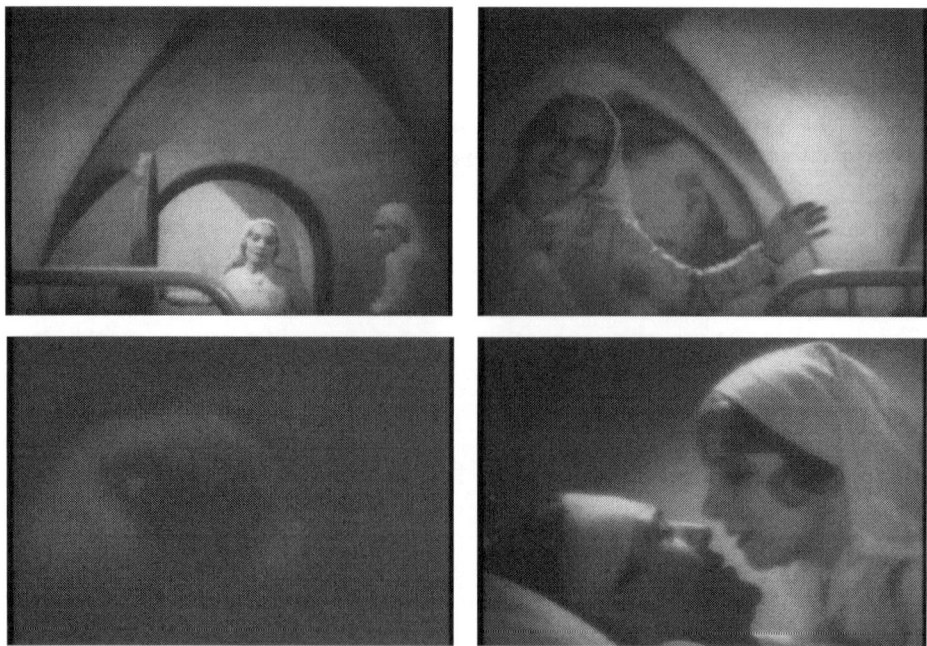

Figures 11–14 *A Farewell to Arms.* Catherine and Frederic are reunited

Hollywood Soundscapes

approaches and leans over to embrace him, she fills the whole frame, and the murmurs of the lovers reuniting fill the soundtrack (Figures 11–14). Indeed, Harold Lewis, the sound recordist on *A Farewell to Arms* (cited earlier), maintains that the sound recording for the film was designed to match the 'low key' of its drama: 'some of the most effective scenes were recorded at an extremely low key and played in whispers'.[45] In this sequence, dialogue style, vocal performance and sound recording practices interlock as expressive elements in rendering the story.

Later in the film, the narration of the lovers' parting privileges Catherine's feelings, emotions and experience. During Frederic's recovery, the pair spend a blissful period together in Milan, but when the sister at the hospital finds bottles hidden in Frederic's room, she ensures his convalescent leave is cancelled, and he is ordered to return to the front. As their last evening together draws to a close, they hear the whistle of Frederic's train signalling its imminent departure. The sound of the whistle shifts the mood of the scene; even though Frederic tries to convince Catherine that the whistle only signals that the train is being prepared for its onward journey, it sets the deadline of their parting and throws a shade over the last few minutes they have together. The dialogue emphasises the theme of the temporal: Frederic recites lines from Andrew Marvell's 'To His Coy Mistress' – 'But at my back I always hear/Time's winged chariot hurrying near' – and Catherine draws attention to the rain, an ambient sound background that, in its continuous duration, contrasts with the whistle but empathetically matches the characters' mood.[46] When the whistle is heard again, the couple must bid goodbye. Frederic insists on going to the station alone, and at the point of parting Catherine is so choked with emotion that she cannot speak. As her voice breaks, the train whistle sounds again, taking on an expressive function in its tonal closeness to a cry, and underlining the moment of parting.

Catherine waits until Frederic has gone on, and then follows him to the station where, unbeknownst to him, she watches him leave. The audiovisual staging of the moment shows an integration of film elements to underline the pathos. The diagonal staging of the movement of the soldiers walking away slowly in the background, as Catherine looks on, is rhymed, but varied, in the next shot of her watching the train move diagonally in the foreground off screen. The train's off-screen movement is established by the building of grinding mechanical sounds, the increasing beating momentum of its departure, and the rhythmic pulsing of light from its carriage windows that plays across Catherine's face.

In addition to the subtle integration of sound already discussed, *A Farewell to Arms* implements audiovisual montage as a storytelling device at two key points in its narrative. The first montage conveys Frederic's journey from the front to be reunited with Catherine. The couple have been separated since Frederic boarded the train in Milan. Unbeknownst to Frederic, Catherine is carrying their child, and after he leaves Milan she moves to the small town of Brissago for the duration of her pregnancy. The lovers write to each other, but their correspondence is intercepted by the jealous Rinaldi. Eventually, Frederic discovers Catherine's letters and travels to find her.

Frederic's journey to Milan through the war-torn country is covered in a five-minute montage. It compresses his journey, and sets his experience and desire to find Catherine against the wider backdrop of the collective experience of soldiers and displaced civilians during the retreat of the army. Visually, the montage is organised according to graphical and dynamic patterns. Early in the montage, the relationships between a series of shots foreground the human price of war. The montage sequence links images of wounded, dying and dead servicemen, graphically matching the composition of a wounded soldier slumped in an arched doorway with the figure of a cross. The montage also foregrounds the disrupting and displacing effects of war. Soldiers and civilians are depicted in transit. The movements of soldiers, and of civilians, are presented with consistent screen direction, from right to left, and this matches Frederic's direction too, lending a sense of scale to his journey. Sonically, the montage is underpinned by score, and overlaid with sound effects which are synchronised with images of bombs and fire wreaking destruction on houses and towns. Rhythmically, the music builds from drums that beat to the movement of servicemen at the beginning of the montage, to a crescendo of tension cues instrumented by strings and flaring brass signalling the final action in the montage: Frederic escaping across a river while under enemy fire.

It is evident from archival sources on the film's production that this sequence had been carefully designed. The papers on the story development for *A Farewell to Arms* include a sequence plan for the montage, called 'The Retreat', in which the outline of the sequence structure and its desired effects is specified as follows:

Sequence N – The Retreat

This episode of the story is to be impressionistic rather than realistic, stylized rather than literal. Three elements are to be considered in relation to it:

    The music
    The cutting
    The camera angles

The music is pure underscoring. A modernistic composition beginning low, slow, as panic is born and mounting to the crashing, whirling nightmare of the flight. All sound effects will be in musical terms. Thus you will see men shout to each other, shells burst, airplanes swoop, but you will hear only music. It will be as if the music drowned every other sound, yet reproduced them in the same way.

In the cutting a montage will be employed, graduating from equal cuts of normal length to rapid flashes as the climax is reached. Thus, along with the music a sort of optical crescendo will be obtained.

The camera angles are to be deliberately distorted. They will be low or high or oblique but never normal. In lighting as well as in composition an effect of nightmare will be sought.

All this until the conclusion at the bridgehead is reached, when the music will fade into the sounds of troops, animals and equipment in flight across the bridge, culminating in the sharp dialogue of the battle police as they drag officers from the line and execute them.[47]

'The retreat' sequence in *A Farewell to Arms* offers an example of montage being deployed to intensify the narrative momentum in the early sound film. Montage, along with transitional devices such as fades, wipes and lap-dissolves, was widely discussed by a range of Hollywood crafts in the early sound era. Montage was conceived of as a device permitting filmmakers to manage pace and tempo, to condense narrative exposition, and to avoid the 'dragginess' of the early sound film. Tamar Lane saw montage as a 'mixture of brief scenes, or impressions ... In montage, it is the effect of the shots *as a whole* that counts, rather than the stressing of any particular incident.'[48]

As noted earlier, screenwriters advocated organising the sound film screenplay in sequences as units within the overall story. This organising principle facilitated the setting of the appropriate tempo within a sequence. Screenwriting manuals also advised on techniques to be used to make transitions between sequences, and to compress or condense sequences. In her analysis of film style in the early sound period, Nancy Wood observes the more frequent use of transitional devices. These devices had 'efficacy in "eliminating detailed action" from overly-long scenes', while 'the liberal use of the lap dissolve was ... [an] ... antidote to the drag of the sound film' in both a temporal and a narrative sense.[49]

Best practice for using devices such as transitions, dissolves and montage was discussed at an Academy Technicians Branch meeting in September 1934. Representatives from different studios presented papers on transitional devices from the standpoint of their craft.[50] Anne Bauchens, an experienced editor at Paramount Pictures, asserted that the choice of transition to be used should be governed by 'the subject matter of a picture and its tempo'.[51] She noted that wipes, dissolves and pans had superseded 'the old time fade-out' to the extent that it 'is now used only to designate a long time lapse or a very complete change in situation'.[52] Bauchens discussed examples of the use of montage as a device to speed up the story presentation in *A Farewell to Arms* and in *Cleopatra* (Cecil B. DeMille, 1934), and transitional devices to make thematic links between sequences in *Dishonored* (Josef Von Sternberg, 1931) and *Belle of the Nineties* (Leo McCarey, 1934).

Loren Ryder, Head of Sound at Paramount studios, delivered a paper jointly prepared by sound representatives from the major studios. The paper outlined how sound could be handled for transitional shots, along with best practice in the dubbing of sound effects. Ryder *et al.* argued that the usual practice was to time the fade or dissolve of sound to match the picture dissolve, but the paper outlined some other effective forms of practice, which included the uses of off-screen sound, sound bridging and the timing and volume of sound in transitions. Ryder *et al.* offered some illustrations of the uses of off-screen sound:

> During black-out, situations are frequently built up by the continuance of sound or even the introduction of new sounds during or between the fades. For example, we may have a fight too gruesome to show, where a man is killed by a beast, in which the picture will frequently be blacked out as the man goes down and the sound of the man's last groan be used as an index to what has happened.[53]

They suggested instances where sound fades may lead the picture, and how they function in relation to story:

> Fade-ins depicting action, as of a railroad locomotive, are frequently given increased tempo by letting the audience hear the train before it is seen. The distant whistle carrying after the

picture of the train fades from the screen gives a nice effect ... Just as sound fades should assist the start or end of an episode, sound dissolves should be handled so as to give the feeling of story progression during the dissolve.[54]

Throughout the 1930s and into the 1940s, craft commentators such as Tamar Lane and Barrett Kiesling, and trade publications such as *American Cinematographer*, continued to write about the story applications of lap-dissolve and montage; the accounts frequently highlighted the innovative work of Slavko Vorkapich, of MGM, as an influence on wider Hollywood practice.[55] Vorkapich had overseen the creation of many montage sequences, such as in MGM's *Viva Villa* (Jack Conway, 1934), *David Copperfield* (George Cukor, 1935) and *Maytime* (Robert Z. Leonard, 1937). Vorkapich was certainly influential, but he was not the only proponent of the montage device, which was used by other studios too. A montage features in *One Night of Love*, discussed in Chapter 2, portraying Mary's (Grace Moore's) rise to success as an opera star in compressed form. This sequence was made several years before the oft-cited opera montage in *Maytime*, and suggests that innovation in devices such as montage were widely shared.

As these storytelling devices evolved in the early sound period, the crafts of screenwriting, optical effects and sound interlocked and combined to produce the appropriate sequence and story 'treatment'. Sound proved integral to lap-dissolve and montage sequences, and flexible conventions developed to deploy sound in a range of highly effective ways. In lap-dissolve sequences it might be deployed subtly, to carry audience attention across the transitions, or more overtly in the narration, to foreground a 'development' of plot, or a deepening of information about character interiority, or backstory.

RANDOM HARVEST (MERVYN LE ROY, MGM, 1942)

MGM's *Random Harvest* provides examples of how sound underpins conventions in characterisation, character interiority and the different moods and modalities of narration. The film features sequences in which sound devices and techniques, such as the layering of sound effects and the flow of sound within lap-dissolve sequences, contribute to communicating characterisation and the creation of intrigue and pathos.

The film was an adaptation of James Hilton's 1941 novel, and is a romantic drama with a complex plot which moves through love, loss and reunion. World War I veteran Smithy (Ronald Colman), suffers from amnesia brought on by shell shock. He has lost any recollection of his former life and identity as wealthy Charles Rainier. As Smithy he is confined to a veteran's hospital which specialises in rehabilitating veterans. The narrative moves through Smithy's recovery, his meeting with Paula (Greer Garson), their marriage, and then their separation when Smithy/Charles has an accident which reverses his amnesia: he recovers his memory of his pre-war life and identity, but loses his memory of his time with Paula. The narrative dramatises how Smithy's shifting memory affects Paula; she traces Smithy/Charles and stays close to him by taking on the role of his secretary Margaret, later becoming his wife in a mutually acknowledged marriage of convenience. The plot gradually circles back to the couple's true emotional

Hollywood Soundscapes

reconciliation and Rainier's recovery of the memory of 'Smithy', and his memory of his love for Paula.

The film opens with Smithy in Melbridge Asylum where he is being treated for the effects of his war experience. His trauma affected his memory and caused him to all but lose his ability to speak. Early scenes in the film evoke sympathy for 'John Smith'; it is clear that he is working to overcome the debilitating effects of his shock, and is trying to engage with the staff at the asylum. In an affecting scene he is brought to meet an elderly couple who are seeking their son who has gone missing in action, but despite Smithy's evident hopes, as soon as they see him they realise their search has been fruitless.

The narration of the film has a subtle and shifting relationship to characterisation, and one that is consistent with Smithy's situation as an amnesiac. The opening titles of the film have a directive and expository voiceover establishing the setting of the film in the asylum at the end of the war. The narration transitions into the main story with a forward-moving tracking shot towards the doors of the asylum. The movement is brief, but it is overt, and it takes the audio-viewer from a more remote position to one closer to the space of the characters; it shifts the modality of the narration, from distanced to more proximate to the characters and their concerns.

In narrative theory, modality is defined as the degree to which the narrative provides information, and the extent to which it might place a reader, or viewer, close to, or separate from, character.[56] It is commonplace to match the concept of literary 'perspective' with filmic 'point-of-view', but formal techniques, such as optical point-of-view, are not the only devices that a filmmaker might deploy to place film narration proximate to character; framing, reaction shots, performance and other elements, including sound, might be used to extend, or withhold, narrative information about character. Furthermore, as Murray Smith has argued, the narrational processes that elicit audience engagement with fictional characters are diverse, and exceed a simple matching of optical point-of-view with 'identification'.[57] Smith proposes a more nuanced way of understanding different levels of engagement with characters, depending upon the extent to which the narration communicates information and cues the audio-viewer to 'make inferences [and] formulate hypotheses' about the fictional character, their experiences, feelings and thoughts.[58]

These concepts are salient in understanding the modality of the narration in *Random Harvest*. After the opening mobile shot, described above, locates the action in the asylum, the narration gradually becomes 'aligned' with Smithy, prioritising his story over the other inmates through the organisation of the formal elements. There is interplay between the framing of the shots, which centre on Smithy, and on Colman's performance through facial expressivity, control of voice and gesture.[59] Sound has a function in moulding the narrational modality of the film, and this is evident in the audiovisual style of the sequence in which Smithy leaves the asylum, goes into Melbridge and meets Paula.

The sequence opens with Smithy taking an evening walk in the grounds of the asylum. It is a foggy night, and he is greeted by, and briefly converses with, one of the wardens. As he walks, his attitude is contemplative, and he practises talking, rehearsing aloud the 'social' register of incidental small talk that is a signature of 'normalised' discourse: 'I'm alright, *thank* you … Coat's very warm … like to walk' (Figure 15). As

Figures 15–16   *Random Harvest.* The sounds of the Armistice Day celebrations pervade the soundscape

he continues to walk, the soundscape shifts tonally and narratively. From the quiet ambience of his footsteps, accompanied by the low volume underscore, the soundscape suddenly becomes filled with insistent diegetic signal sounds: bells toll and a factory siren blares out, celebrating the end of the war. But Smithy's, and the audience's, understanding of the significance of the sounds is not instantaneous. The off-screen bells and siren sounds pervade the diegesis, and envelope Smithy, before the source and cause for their sounding become clear. Momentarily, it is possible for the audience to interpret their source as inside the asylum, perhaps sounding as a warning of an inmate's misadventure or escape. Alternatively, with the background knowledge that he has suffered trauma in battle, it is also possible to be cued to interpret the sounds as internal and subjective, as Smithy's auditory flashback. In Michel Chion's terms, the sounds are initially acousmatic, but as Smithy's audition becomes more obvious, they are deacousmatised and their sources are 'spatially magnetised' and placed within the on-screen space.[60]

This momentary delay in resolving the sounds, their source and their significance is evidently experienced by Smithy, and is just one example of how the narration offers the audience multiple levels of knowledge with which to position his character in relation to events. The gap, or distance, between Smithy and the unfolding events is represented visually as he stands by and watches wardens from the asylum running joyfully out of their office to celebrate the Armistice (Figure 16). A framing of Colman/Smithy looking on is a repeated choice in the film, and is used several times later in the sequence: as Smithy shelters from the noisy crowd in the tobacconist's shop (Figure 18), as he stands at a railing at the side of the street (Figure 20) – again to separate from the chaos of the crowd – and as he watches Paula's music hall performance, separated from the main audience in his vantage point on a balcony in the wings of the stage.

The narration signals that Smithy experiences the noise of the Armistice celebrations as chaotic, frightening and oppressive. The mixing and balancing of the sound elements, and their development and calibration during Smithy's journey through Melbridge, function to convey the weight of the atmosphere on him. As he walks towards and through the open asylum door, the sound effects and tension cues in the score are balanced, and already at a medium to high volume level.

Smithy's movement out of the bounds of the asylum is scored with a steadily rising theme instrumented with brass, and, as he steps out into the street, with a roll of drums that marks the moment, and provides a temporary pause in the scoring.

Hollywood Soundscapes

Figures 17–18   *Random Harvest.* Smithy's disquiet is at odds with the joyful tone of the Armistice Day celebrations

Once the action cuts to the town, the sound mixing prioritises diegetic sound; we hear the blare of factory sirens, and the shouting and singing of the crowds (Figure 17). The volume levels of all these sound elements are raised to high, and the sound mix is very dense. The density edges, at moments, into distortion, as the mix conveys how the competing sounds are heard by Smithy as he moves through the streets; at certain points the sound mix has a tonal underlay of ringing which, we infer, is a mark of Smithy's underlying psychological disquiet. The overall mix of the soundtrack holds together the diegetic sounds of the Armistice Day celebrations, whilst the leitmotif which expresses Smithy's feelings is 'metadiegetic', indicating character interiority.[61] The narration is thus filtered, or channelled, through Smithy's experience of the noise. His 'point' of audition is not exactly located (as it might be in, say, a chase sequence); nevertheless, the sound mixing evokes Smithy's 'zone of audition' and his experience of the enveloping, overwhelming sound is registered emphatically.[62]

In order to escape from the noise, Smithy ducks into a tobacconist's shop (Figure 18). His hesitant speech and startled expression raise the suspicions of the woman behind the counter; she realises that he is an inmate from the asylum. As the woman goes to telephone the asylum, Paula enters the shop and befriends Smithy (Figure 19). She suggests they have a drink to steady his nerves, and then takes him with her to the music hall where she is performing. As noted, Smithy watches from a distanced vantage point. At the end of Paula's act the audience, celebrating the end of the war, noisily flood onto the stage; Smithy, overwhelmed by the noise, and ill with flu, passes out.

Figures 19–20   *Random Harvest.* After meeting Paula at the tobacconist's, Smithy re-enters the chaos of the street, but retreats to an enclave to get out of the crowds

This ends the sequence of Smithy's transition from the asylum to the outside world. Paula takes care of him, nursing him back from illness, and then arranges for them to move to a quiet village in the country. The narration shows Smithy gradually gaining confidence, and the relationship between Smithy and Paula strengthens. Smithy gets some freelance work as a writer, the couple get married and their son is born. Smithy hopes to support the family by writing, and secures an interview for a position at the *Liverpool Mercury* newspaper. He travels to Liverpool for the interview but is knocked down while making his way to the *Mercury* offices. When he comes around from the accident, he has lost his memory of being 'Smithy', and his time with Paula, but recovers his memory of his former life as Charles Rainier, his identity before and during the war, up to the time he is stretchered out of a trench to hospital.

The build-up to the accident is paced slowly; Smithy is shown leaving his hotel and setting off for the interview. Smithy's walk is framed in three tracking shots, with a consistent screen direction of right to left. The city streets are busy with people, and the background urban environment is fabricated with sound effects: a low rumble of traffic noise, higher-pitched car horns, and the yells of a paper boy selling the *Liverpool Mercury*. Smithy asks the paper boy for directions, and as he steps out of the frame to cross the road, the screech of brakes and a pedestrian calling 'Look Out!' mark the moment of his accident, which is off screen. A series of shots of traffic coming to an abrupt halt follow, and then, rather than cutting directly to Smithy, the narrational position shifts back from the event, creating suspense as to his condition, before moving in with the crowd who surround him.

The narration shifts mode, becoming subjective as a brief lap-dissolve sequence renders Smithy's experience and the recovery of his memory of the war (Figures 21–23).

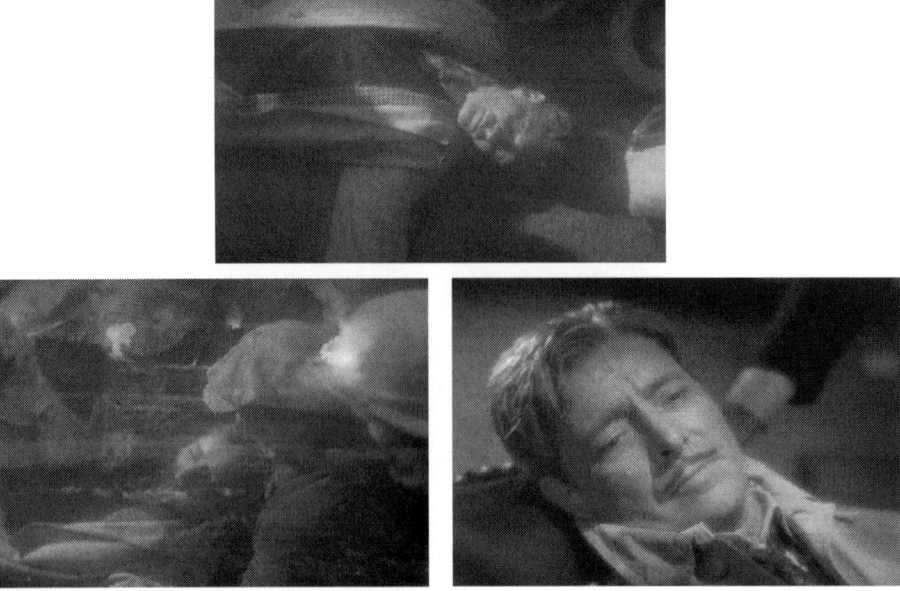

Figures 21–23   *Random Harvest.* Smithy's accident and the lap-dissolve sequence that brings his memory back

The lap-dissolve shots are accompanied by the sounds of war, which are mixed to bleed into each other expressionistically and which suggest his auditory memory rather than concretely establishing a location or specific event.

Smithy is taken to a pharmacy, where he recovers consciousness but cannot remember why he was in Liverpool. He picks up his life as Charles Rainier, returns to his family, who had thought he had been killed in action in the war, and takes on the family business. As summarised earlier, Paula traces Smithy/Charles and works for him, all the time hoping that Charles will remember her, and recover his identity as Smithy.

The sequence in which Charles recovers his memory of being Smithy portrays his gradually surfacing recollections through a strategy of repetition. Charles has to go to Melbridge to pursue some business interests there. There is labour trouble at a large factory, where he manages to smooth relations between management and workers, and is celebrated by cheering crowds of workers. Charles and his assistant have a drink at the Melbridge Arms, the same pub where Paula had taken him the night they met. After their drink, they leave for the station, but on the way Charles wants to buy cigarettes and instinctively heads directly for the tobacconist's shop, even though he thinks he is unfamiliar with the town. His feeling of déjà vu grows stronger, and the narration underlines this for the audience: the audiovisual structure prompts audience recollection in replaying and reworking earlier shots and sound. The set-ups for the action mirror the earlier sequence, and the soundscape, noisy with the celebrating crowd, echoes the Armistice Day scene. The sound effects are keyed on two levels: objective, portraying diegetic sounds in the narrational present, and subjective, auditory fragmented sounds from Armistice Day, which are heard at a lower volume level. The sonic signature of reverberation they are given indicates they are internal, representing the auditory sense memories that Charles feels are returning. The order of the locations Charles visits, though, is reversed from Armistice Day, and this builds and intensifies audience expectation about when he will fully remember his past. This expectation is finally fulfilled when Charles is returned to the origin point of the plot; standing outside the asylum, at last he recalls Paula. The final scenes of the film reunite the couple at the location of the cottage where they lived when they were first married.

COMMANDING THE SOUNDS OF THE UNIVERSE: SOUND TECHNIQUES AND PRACTICES FOR CRAFTING SOUND

The sequences from *Farewell to Arms* and *Random Harvest* discussed above demonstrate the command of an array of effective sonic conventions by sound technicians. These conventions were underpinned by a range of techniques and practices allowing for subtle balance and mixing in the soundtrack, and for the careful placement of sound effects in the post-production phase. Techniques for manipulating sound in post-production had been in place from the early sound era, when re-recording, or 'dubbing', as it came to be termed, evolved as a solution for managing sound quality in post-production.[63] From 1929, sound personnel were discussing re-recording as a practice, and by 1930 there was growing attention to the creative potential that re-recording offered. Dubbing was identified as a research priority by the Academy and the research service sector, because of the control that it offered over sound.[64] The dubbing process also fitted into the organisation of production labour as increasingly divided and specialised during the 1930s.[65]

From the standpoint of sound technicians, the production process typically had several phases.[66] When a film project was ready to go into production, the producer's office sent the final shooting script to all key craft departments. Senior members of the Sound Department, usually the director of sound and an experienced sound mixer, studied the script to determine the requirements in terms of production sound recording personnel, equipment, and to assign a sound crew. Usually the crew was composed of four technicians: a production sound mixer (the most senior member of the crew), a sound recordist, an assistant and a maintenance technician. The primary focus of production sound recording on set was capturing dialogue, but if the script or story scenarios required specific or special sound features, plans might be made at this stage to obtain the sound effects that would be necessary for the finished film. In such instances, lists of the required effects were made, some of which might be recorded in the course of production shooting. If stock or library sounds were suitable, those might be used, or 'wild' soundtracks might be recorded by Production Sound personnel, independently of the camera. Recording wild was a common feature of location sound recording, employed to capture the ambience or 'soundmarks' that being on location afforded.[67] I discuss examples of wild sound recording in some of the production case studies examined in Chapter 4. Capturing wild sound seems to have been a priority at particular studios, and a number of sources suggest that this was so at Warner Bros.

During the shooting phase, the sound crew assigned to the production reported to the sound stage, or shooting location, ahead of the main company in order to set up and test equipment. It was common for the sound crew to report an hour before the main crew, even earlier if the day's shooting required a particularly complex set-up of equipment. Microphones would be placed, or mounted, on booms, power and signal cables connected, and tests made on the motors driving the sound recorder, the circuits that synchronised the sound and camera and the transmission from the stage microphones to the sound recorder.

Once the main company were on set, preparations for a take would begin. If a scene required a complex co-ordination of camera and boom movement, a technical rehearsal would take place with stand-ins, and then a rehearsal for the actors might follow. When the director was satisfied with the rehearsals, he would signal to the production sound mixer that he was ready for a take. The mixer would then signal to the sound recordist to start the sound recorder motor running, and once the sound system was 'up to speed', the sound recordist would signal to synchronise the camera and the action so the take could begin. During the take, the production sound mixer monitored the quality of the sound recording, and of the dialogue performance, and if necessary could mix the sound inputs from different microphones. The takes were usually logged on a report of the day's production. If a take was 'no good', because of either sound quality or equipment failure, this would be logged: for example, the note 'ngs' connoted 'no good – sound'. Similarly, takes that were 'no good' from the standpoint of 'action' or 'camera' were also logged. The best takes were selected to be 'printed', or developed, for reviewing. Usually back-up takes were 'held'.

At the end of a day's shooting, the negative film on which the sound was recorded was forwarded to the laboratory for processing. These 'rushes', the takes of sound and picture, were reviewed; usually the film's producer, director and often the directors of sound and camera would be present at these reviews, and were accountable for any recurrent or significant problems in sound and image quality. At most studios, the process of making a preliminary assembly of the film by the Editorial Department occurred as specific takes from the review process were approved by the producer and director. Sound and image tracks were edited separately but kept in sync. Refining the film through editorial involved a process of regular review, with producer and director present at reviews and with cutting notes taken and distributed to editorial and sound. The need for any retakes was usually identified during this review process. The film was 'spotted' for sound effects and music: that is, the points at which additional sound effects or score were to be placed were identified. From the 'spotting' session, detailed lists of sound effects were generated, as well as the precise timing 'cue' for their insertion into the film.

During the dubbing phase, the specified sound effects were placed and edited into the soundtrack and balanced with the dialogue. Recording of the score took place in the later stages of post-production; this was also guided by using precisely timed cue sheets and the 'click track' system. Once the film was edited, dubbed and scored, the final review stages took place, with producer and director giving the senior sound technicians instructions about the balance of the soundtrack and volume levels for specific scenes or sequences. The final re-recording stages permitted alterations in balance to be executed and for the release print to be finalised.

Sound technicians conceived of dubbing as a creative recombination of sounds and regarded the fabrication and mixing of sound effects as analogous to special image processes in cinematography.[68] Dubbing was similar in function to the fabrication of process shots in the laboratory for specific scenes or sequences of a production, and it came to occupy a parallel place in production schedules. In a lecture from the Academy's first School of Sound, Kenneth Morgan (from ERPI) wrote that:

> The artistic and commercial advantages of the superimposition and combination of sounds recorded at different times and places are, if anything, even greater than those of trick photography, so that the art of dubbing has developed with great rapidity and is already a fundamental part of the production of sound pictures. A sound recording and reproducing system recreates with artistic illusion at a later time the auditory sensations which would be experienced had the listener been present when the original sounds took place. Sound pictures introduce the added feature of synchronization and the localization of a definite viewpoint, and in some instances employ unnatural sound emphasis for dramatic reasons.[69]

The studios quickly adopted dubbing as a widespread practice. Morgan estimated that by 1931, 'most pictures released are now 50 to 100 per cent re-recorded',[70] and went on to state that:

> The dubbing process must be recognised as the most expedient technical, economic and dramatic asset in sound production. It permits production to proceed without delays that otherwise might be necessitated if all the sounds had to be recorded at once. It facilitates the

editing of pictures, especially the attainment of uniform level and proper balance of sound. It is an acoustical art in itself, and represents a new form of composition in sound where the artists' keyboard commands the sounds of the universe.[71]

Morgan's view is echoed in a number of articles through the 1930s. George Lewin (of Paramount) described the practice of dubbing in 'characteristic' sounds, like street noises for urban settings, and revealed that dubbing crews at Paramount often numbered between ten and twelve men, indicating the scale of the task, and of the studios' investment of personnel in these specialised roles.[72] Carl Dreher (Head of Sound at RKO) also likened dubbing to 'special process' photography, and argued that it could not only replicate a sonic setting, but could actually *construct* a background through sound:

[In special process photography] the blue cloth against which the foreground action is photographed corresponds to the silent background of dialog in sound. In re-recording, any desired sound background may be supplied, just as in special-process photography any desired visual background may be supplied ... In some cases, the special audible background can be secured *only* by re-recording.[73]

Dreher focused on the control that dubbing permitted, allowing for the precise synchronisation of particular sound effects and exact volume calibration.[74]

These benefits of dubbing as a practice led to the development of new apparatus, offering refinements in the dubbing process and allowing a wide array of sounds to be mixed into the final track; Nathan Levinson (of Warner Bros.) termed this final track a 'composite', capturing the sense of weaving, and composing, a range of sounds.[75] Dubbing practices and technologies were adapted by different studios, and consequently there were slight variations, or what we might think of as 'practice preferences' created by different studio groups. Homer Tasker (of Universal) described apparatus facilitating better preparation for dubbing, and more accurate synchronisation.[76] The equipment could accommodate six soundtracks, each with an output control allowing the dubbing mixer to combine and weave together the sound inputs. Tasker wrote that the mixers '"build" the soundtracks to provide supplementary effects and music required for a complete dramatic presentation of each reel', suggesting a division of labour at Universal, with a mixer working solely on sound effects for a reel at a time.[77] Edwin Wetzel, a Dubbing Mixer at Universal, described the practice of 'spotting' the film for sound effects, after which the Sound Effects Department would refer to Universal's sound library to plan which effects might be drawn from stock, and which will be 'especially recorded' – in other words, created to synchronise with the action.[78] He also described the process of layering and overlapping sound effects in order to direct audience attention, and to balance with music and dialogue.

At Disney Studios the task of mixing sound for animated cartoons could be complex, as it involved more sound cues than the average sound feature at other studios. The Disney Sound Department had devised a way of managing the mixing of multiple sound cues. Instead of handling the multiple cues by mixing the sound effects, the music and the dialogue into separate 'composite' tracks, or by mixing the sounds in short sequences, the studio innovated a sound mixing set-up which permitted music and sound effects to be mixed simultaneously by a team of dubbing mixers.[79] Head of

Sound, Sam Slyfield, described a system in which the dubbing mixers were co-ordinated by a conductor signalling when the specific cues should be inserted. Slyfield estimated that this set-up allowed Disney's Sound Department to mix and balance 'hundreds' of sound cues in the same operation.

At MGM the practice was not to make a 'composite' track of pre-combined and 'layered' sound effects, as was the preference at Warner Bros., but to mix all the effects tracks simultaneously. This was made possible with the innovation of sound mixing apparatus in the early 1940s – a potentiometer – which allowed for the very precise control of up to eight soundtracks at once.[80] The new feature of this potentiometer was its control panel; rather than rotating a dial for each input, the mixer slid a control up and down in a linear motion, allowing several potentiometers to be operated simultaneously, and for exact and subtle adjustments to be made to the sound mix. By 1944 it was common for MGM to combine between fifteen and twenty tracks into a final soundtrack.[81] In 1948 MGM renewed their re-recording equipment with newly designed apparatus which allowed for precise but time-efficient rehearsal of different sounds to co-ordinate with the image, while the Sound Department also incorporated mechanisms to facilitate the equalisation of the soundtrack.[82] Wesley Miller and C. Crane, of MGM's Sound Department, cited earlier, accorded re-recording a key role in production:

> [Re-recording] … reflects the sound engineer's ingenuity in finding answers to many problems, suggestions, and inspirations presented by all of the other individuals and groups who contribute to the final product. It is also the place where the soundman ceases to be an engineer and becomes a controlling and creative force in the successful presentation of the product to the public. To an increasing degree the interpretations of the producer, the director, the musician and the editor are dependent on the re-recording processes and upon the skill and understanding of the re-recording mixer.[83]

It is clear from the perspectives cited above that the establishment of re-recording and dubbing as a key part of the post-production phase gave sound engineers a mode of precise control over the placement and balance of sounds overall. This precision allowed sound mixers, often in discussion with a film's director or producer, to vary, balance and contrast sounds, silences, dialogue and music to craft the soundscape to fit a wide variety of narrative scenarios and settings.

SOUND EFFECTS AND THE FABRICATION OF THE SOUNDSCAPE

As dubbing developed as a widespread practice, the studios innovated ways of producing and archiving sound effects. From the early sound era, sound departments began to collect sound recordings and developed ways of creating special 'synthesised' sounds.[84] The process of creating sound effects to fit a particular action, or sequence, is now widely referred to as 'Foleying' sounds, a task undertaken by 'Foley artists'. The process acquired its name from Jack Foley, who specialised in creating sound effects at Universal Studios. Valuable background research on Foley himself, and on the evolution of Foley craft in the post-studio era, has been undertaken by David Yewdall, Vanessa Theme Ament, Benjamin Wright and Lucy Donaldson.[85] The term 'Foley sound' now has an established currency, but the practices of making sound effects to fit the tempo and mood of action were not the sole innovation of one sound man; these practices have mixed and intermedial origins, and were innovated in shared contexts of sound craft. Stephen Bottomore and Rick Altman trace the practices of making 'live' sounds to the early cinema period; live sounds accompanied the exhibition of some early films, and the practices of fabricating them were drawn from theatre, where 'sound effects boys', or 'trap' drummers, used specially designed instruments and apparatus to supply a wide range of elemental, mood and action-enhancing sounds.[86] Radio historians, such as Neil Verma, Richard Hand, Robert Mott Jesse Schlotterbeck and Frank Krutnik, have also established the important cross-industry influences between sound effects practices in live radio drama and sound effects for film. These influences were underpinned by the flow of sound personnel from the radio industry to studio sound departments, and by synergies in programming, particularly radio versions of the majors' big releases.[87]

In his Oral History, Walter G. Elliott, who joined RKO's newly formed Sound Effects Department soon after the studio's formation, recalled creating 'live' sound effects 'right on the set' in the transitional sound era. He attributed his success with making sound effects to his sense of timing, and related an occasion when he had to make sounds to match on-camera action in *Seven Keys to Baldpate* (Reginald Barker, 1930): 'One of [the characters] had to fall downstairs, so I had to do the fall downstairs offstage in time with the man who was doing it on set.'[88] During the late 1920s, Elliott worked on creating film sound effects for RKO, and radio sound

Figure 24 'Prehistoric Monsters Roar and Hiss for Sound Film', *Popular Science Monthly*, April 1933, pp. 20–21

effects for NBC. He also worked with Murray Spivack, Head of RKO's Sound Effects Department, on the fabrication of spectacular and unusual sounds for *King Kong* (Ernest B. Schoedsack and Merian C. Cooper, 1933), a production that has become widely celebrated as innovative in the creation of its soundscape.[89] Their work on creating the sounds was covered in an article in *Popular Science Monthly* in April 1933 (Figure 24).

In separate Oral Histories both Elliott and Spivack recalled making the sounds which, with the skilfully conceived visual effects, build to a vivid recreation of the monsters of Skull Island, where the adventurers encounter the giant gorilla, Kong. Spivack recalled that the Sound Effects Department had received a copy of the script for *King Kong*, from which they created a list of the effects required. On reviewing the list of prehistoric and fantastical creatures, Spivack's response was, 'I knew I had to concoct sounds' but that he 'didn't want any cartoon sounds. I wanted something ... believable.'[90] Spivack remembered a mixed approach to sourcing, and shaping, the sounds needed. He recorded a range of animal sounds at a local zoo, but wanted to mask their familiarity, and so he slowed down the roar of a lion to half speed, causing the pitch to drop, and lengthening the playing time of the sample. He experimented with playing some animal sounds backwards, and, by recombining them, shifted them away from the realm of the familiar; Spivack recalls: 'I made all sorts of shadings'.[91] As well as morphing animal sounds, Spivack and Elliott created and recorded sounds by vocalising noises, performing and producing physical actions, and using sound effects props, as illustrated in Figure 24. Spivack recalls producing Kong's 'love grunt' – the sound he makes when he sees Ann Darrow (Fay Wray) – by vocalising it, and then slowing it down and re-recording the low sound.[92]

The special sound effects for *King Kong* were added to RKO's growing sound library, a collection overseen by Walter Elliott. All the major studios created libraries of sound effects that sound editors could call upon. In 1930 H. G. Knox (of ERPI) reviewed the progress that had been made in sound practices after the transition to sound, and remarked that:

> already libraries of sound are growing. On one endless loop of film may be recorded an airplane engine, on others a railroad train, machine-gun fire, dishes being washed, crowd noises and whatnot. When appropriate these loops – more than one at a time if you wish – may be dubbed into the new record. They may be fed into the recording machine while the microphone is having its say or they may be added to the record later on. Once mastered, and a complete library of effects is on hand, you must admit the sound technicians have their fun.[93]

Sound effects were often sourced from current production recordings, and it was common practice for sound footage recorded on location, and special recordings of 'wild' sound, to be added to the library.[94] Within a few years of the transition, the array of sounds in Hollywood's sound libraries was vast, and included not only spectacular sounds, such as the avalanche heard in *Spawn of the North* (Henry Hathaway, 1938), discussed in detail below, but many quotidian or 'incidental' sounds that added liveliness and presence to even 'unremarkable' action. Milo Lory (of MGM), who worked on dubbing in the early sound period, and was later a Sound Effects Editor, described 'the tedious work of replacing cup set-downs, and the clothes rustles, and the footsteps to give [the action] ... realism, that's what the sound effects editor did'.[95] He declared that the MGM library included 'everything from a garter snap to an atomic bomb'.[96] The MGM sound librarian Mike Steinore carefully indexed effects under the name of their subject, and logged the title of their original provenance. Lory relates: 'Under G, there were gunshots: pistol shots, rifle shots, shotguns, machine guns.'[97] At Twentieth Century-Fox, sound librarian Carl Effinger estimated he had thousands of effects in his library, from the buzzing of a fly's wings to the very loudest explosion.[98] The Warner Bros. sound library was under the supervision of Hal Shaw, who also supervised the studio's Dupe Department. An article in the studio's house magazine, *Warner Club News*, detailed the extensive collection, which included machinery noises, unusual animal sounds, weather sounds, 'bells from different parts of the world', and so on.[99]

As well as adding sound effects during the re-recording process, the post-production phase allowed sound editors and mixers to use reverberation to alter the character of recordings. This was a widespread practice across different studios. For example, one of Warner Bros.' sound engineers, L. T. Goldsmith, described using an '"echo chamber"' to 'simulate voice sounds in large halls, caves etc., and to add reverberation and life to some kinds of music',[100] and other sources describe similar processes.[101]

Adding reverberation in post-production, rather than recording with spatial perspective during production, made sound more flexible, and made production recording manageable and expedient. These practice principles meant that sound technicians could meet the requirements of 'good' production sound recording (characterised by clear, intelligible dialogue) but 'add' the enhancement and story values that reverberation offered for specific scenes or sequences. As Rick Altman outlines, although senior sound experts in the technical culture, such as Bell Labs' Joseph Maxfield, repeatedly exhorted sound technicians to adopt microphone set-ups which would privilege spatial fidelity, within production contexts sound technicians had to work with microphone placement set-ups that fitted with the combined demands of camera position, set design and other agendas, alongside the need for sound quality.[102] Altman notes that during the classical studio period, reverberant sound – that is, sound that indicated a spatial position within the narrative soundscape – gradually began to take on a specific role in indicating point-of-audition:

> point-of-audition sound is identified by its volume, reverb level, and other characteristics as representing sound as it would be heard from a point within the diegesis, normally by a specific character or characters. In other words, point-of-audition sound always carries signs of its own fictional audition.[103]

Hence reverberation shifted from being an abstract quality of 'good' sound to being invested with 'story values'. To illustrate how the sound practices and techniques explored above were 'keyed' to specific genres and stories, and to demonstrate how sound effects, and special processes such as reverberation, were used to underpin setting, build story values and appeal to the ear of the audience, I want to turn to particularly effective uses of sound in Paramount's *Spawn of the North*.

Hollywood Soundscapes

SPAWN OF THE NORTH (PARAMOUNT, 1938): SOUND EFFECTS AND THE SONIC SPECTACLE OF DISASTER

Spawn of the North is an adventure film set among the Alaskan fishing community during the salmon spawning season.[104] It tells the story of a conflict that arises between two friends who have known each other since boyhood. Jim Kimmerlee (Henry Fonda), who fishes lawfully in the Alaskan territories, suspects his friend Tyler Dawson (George Raft) of collaborating with a group of Russian fish pirates, led by Red Skain (Akim Tamiroff), to raid the fish traps of the local fishermen. Tyler's involvement with the fish pirates leads to a run-in with Jim, who badly wounds Tyler during the fight, and their friendship seems at an end. But when Jim crosses paths with Tyler and Red on a fishing trip to the ice fields, Tyler demonstrates that his feeling for his friend has endured. He locks Red in the cabin and takes over the wheel. Watched by Jim, Tyler's sweetheart Nicky (Dorothy Lamour) and Jim's girlfriend Dian (Louise Platt), Tyler steers the boat towards glacial cliffs, sounding the horn to create an avalanche in which he and the pirate are obliterated.

In its style and scale of production, *Spawn of the North* exemplifies a shift in the major studios' production policies in the late 1930s, noted by Sheldon Hall and Steve Neale, towards higher-budget productions as the industry emerged from the more straitened times of the Depression, and audiences for pictures increased.[105] *Variety* noted the shift to 'heavy schedules' of production for the majors, and an emphasis on 'A' features in the 1938–1939 cycle, whilst the trade featured *Spawn of the North* as exemplifying Paramount's production strategy that season.[106] At $1,454,782, *Spawn*'s final production costs put it firmly in the 'A' zone of production.[107] The film also typifies the 'mechanizing trend' in the studios, whereby 'entertainment values' of spectacular action and settings were achieved through the application of special processes, specialised technical expertise and engineering solutions to specific scenes and sequences.[108] The settings and action in *Spawn of the North* were synthesised from a combination of location footage, action shot in a specially constructed tank on the Paramount lot, work with miniatures, and special processes for both image and sounds.

In *Spawn of the North* the scapes and spaces of the Alaskan sea, ice and landscape are powerfully and carefully evoked through judicious sequencing, and mixing, of sound and visual effects. Similarly, the experience of the fishermen and their feelings for the territories in which they sail and fish are vividly rendered. A sequence which sets the tone for the encounter between the fishermen and their challenging environment unfolds as they prepare for the salmon run. The fishermen chip ice from the bergs near the fishing grounds to preserve their catch. The sequence opens with Jim and his shipmate Lefty (Fuzzy Knight) on their boat chugging steadily towards huge ice cliffs, where a glacier meets the sea (Figure 25). Lefty spots a large berg still partially attached to the cliff and, rubbing his hands with glee, clears his throat, humming a little musical scale to warm up his voice. It transpires that the fishermen habitually use the power of sonic vibrations and sing loudly to dislodge the ice. As Jim and Lefty approach, they spot other fishermen there, Tyler and Red, and two of Red's associates, Dimitri (Vladimir Sokoloff) and Ivan (Duncan Renaldo). They call across the water, their voices echoing off the ice and giving a sense of the character of the space. They egg Lefty on, calling out and arguing over what song he should let loose with to break off the ice.

'Mighty Like a Rose', 'Pagliacci', 'Mr Dooley' and 'Mother Machree' are all variously suggested. Lefty tries out a line from 'Mother Machree',[109] and with a rumble the ice starts to crack. 'Turn it on,' the fishermen yell, and Lefty belts out the song, coming to a crescendo with a long-held high note which echoes off the water and ice (Figure 26). The others applaud his rendition by cheering, sounding their boat's whistles, ringing bells and creating a percussive chorus by clanking anchor chains and banging on tin pots and pans (Figure 27). These sounds build to a cacophony of noises, and the iceberg splits off with a terrific rending, splitting, rumbling and crashing (Figure 28). The hubris of their celebration at their influence over the ice is quickly tempered as Dimitri's boat, which is too close to the avalanche, is damaged and he has to be rescued by Tyler and Jim.

The audiovisual design of the sequence clearly dramatises the power of sound as an invisible but almost tactile force. The sequence does not simply deploy or replay these sounds of nature; it orchestrates a chorus between the human-produced sounds of the voice and its environment.

The sequence has a range of features; it is impactful not simply because of the volume dynamics of the sounds at its climax, but also because of the strong role that sound plays in constructing the setting of the story. The extensive use of reverberation in the dialogue and song distinctly evoke the strangeness and wildness of the fishing territories. The post-production addition of reverberation to voices and effects reinforces the strangeness of the iceberg fields, and creates an echo chamber of ice and water. The dimensions of the ice have awesome scale and presence, but are dangerously mutable, and the film's soundscape has a shifting morphology. The action of the scene foregrounds the potency of sound vibrations in this precarious environment.

Figures 25–28 Reverberation and the spectacular crashes of the avalanche in *Spawn of the North*

Hollywood Soundscapes

As Jim and Lefty sail up to the ice, they talk in whispers, carefully tuning down their voices so as not to disrupt the balance of the ice. Spatial qualities are also suggested through sound. The echo added to the voices, and the pacing in the cutting of the shot sequence (as the fishermen respond to each other across the water), renders a sense of sonic duration, the time it takes for sound to travel across the sea's surface. There is a distinct contrast between the harshness of the environment and climate, and Lefty's sentimental song. 'Mother Machree' is an Irish folk song celebrating the constancy of maternal love into old age, and has a chorus which builds to an emotional peak and ends on a high musical pitch. Thus, while it is different in tone to its setting, the song's denouement makes it structurally suited as a catalyst for the avalanche.

The avalanche sequence is part of a wider expressive use of sound in the film. Less overtly cataclysmic, but highly effective uses of sound are woven through the film. An episode where Jim and his law-abiding associates take on Red's pirates provides a contrast. Jim's men find Red's cronies – Ivan and Dimitri – stealing from fish traps, and engage them in a bloody fight, resulting in Ivan and Dimtri being killed. Jim's group take their bodies to Red's remote fishing cabin. When they arrive, Red and his gang are drinking and playing cards, and one of them softly sings a Russian folk song. The celebratory mood is broken with the quiet entry of Jim and his men.

The sounds of this scene are designed according to a principle of minimalism. There is no underscoring, and the sound effects that are chosen are deployed against a pregnant silence that is invested with the tension of the potential conflict between the competing groups of men. The dialogue is pared back and elliptical; Jim's men simply say they 'found' Red's men at the traps and 'decided to bring them back', before they bring in and lay down the dead bodies of Dimitri and Ivan. Red and his gang watch but don't audibly react. The silence is broken by the raw cawing of Dimitri's pet crow as it flits across the room and crouches on Dimitri's arm, seemingly puzzled about not getting a reaction from him. The men turn and leave in silence; as Jim turns away from the room, the silence is broken again, this time by the barking of Slicker, a tamed sea lion that Nicky treats as a pet. Slicker has a bond with both Jim and Tyler, and early scenes of the film exploit comic interplay between the men and the cheeky sea lion. In the most expressive line of the scene, Jim wearily tells the animal: 'This is the last place in the world I wanted to see you.' This line displaces the freight of tension in the scene onto the seemingly inconsequential, and safe, interaction between man and beast. Jim's disappointment, though, is justified. From off screen comes the sound of Tyler singing, the sound betraying his presence in the cabin and his allegiance to Red's gang. In this sequence both the cawing crow and barking Slicker are deployed as expressive and empathetic sound effects. As noted, the sounds break the silence between the men, but further, they come from a different world, the realm of the natural, and in the context of the sequence, these sounds seem to gain a communicative function absent from the sparse dialogue. The design of this sequence, then, contrasts with the high-volume dynamics of the avalanche, but the sounds are put to the service of a similar thematic nexus between the fishermen and the wild territories, and creatures, they encounter.

The connection between man and environment is played out in the film's final sequence, in which Jim and Tyler see each other for the last time. Tyler's death is ennobled by his fusion with the wilderness as he drives his boat, full steam ahead, into the glacier that flows into the fishing grounds. The sound design of the sequence has similarities to that of the earlier avalanche; though during the build-up to Tyler commandeering the wheel, there is an added sound element: Dimitri Tiomkin's score augments the tension and suspense. As Tyler heads for the glacier, the score also underlines the emotions of those watching – Nicky and Dian on one boat, and Jim on another. In the finale, though, the soundtrack is given over completely to the splintering and crashing of the ice.

Variety's preview of the film noted its 'exciting and tempestuous action' and the 'lavish production and smart showmanship', and predicted strong box-office returns.[110] *Spawn of the North* did indeed perform strongly, giving Paramount its biggest opening gross of the season.[111]

Spawn of the North typified a trend for films that, with their emphasis upon spectacular values, tested the limits of sound reproduction in the exhibition field. As discussed in Chapter 2, from the mid-1930s onwards Hollywood's sound technicians defined the limited volume capacity of sound reproduction equipment as a problem for the technical cultures to solve in order to present films with the appropriate impact. In preparation for *Spawn of the North*'s release, Loren Ryder, Paramount's Head of Sound, met with the chief projectionists of Paramount's theatre circuit to brief them on the special projection treatment required to ensure the film's spectacular sound sequences played to best effect, but without overloading the speakers and causing distortion.[112]

The vivid rendering of the cataclysmic avalanche in *Spawn* was part of a wider production cycle of big-budget disaster films in the latter part of the 1930s.[113] The cycle was initiated by the success of MGM's *San Francisco* (W. S. Van Dyke, 1936), which featured a spectacular and extended earthquake sequence. Fire, flood, hurricanes and other catastrophes were highlighted through the use of special effects (including, centrally, sound effects) in films such as Twentieth Century-Fox's *In Old Chicago* (Henry King, 1937), Samuel Goldwyn/United Artists' *The Hurricane* (John Ford, 1937), Warner Bros.' *The Sisters, The Rains Came* (Clarence Brown, 1939) (also from Twentieth Century-Fox) and Paramount's *Typhoon* (Louis King, 1940). The virtuosity of the sound craft in these films was recognised at the Academy Awards. The sound departments of MGM and United Artists won Academy Awards for Best Sound Recording for *San Francisco* (1936, 9th Awards) and *The Hurricane* (1937, 10th Awards) respectively. *The Rains Came* was awarded the 1939 (12th Awards) statuette for Best Special Effects.

The post-production sound work on *Spawn of the North* was undertaken by Loren Ryder (Figure 29) and Louis Mesenkop. As a senior sound engineer, Ryder was part of the wider technical culture, discussed in Chapter 2. He was an SMPE member, and served on the Academy's Technical Branch for Sound. In these wider networks, he advocated for 'cooperation between story construction

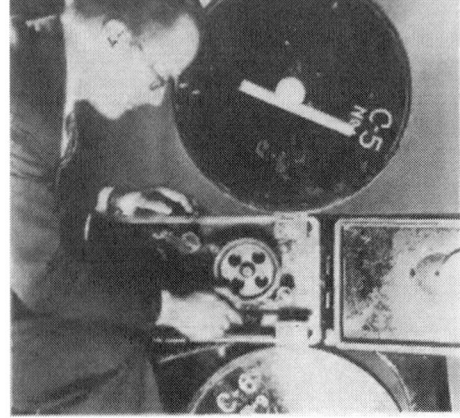

Figure 29 Loren Ryder, Paramount's Director of Sound, from 'Sound's Interesting', *Cinema Progress*, May–June 1938, p. 4 (Image Source: Media History Digital Library)

and sound', arguing that 'technical knowledge can assist [producers] in obtaining a better dramatic result', and emphasised that sound could be used to make 'our audience feel they are part of the dramatic story that is being told'.[114] This impulse to involve the audience is certainly clear in *Spawn of the North*. The interplay of visual and sound effects to construct the spectacular sequences demonstrates the extent to which sound technicians were able to deploy specialised technical processes of sound work flexibly and to interlock their work with that of other crafts. In *Spawn of the North* there is a strong interplay between the use of photographic effects, miniature work and the post-production sounds that fabricate the Alaskan territories.

CONCLUSION

From the broad range of sources I have synthesised in this chapter, it is evident that during the 1930s and 1940s Hollywood's sound technicians developed an aesthetic understanding, moulding and fabricating sound to give it 'story values' and 'ear appeal'. They were able to deploy flexible conventions for creating soundscapes appropriate to the narrative needs of different genres – as the sequences analysed in this chapter demonstrate. These shared conventions formed a framework for sound work, but the choices that sound technicians made in their day-to-day work were finely calibrated to balance the use of practice conventions within the contexts and constraints of specific productions. The next chapter draws on archival sources of productions as a way to examine the fine-grained decisions that sound technicians made as part of their daily work. In doing so, I move from the craft-level shared conventions of sound work examined in this chapter, to the micro level of sound work in specific contexts and production cultures.

4

Crafting the Sequence: Sound Work and the Dynamics of Production

Filmmaking ... is an avalanche of minute choices.

David Bordwell, *On the History of Film Style* (Cambridge, MA, and London: Harvard University Press, 1997), p. 149

INTRODUCTION

The previous chapter analysed aesthetic discourses on sound and explored how an array of flexible conventions for sonic storytelling emerged in the early sound era in which sound interlocked with other crafts. These were appropriate to different genres and moods of the studio era sound film. As David Bordwell, quoted above, suggests, the choices and decisions shaping the filmmaking process are legion. This chapter looks more closely at the material practices and processes of sound work in the Hollywood studio system by undertaking a fine-grained examination of the decisions that underpin the construction of a sequence. A range of factors influenced this work, from the broad economic context of the film business, the technologies and sound standards that technicians worked with, through the management of work at different studios, and to the demands of individual productions. The combination of these factors comprise the historical production cultures shaping sound in the studio period.

This chapter examines three production case studies: Warner Bros.' *I Am a Fugitive from a Chain Gang* (Mervyn LeRoy, 1932), RKO's *Alice Adams* (George Stevens, 1935) and Warner Bros.' *Cheyenne* (Raoul Walsh, 1947). The choice of these films allows me to balance formal analysis of selected sequences with insights gathered from archival and primary sources about their production. The choice of case studies was governed by a wish to contrast different kinds of sequences, and to examine sound work at different moments during the studio era. The selection of case studies was also influenced by pragmatic factors, particularly by what is available in the archival record.

Archival work always confronts the challenge of forming a picture from fragmentary and incomplete sources, and this is particularly true in studying production at the 'ground level', where records of the day-to-day decision-making that constitute this craft labour were often not preserved, or were logged briefly and synoptically. I have chosen case studies where I have been able to find traces of sound work, but inevitably it is impossible to track every decision. The sources I have drawn upon are diverse, and comprise documents such as scripts, production planning documents, production work logs, editing notes, correspondence, legal contracts and so on. Some of these documents, such as daily production reports, form the traces of sound practice; others, such as budgets or contracts, elucidate the frameworks, constraints and hierarchies within which sound work was situated. In drawing upon archival sources to trace sound practices, I have tried to correlate between the material practices of sound work on particular film sequences, the contexts of specific production cultures, and the textures of sound style in the finished sequence. This method of correlation illustrates how craft-led decisions shaped film style within the process of production for specific films, and particular sequences, and elaborates a picture of how sound fitted into the dynamics of production labour in the studios. These decisions were, of course, shaped by the conventions I have examined in Chapter 3, but attention to ground-level decisions, and to individual productions, moves the history of sound from a generalising account of sound broadly determined by technologies and standards to the micro levels of production. Working on history at this level reveals that sound technicians had a repertoire of devices to draw upon, and they innovated to solve problems in style while working within the constraints of particular productions and work cultures. The material processes of sound recording, mixing, editing and re-recording were executed according to subtle, shifting, nuanced and contingent decisions and choices which evidence creativity within constraints.

STUDIO STYLE AND SOUND STYLE: SOUND, ACTION AND POINT-OF-AUDITION IN *I AM A FUGITIVE FROM A CHAIN GANG* (MERVYN LEROY, 1932) AND WARNER BROS. IN THE EARLY 1930s

'Every swish of the lash SCREAMS the horror of the chain gang'
Warner Bros. poster design, *I Am a Fugitive from a Chain Gang*
Pressbook, Warner Bros., 1932

[*I am a Fugitive from a Chain Gang*] ... depicts its grim background vividly. The prison and prisoners are depressingly effective, with the clanking of chains, the baying of bloodhounds and shots of the long cell room lending a realistic atmosphere.
Review, Rose Pelwick, *New York Evening Journal*, 11 November 1932

Warner Bros.' low-budget box-office hit *I Am a Fugitive from a Chain Gang* has been seen as typifying the Warner Bros. 'house style' and business strategy in the early 1930s.[1] The studio's position, relative to the other majors, shifted following the transition to sound, and its business strategy was influenced by the 1929 Wall Street Crash.[2] Economic historians Douglas Gomery, and John Sedgwick and Michael Pokorny analyse the studio's move from a 'modest second level producer' to a vertically integrated company that was one of the Big Five studios.[3] Warner Bros. achieved this through a series of strategic partnerships and acquisitions, increasing the company's assets from $5 million in 1925 to $230 million by 1930.[4] However, as the economic downturn of the Depression began to affect the American leisure economy between 1929 and 1933, Warner Bros., and the other majors, had to manage resources in a much less buoyant economy. The major studios had extended their borrowing to vertically integrate their operations, and to refit movies theatres for sound exhibition, and consequently were vulnerable to the downturn.[5] While different studios evolved specific strategies for responding to the Depression, common principles underpinned the management of Hollywood's major motion picture companies in the early sound era. These principles are defined by Tino Balio as rationalised business operations and regulated production regimes, and were oriented to the goal of long-term stability typical of 'modern business enterprise' in the 1930s.[6] As Sedgwick and Pokorny note, Warner Bros. was already stringently managing its budgets in the 1920s, and was, as Nick Roddick argues, in tune with 'the new cost conscious budgeting and meticulous planning that would characterise the studio system through the 1930s'.[7]

Other critics have seen the film's portrayal of the brutalities of the penal system, which was a social issue with distinct currency at the time of its release, as evidence of the studio's 'social conscience'.[8] The prison film had proved attractive to audiences during the early 1930s, forming a successful production cycle illustrated by titles such as MGM's *The Big House* (George Hill, 1930), Columbia's *The Criminal Code* (Howard Hawks, 1931), Paramount's *Ladies of the Big House* (Marion Gering, 1931) and *Hell's Highway* (Rowland Brown, 1932), a chain-gang film that RKO released just six weeks before Warner Bros.' *I Am a Fugitive from a Chain Gang*.[9]

The riveting effect *I am a Fugitive from a Chain Gang* has on many audio-viewers, and its vivid presentation of its protagonist's experience, is attributable in large part to its sonic style, as noted in Rose Pelwick's review from the *New York Evening Journal*, cited above. The impactful style of the film has often been ascribed to the above-the-line talent constituted by producer Darryl Zanuck and director Mervyn LeRoy.[10] Undoubtedly, they were both important figures in shaping the project and its narrative, but the fine-grained details, which contributed to the subtleties of the film's style, were the responsibility of a wider group of below-the-line workers. By analysing the production background to a key sequence from the film from the 'ground level', I will foreground how the practices, techniques and devices deployed by Warner Bros.' sound and editorial personnel contributed to crafting the film's style. This will demonstrate that attention to the material practices of production crafts allows a richer, more complex and nuanced picture to emerge of how craft and creativity were exercised in the studio era. The film's tough, fast-paced story was 'ripped from the headlines', adapting the real-life events faced by Robert Burns, a World War I veteran from the South. Burns fell on hard times on his return from the war to civilian life. After committing a petty crime, he served time on a Georgia chain gang, escaped, rehabilitated himself, was betrayed to the authorities, returned to Georgia to complete his sentence and, sensationally, escaped for a second time. He was still at large when the film was released.[11] Burns wrote a vivid and unvarnished memoir, *I Am a Fugitive from a Georgia Chain Gang!*, which was serialised in *True Detective* magazine in early 1931 and subsequently published as a book in 1932.[12] Warner Bros. bought the rights to Burns' story in February 1932.[13]

The film adaptation of Burns' memoir is vivid in its evocation of settings and visceral in its inflection of action. The style of the film is organised to portray the experiences of Burns' on-screen surrogate character Jim Allen (Paul Muni) directly and intensely. Within the overall design, sound effects and sound editing contribute to realising this intensity, and provide repeating patterns and distinct motifs which are woven through the film. The screenplay of the film was written by Sheridan Gibney and Brown Holmes, both of whom were contract screenwriters at the studio. Producer

Darryl Zanuck had input into shaping the screenplay at particular points during story development. It is structured very distinctly into sequences, a strategy which, as discussed in Chapter 3, offered a way to organise the story to maintain pace and flow in the early sound film. Sound effects provide pace and characterise setting within sequences, and create linking or punctuating techniques in scene transitions and lap-dissolve sequences. It is useful to outline some of the ways that sound devices are established in the first part of the film, before going on to discuss the production and construction of Jim Allen's sensational escape and chase sequence in more detail.

The film opens with a sound bridge, using a signal sound that becomes a motif throughout the narration. A low-pitched ship's whistle sounds as the film dissolves from the title sequence to the action proper. The ship bears Jim and his combat comrades back from the war in Europe. The whistle is the first sounding of a signal motif that plays throughout the film's narrative soundscape, a motif that undergoes complex tones and modulations, and which builds character and story connotations. Signal whistles are by turn associated with transport; with journeys and movement; with instruction, routine and discipline; and with warnings and danger. This tonal play sonically dramatises the tensions between movement and stasis, freedom and confinement, which are central to the film. As Jim and his companions alight from their ship, they are fêted with the music of a parade band and a cheering crowd, but his final arrival in his home town is more subdued. Jim is greeted by his mother (Louise Carter), brother (Hale Hamilton), erstwhile sweetheart Alice (Sally Blane) and, to his discomfort, his employer Mr Parker (Reginald Barlow). To Jim's dismay, his overbearing brother, Reverend Robert Allen, and his anxious mother pressure him to return to his job at Parker's factory. Jim tries to convey that service has changed him: 'I don't want to be spending the rest of my life answering a factory whistle instead of a bugle call ... I want to get out, away from routine', a line of dialogue which underlines the resonance of this sonic motif as well as portraying Jim's antipathy to the monotony of factory work that foreshadows the punishing routine of his time served on the chain gang.

Jim's resistance to routine motivates him to leave his factory job and travel to seek work in the construction business. He gets temporary jobs in Boston, then New Orleans, then Oshkosh near Lake Winnebago; his travels by train, boat and truck are presented in short lap-dissolve sequences punctuated by sound effects of travel. When work dries up, Jim bums a ride on a train, and eventually ends up walking along a dusty railway track, the sound of his scuffling footsteps suggesting his weariness. Unable to get work, or to raise money on his war medal from a pawnbroker – who already has a case full of medals from 'forgotten men' – Jim falls in with companions he meets at a doss house and becomes involved in the robbery of a diner. Caught with stolen money in his hand, he is sentenced to hard labour. The sequence of movement and change draws to a close with the verdict in Jim's trial, and a remarkably overt audiovisual transition renders what his prison term means. A close-up shot of the judge banging his gavel dissolves to a close-up of the prison blacksmith pounding the rivet on Jim's leg irons. The image dissolve graphically and rhythmically matches the actions of judge and blacksmith, portraying Jim's legal sentence and the physical realisation of his confinement. The sound cutting matches the gavel and hammer sonically and metrically, precisely maintaining the interval of beats across the cut while the different instruments of power retain distinct sound signatures.

The harsh metallic ringing of the blacksmith's hammer marks a shift in the story's setting, and setting comes to the fore in the narrative. Setting is often a neglected element in discussions of narration, frequently dismissed in analysis as simply background. However, as Gerald Prince points out, setting can have a range of narratological functions:

> Setting maybe textually prominent or negligible, consistent (when its features are not contradictory) or inconsistent, vague or precise, presented objectively or subjectively ... Furthermore, it can be utilitarian (every part of it has a function in the action), symbolic (of a conflict to come, of a character's feelings), 'irrelevant' ('realistic': it is presented simply because it is there, as it were), and so forth. Finally, its features may be introduced contiguously (a description can then be said to obtain) or scattered one by one through the narrative.[14]

Prince's definition designates literary setting, but it is clearly relevant and applicable to how filmic settings are both planned and rendered through cutting and sound design. Setting in the prison film is particularly 'textually prominent', and the genre frequently exploits the details of highly regulated settings, and the manner in which a new character is initiated into inflexible routines. Such textual prominence is a feature of other prison films, and is evident in MGM's *The Big House* and Howard Hawks' *The Criminal Code*.

In *I Am a Fugitive from a Chain Gang* the textual prominence of the setting comes to the fore through the carefully rendered soundscapes of the prison camp, and the quarries and valleys where the prisoners labour. These are characterised by background or keynote sounds: of clanking chains that accompany the prisoner's every movement, and the monotonous swinging of their hammers and pickaxes as they work. The sound patterns give a specific emphasis to these settings; the control of inmates' communication means that dialogue is restricted, and sound and action take on primary narrational functions. An interplay between signal sounds and keynote sounds regulates the actions of the prisoners at the camp: a prison guard clashes a large metal triangle to wake the convicts; they follow a set routine as the long chain that secures them together while they sleep is arranged for their daytime hard labour. Once the inmates are out in the quarry, a steam whistle signals the start of the day's work and the repeated beat of the prisoners' pickaxes forms the background keynote sounds.

The film's soundscape is stratified into the signal commands of the guards and the keynote sounds of work. The sounds are divided between figure and ground, a division which articulates the power relations of guards to prisoners. The regulation of the inmates' daily lives is echoed in the unchanging rhythms of diegetic sound. This is created by the choice of post-production sound techniques. In sequences portraying the gang at work, the sounds of labour are looped, creating a sonic background without distinct direction and development. As detailed in Chapter 3, sound loops were created by sound effects editors to join a sequence of undifferentiated or continuous sound. Looping was a common sound practice to 'fill in' sonic backgrounds; ambient sounds such as crowd noise, the low hum of urban environments or wind noise were frequently looped. MGM Sound Effects Editor Milo Lory recalls using the practice, noting that it was useful in creating a steady and constant sound background.[15] The looping of the sounds of labour in *I Am a Fugitive from a Chain Gang* emphasises regularity, and the cadence within which the prisoners are trapped. The sound design further exploits this unchanging sonic pattern; it infers a feeling of unmarked duration by bridging sound over dissolves between different periods of action. The uniformity of the prisoners' experience is also underlined in a lap-dissolve sequence: shots and sounds of hammers being swung are superimposed over a calendar, each beat marking another month of hard labour.

Establishing this distinct pattern to the prison routine through the sound design, in concert with wider narrational elements, fosters audience attention to patterns of action, and to the potential for the pattern to be broken. Finding weaknesses in the system which might lead to escape and flight is a staple of the prison film. As noted earlier, Jim's hatred of routine is established early in the film, and the effect of the monotonous labour, and the brutal treatment of the prisoners by the guards, makes him resolve to escape. He persuades one of his fellow inmates, Sebastian (Everett Brown), to strike his shackles, bending them so that he can slip them off. Jim bides his time, and, aided by his confidant 'Bomber' (Edward Ellis), he seizes the moment to escape; he runs through woodland, snatches clothes from a laundry line at a shack in the woods, and dives into a swamp, hiding below the water until the guards and dogs give up the chase.

Jim's flight, the chase by guards and bloodhounds, and his hiding in the swamp break the earlier rhythms effectively by varying the patterning of sounds. The sequence is structured with the precise use of four contrasting sound devices: looped sounds to create background; the placement of stock sounds and sound effects to punctuate actions; a use of wild sound for the chase sequence; and, at the close of the sequence, strong contrasts between sound and silence to localise the action very strongly with the fugitive protagonist.

The sequence begins with a dissolve to the chain gang working on a section of rail-road (Figure 30). Looped sounds of hammers and picks form a sonic background; in the foreground Jim and Bomber whisper, consulting on when Jim should ask the guard's permission to 'get outta here' (relieve himself in the bushes) (Figure 31). As the action cuts between Jim slipping off his shackles and the guard watching the gang, a different principle informs the sound cutting (Figure 32). The volume of the hammers is manipulated to match the position of the guard – when he is in shot, the volume of the hammer blows is higher, indicating his proximity to the chain gang, whereas when the action

Figures 30–31 *I Am a Fugitive from a Chain Gang*. Looped sounds provide the monotonous background, or keynote sounds, of the chain gang labouring

Figures 32–33 *I Am a Fugitive from a Chain Gang.* Jim wriggles out of his leg irons and takes flight through the woods. Sound effects – the guard's gun and an off-screen steam whistle break the sonic pattern as 'signal' sounds stand out from the background

depicts Jim, the hammer blows are quieter, indicating Jim is further away. This matching is a norm of narrative motivation, and the shift is quite understated, but sound is central to marking proximal relationships in the space of action.

Bomber is able to distract the guard's attention by asking for help, and Jim starts to run. A gunshot and the guard's steam whistle raise the alarm and break through the regular keynote sounds of labour (Figure 33).

Figures 34–37 *I Am a Fugitive from a Chain Gang.* Cross-cutting and wild sound are used for the chase through the woods, adding variety, pace and movement to the sequence

Hollywood Soundscapes

The guards, and their bloodhounds, give chase. The chase sequence, through a wood and down to a river, is dynamically structured by cross-cutting between Jim and the guards (Figures 34–37). Again, volume contrasts infer proximity/distance as the baying of the hounds is heard differently from the guards' position and from Jim's. The sounds of the hounds baying are not looped; there is variety in their barking, and a rising excitement as they follow the scent, building to a crescendo as they get nearer. This build in animal sound gives a direction and a 'vector' to the chase. Michel Chion notes this capacity of sound, writing that sounds can '"*vectorize*"or dramatise shots, orienting them toward a future, a goal and a feeling of imminence and expectation. The shot is going somewhere and it is oriented in time.'[16] The character of the bloodhounds' bark is also defined against the higher-pitched yapping of a terrier, which snaps at Jim as he snatches clothing from a clothes line at a shack in the wood.

The sequence closes by tying sound completely to Jim's point-of-audition (Figures 38–41). As the bloodhounds gain on him, Jim splashes waist deep into the swamp. Desperate to hide, he breaks off a shoot of bamboo to use as a breathing straw and plunges below the surface, and as he does so the soundtrack is silenced. The dramatic sonic contrast between close-up baying of the hounds, which reaches a crescendo at the edge of the swamp, and the silence below the water level, signifying Jim's immersion, is reinforced several times in the cross-cutting above and below the surface of the water, and builds suspense as to whether he will be captured, before the guards give up the chase.

Figures 38–41 *I Am a Fugitive from a Chain Gang.* The sequence closes with strong contrasts baying bloodhounds accompany action above the water, but there is silence when the action is below the surface and hence the action is localised from Jim's point-of-audition

Researching the development and production process of *I Am a Fugitive from a Chain Gang* allows us to trace the flow of story ideas (from script, through shooting to post-production), and to contextualise the construction of the flight sequence in relation to the studio's wider production strategy at the time. As noted, Warner Bros. were a cost-conscious company and, suffering losses in the 1930–1931 season, the company reduced its average budgets, from $315,000 per film in 1930–1931 to $208,000 for 1931–1932.[17] *I Am a Fugitive from a Chain Gang* had a budget of $195,845,[18] and final negative costs of $228,000.[19]

A breakdown of the budget gives an overview of where the major costs of the production lay (Table 1). The largest proportions of the budget's direct costs were on story and screenwriting, star salary, director and set construction; other production areas, such as camera and sound, constituted a much smaller proportion.

Story development began soon after Warner Bros. acquired the screen rights to Burns' memoir, and the script moved through four major drafts before a final version was produced on 23 July, with revisions on 28 July 1932, just one day before shooting began. The early drafts of the story, undertaken by screenwriters Sheridan Gibney and Brown Holmes, evidence careful thinking about how sound might be exploited.[20] Holmes' treatment suggests using the expressive audiovisual transition from a judge's banging gavel that sentences Allen to hard labour, to the ringing of a blacksmith's hammer as Jim is shackled at the camp, discussed earlier.[21] The Holmes–Gibney screenplay also integrates sound as a marker of prison routine, and brutality: the clanking of the house chain that ties the prisoners together is described, as well as the off-screen sounds of the lash that Allen endures and which the other inmates listen to.

As the script moved through the development phase, and through story conferences with Zanuck, the pacing of events was tightened and the suspense of Allen's first escape heightened. Notes from the story conference of 7 June 1932 give suggestions for the escape sequence discussed above. The notes specify the number of guards following Allen, and the suspense created as he hides underwater and breathes through a bamboo stalk.[22] In the final shooting script, the escape sequence comprises scenes 143–178, and directions for the mood of the action include detailed descriptions of sound effects, such as: 'the dogs coming on, yelping' and 'the dogs are just a few yards behind Jim Allen now, howling louder'.[23]

Archival sources in the Warner Bros. production files allow us to see how work was planned and how resources were allocated as the project moved from script development into the shooting phase. A brief comparison between the areas of camera and sound is helpful in establishing how sound roles had been integrated into production in only a short time since the transition. The total direct costs for camera were $3,755, and comprised salaries for Director of Photography, Sol Polito, a second cameraman, two assistants and a stills man.[24] The total direct costs for sound were lower. Sound operating costs for the film were budgeted at $900, with sound operating salaries listed at a flat $1,400. There are fewer details in the budget for different sound roles than there are for camera, although, as the production papers reveal, there was a team of production sound recordists working on the film most days, with one notable exception, which I will detail later.

Table I *I Am a Fugitive from a Chain Gang*: Budget breakdown by area of activity

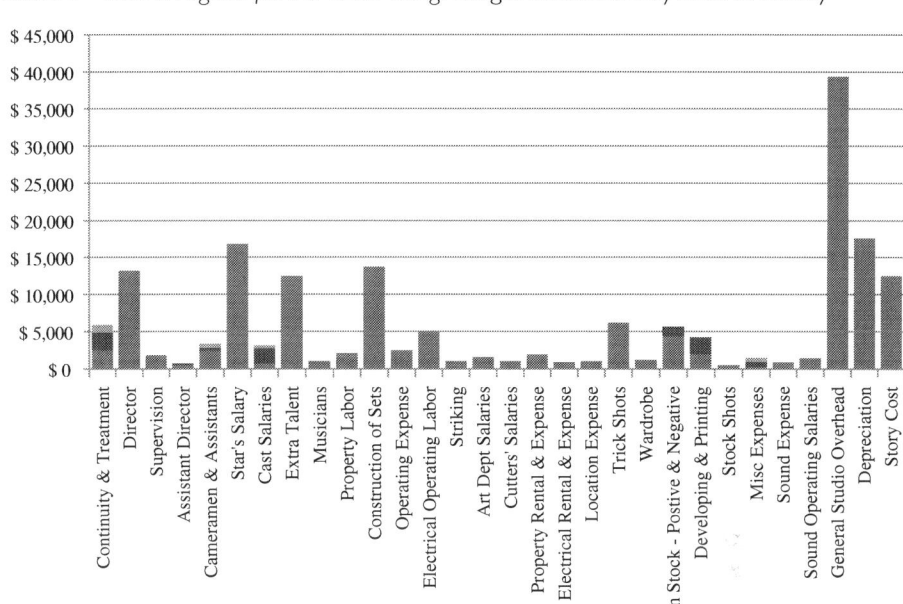

By tracking through the production papers to see how the component shots and sounds of the sequence were planned, filmed and recorded, it is possible to trace the construction of sound with the appropriate 'story values' for the sequence. Correlating the Daily Production and Progress Reports with the script scenes of the escape and chase – scenes 143 to 178 – reveals the organising principles of the production: how labour was deployed and how different areas of knowledge were brought to the crafting of a sequence.[25]

The shots of Allen getting permission to go into the woods, shots of him hiding there and being chased by the guards and dogs were taken over three days: 10, 11 and 12 August 1932 at the Warner Bros. ranch. The underwater shots that form part of the crescendo of the escape were filmed on 3 September in one morning's session in a glass-sided tank on Warner Bros.' backlot. The production planning shows that scenes to be filmed were allocated by location, which we might expect, but closer examination of how the principal shooting and sound recording unfolded reveals that there was also further planning and division of activity and labour according to talent and to technical specialism.

The scenes of the escape and chase were shot in rough continuity, but with the scenes of the sequence centring on Muni given priority each day. On the first day of production at the ranch, dialogue scenes between Muni (Allen) and the guard, and Ellis (Bomber) were completed first.[26] On the second day at the ranch, the chase scenes involving Muni were completed first, with the remainder of the chase shots delegated to a second unit, led by Fred Jackman, Head of Warner Bros.' Technical Department.[27] On the third and final day at the ranch, Muni's last few chase shots were taken (the shots of him grabbing the bamboo stalk and disappearing under the water),[28] as well as the scenes of the guards and dogs on the riverbank.[29] In addition to these shots (which completed the coverage of the chase sequence), the company filmed a series of script scenes of Allen hitching a lift into the city.[30] These scenes are not in the final film, and the action in the finalised sequence dissolves from Allen wading through the water to a night-time cityscape filled with flashing neon accompanied by stock 'city' sound effects.

Analysis of these production sources reveals meticulous planning and an exacting and economical production regime. As historians of Warner Bros. have noted, the Production Office set their directors a daily target of scenes to shoot, and kept track of how many 'OK'd takes' of usable film and sound footage had been taken per day.[31] Mervyn LeRoy comfortably achieved his target of thirteen and a half scenes per day, and in fact on the three days that the company were at the ranch, he exceeded the target, and shot a number of additional scenes. These comprised alternative set-ups of scenes involving Muni, and thus provided a variety of angles of the action and star performer.[32] These extra scenes allowed latitude for a range of choices to be made during editing.

During the three days of shooting at the Warner Bros. ranch, the sound was recorded by a crew of four men: Sound Mixer C. A. (Al) Riggs, Boom Operator D. H. (Dick) Williams, Sound Recordist H. A. (Ham) Cunningham and Swarts, a Cableman.[33] Accounts of sound recording practice reveal that a crew of four was typical for production sound recording with single camera shooting and mobile microphones.[34]

Some of the sounds of the chase (the baying of the dogs, and movement through the forest) were recorded as 'wild' sound, with some 'wild' shots also filmed of the guards and dogs. This allowed sound and image to be recorded with a dynamic sense of audio and visual movement and to be captured without the technical restrictions of synchronising image and sound at the point of recording. The energy and sense of motion and the development of the chase sequence could then be built up through the selection and weaving together of the production sound, wild sound and stock sound effects in the sound editing phase.[35]

Information from a range of sources suggests that Warner Bros.' Sound Department had a preference for recording wild sound when shooting on their ranch, or on location, rather than creating sound effects later by other means. Production reports for other Warner Bros.' films featuring dynamic action sequences reveal that wild sound recording, often undertaken by a second unit, was a common feature.[36] Of course, in order to capture wild sound, the production tasks had to be planned to allocate enough time for the sound recordists assigned to this. In several accounts about their practices, Warner Bros.' sound technicians made distinctions between 'actual sounds' and 'synthesised sounds' (now known as Foley sounds), putting a premium on the former. In 1937 Nathan Levinson, Burton Miller and L. T. Goldsmith wrote:

> In the early days when sound equipment was less faithful in recording than it is today, the sound of horses' hoofs, railroad trains and lion roars were produced synthetically by means of coconut shells, roller skates on wood, and resin strings. Now almost all sound effects heard in pictures are recordings of the actual sounds themselves – from the chirping of crickets to the peals of thunder.[37]

This distinction was echoed in a 1939 account detailing the collections of sounds for Warner Bros.' sound library. The article, published in *Warner Club News*, responded to a question sent in by a reader of the magazine, asking if the studio's sound effects were 'actual reproductions of sound or [were] the sounds imitated?' The answer was given as follows: 'It will no doubt surprise you to learn that in spite of the stories you read about faking sound effects, the majority of sounds used by Warner Bros. are authentic reproductions and very few of them are faked.' Cataloguing a wide range of sounds, the writer reiterated, 'most of the aforementioned sounds have been actual reproductions'.[38]

The practice preference for recording 'wild' was reiterated in an Oral History recollection by Evelyn Rutledge, one of the few female sound and music editors working in Hollywood's studio era. Rutledge worked at Warner Bros. in the late 1950s, having previously had experience at Columbia. She recalled:

> Warners was good on going out and shooting stuff. They'd take you out, go out into the boondocks, and shoot cars, or they would go on the stage and shoot things that you needed. And then you always get an awful lot from production tracks too. And if you have a good soundman, he shoots a lot of wild stuff.[39]

It is evident from the sources on the recording of sound for *I Am a Fugitive from a Chain Gang* that Warner Bros.' practice preference for recording wild sound was in place from early in the sound era.

The final components of the escape and chase sequence were the underwater shots of Allen. These were recorded at a later date by Fred Jackman's unit, on Warner Bros.' backlot. The Daily Production and Progress Report for that day's shooting verifies that no matching sound was recorded for the shots of Allen hiding underwater (as we have heard, none was needed for these shots). The call for the sound crew (Riggs, Swarts and Williams) was cancelled.[40]

Shooting for the film was completed on 7 September 1932, with the premiere screening on 11 October. In the interim period of just over five weeks, editing and post-production took place, and all of these elements and material from the principal shooting stage were combined and woven together in the editing and re-recording phase. In order to explore the decisions that were made during editing and re-recording, ideally one would want to consult papers that allow us to reconstruct this phase of work, papers such as editorial notes, annotated scripts or cue sheets. However, such papers are not always available, and in the case of *I Am a Fugitive from a Chain Gang*, neither editorial records, nor a script annotated with editor's notes is available for the film, neither are sound mixing reports. We can, though, construct hypotheses about the editing and re-recording process, by comparing what material was recorded with the final structure of the sequence, and with reference to the wider craft conventions discussed in Chapter 3.

As noted, the escape and chase sequence was carefully planned from the script stage. Story conference notes reveal that Zanuck advocated tightening the chase sequence, and document his ideas for Allen to hide underwater.[41] Mervyn LeRoy covered a range of angles on the chase by shooting additional scenes, and the second unit allowed extra flexibility by 'wild' recording. Thus, in the editing and re-recording phases, image and sound footage were available to permit the action to be shaped, inflected, varied and amplified to best fit the 'story values' of the sequence, and the wider film.

This is evident in the differences between the chase scenes in the script and the construction of the chase in the final film. The escape and chase sequence exploits the additional set-ups filmed, particularly in offering 'extra' angles on Allen, and to underline and punctuate specific narrative pivots within the larger chase sequence. For example, Allen's approach to the shack in the woods (three shots in the script) is expanded to six shots in the finished film. This expansion more fully develops a pause in the chase sequence, and varies the alternation of action between Allen and the guards following him. Sound effects – the guard's steam whistle as an alarm, the baying bloodhounds and the yapping dog at the shack – are used to establish the proximity of the guards to the fugitive, to spike the shots with tension, and to give a sense of pace and duration to the chase. The final section of the escape and chase sequence, with Allen underwater, is also expanded from the script.

In the script the action moves between underwater shots of Allen submerged and the pursuing guards in just six shots, with two alternations of action above and below the water. In the finished film the section comprises fifteen shots, and the action alternates between Allen below and the guards above the surface of the water seven times. This expansion to the denouement of the chase serves a range of functions. Firstly, the extra shots considerably extend and amplify the suspense of the sequence by underlining the distinct possibility of Allen's recapture – for example, additional shots of the guards wading through the water and another underwater shot framing Allen in the foreground and a guard's legs in the mid-ground. Secondly, the extra shots complete a pattern of cross-cutting that tie the finished sequence closely to Allen's character and narrative situation. Throughout the chase, Allen's point-of-view and point-of-audition are evoked by eyeline matches as he anxiously looks over his shoulder to the guards approaching. As he sinks under the water, the strong contrasts between silence and sound align the audience with him through point-of-audition. The alternations between Allen below, and the guards above, the water intensify the cross-cutting that has structured the escape and chase sequence as a whole. In the final part of the sequence, the lines of action converge as the distance between the fugitive and the guards closes. The convergence is sonically marked in the increasing volume and intensity of the baying bloodhounds tracking Allen's scent to the riverbank, but the convergence point – Allen himself – is not reached.

The shots and sounds from which the escape sequence is constructed comprise a mixture of different material and distinct techniques. Its dynamic pace, moments of suspense and its evocation of Allen's position as fugitive were achieved by the careful planning of how the different aspects of the sequence should be filmed, and, as noted above, how different sound techniques should be blended and calibrated: production sound (for dialogue recording), sound looping, the use of stock sounds and sound effects, and wild sound recording.

Attention to the 'ground level' work in the escape and chase sequence from *I Am a Fugitive from a Chain Gang* allows a picture to emerge of the interaction between sound men and other crafts, and the confidence with which sound had been integrated into production regimes at Warner Bros. by 1932. The repertoire of techniques from which the sequence was crafted evidences specialisation in a range of roles, and the capacity for innovative yet expedient and cost-effective sound to be brought to the service of the story.

TAILORING SOUND TO STARS, DIALOGUE PERFORMANCE AND MOOD: *ALICE ADAMS* (GEORGE STEVENS, RKO, 1935)

RKO's romantic drama *Alice Adams* was among the most profitable films that the company released in 1935, a year that saw the studio finally emerging from the effects of the Depression, and returning a profit for the first time since 1930.[42] The film also marked a return to box-office form for one of the studio's foremost female stars, Katharine Hepburn, and an upturn in the studio's commercial and critical fortunes. *Alice Adams* was nominated for an Academy Award for Best Picture, and Hepburn for Best Actress. Adapted from Booth Tarkington's 1921 Pulitzer Prize-winning novel, *Alice Adams* has features of the 'prestige' film: a 'big-budget special based on a presold property ... and tailored for top stars'.[43] The film is indeed 'tailored' to Hepburn, and centres upon her portrayal and performance of Alice, a vivacious and intelligent girl whose social ambitions are curtailed by her father's illness and his lack of career drive. The scenarios and events through which the audience witness, and empathise with, Alice's frustration hinge upon the narration of the film conveying the ideals that Alice desires, whilst also illustrating how she must adapt herself to the knowledge she may not achieve them.

The 'tailoring' of the film to Hepburn/Alice is achieved by careful and judicious structuring of audiovisual style so that the film's narration and storyworld foreground Alice's context, feelings and experience for the audience. The process by which the soundscape was structured can be understood by analysing sources relating to the film's production. By comparing how sound effects, source music and score were conceived in its planning stages, and how the balance, interactions and narrative functions of these elements were modified, and settled, in the finished film, we can trace the priorities and modifications of the sound's relationship to story.

Before the principal shooting for the film began, Walter Elliott, Head of RKO's Sound Effects Department, whose earlier work on *King Kong* was discussed in Chapter 3, generated a detailed list of sound effects that he anticipated would be needed in the film.[44] The list for *Alice Adams* comprises thirty-five different effects, specified by set and script scene number. There are two notable features about Elliott's plan. The first is that he had interpreted the script for 'ear appeal', and the effects listed form a sonic pattern designed to serve a range of functions in the film.[45] The plan included quotidian, background sounds, and more individuated sounds to mark the specific settings of the story. For example, 'street traffic and noise', 'sound of lawn mower', 'sound of sewing machine on and off scene' and 'crowd babble and laughter'.[46] Background sounds are defined by Chion as 'territory sounds', and he denotes specific sounds as 'elements of auditory setting'.[47] These sounds form the backdrop, or keynote, of the film's soundscape.

It is evident from the plans for sound that Elliott was attuned to how sound might contribute to characterisation. Along with the plan for incidental sounds, his list included sound effects that would be produced by actors, to be closely linked to character. These effects were paravocal sounds and were more emotive than incidental sounds, thus possessing an 'empathetic' quality.[48] For example, he listed 'girl sobbing on and off scene' and 'loud, angry, indistinct voices (off scene)', but he also lists seemingly incidental sounds in emotive terms. These are suggested for narrative moments where Alice's feelings are particularly foregrounded: for example, Elliott plans a sound effect to accompany Alice hopefully waiting for her beau to arrive as 'clock with a quick, high, nervous note chimes'.[49] Finally, the plan includes sound effects that cue audience attention to significant events by sonically 'rendering' them: for example, 'man pounding on table' and 'body thud'.[50]

The second notable feature about Elliott's effects list was the subtlety with which he conceptualised the spatial qualities of sound effects, sound perspective and sound effect placement, all of which were identified in his plan as expressive aspects of the film's soundscape, even at the planning stage. For example, Elliott specified the placement of a number of effects 'off scene', he emphasised background effects that flowed across several scenes, and he planned for one pivotal sound effect, of Alice sobbing, that would be heard from two different perspectives.[51] Elliott's plan for a variation in auditory perspective is evidence that he made a distinction between the 'story values' of sound's narrative space and the 'ideal' standards of spatial recording that were advocated by senior sound engineers in the period (such as Joseph Maxfield). In other words, sound technicians did not rigidly hold to ideal standards; rather, principles of sound recording and of microphone placement were 'flexible'. Elliott conceived of the soundscape as structured by emotional and narrative hierarchies first, not by fidelity and intelligibility.[52]

During the pre-shooting planning phase of the production, Elliott sent the list of effects to the film's assistant director, Edward Kelley, asking him to help the Sound Department in obtaining some of the effects during shooting; one specific request was that crowd noise should be recorded 'for use in backgrounds over CLOSE-UP shots'.[53] Elliott's memo also noted that the sound recordist on the production (D. A. Cutler) had been issued with the effects list so that he might obtain them during shooting where possible.

Accounts from sound effects editors identify the creation and manipulation of background crowd noise as potentially challenging, hence Elliott's request for the production recordist to record crowd noise. It was common practice to create audio backgrounds using short 'loops' of even sound, such as car noise. Evidently, crowd noise could be more difficult for looping, because any audibly identifiable words, laughter or other vocal expressions created a point that stood out from the background sound of the loop, and might catch the ear of the audience and become noticeable as the loop was repeated.[54]

The range of sound effects suggested in Elliott's list was considerably modified, and in a number of cases reduced later in the production process, once they were incorporated in the balance of the soundtrack between dialogue, sound effects and music. Archival sources on the sound work for *Alice Adams* reveal the decisions taken to modify and balance the elements of the soundtrack. These decisions are evident when comparing Elliott's sound effects list, made at the pre-shooting stage, with records of the re-recording cue sheets for music and sound effects, from the post-production phase.[55] These comparisons show how the practices of placing and editing sound effects interacted with other areas of creative expertise, such as scoring and picture editing, to form part of a larger sonic design that functioned harmoniously to underline the key thematic strands, and moods, of the film.

The strongest of these thematic strands are the tensions Alice feels between her social position, affected by the financial standing of her family, and her desire to be accepted into the high society of South Renford, the small town where the Adams live. The plot of the film repeatedly lays out these frustrations for Alice, and the narrative implies that her family's social stasis lies in Virgil's (Alice's father) lack of ambition and achievement.

These family tensions are clearly outlined as the characters are first introduced at the beginning of the film. The opening establishing shots portray the main street of the small town, before the panning frame picks up Alice entering the florist's in search of a corsage to wear to a party that evening. Reactions shots of Alice in the florist's show her embarrassment as she realises she cannot afford the exotic arrangements. Alice leaves the shop without buying anything but, inspired by violets she has seen at the florist, she handpicks a corsage of the flowers from the park.

At the Adams' house the tensions between Alice's social hopes and family situation become manifest in the introduction of a trope that is threaded through the narrative: that of characters, and audience, overhearing painful truths over which they have little or no influence. This is illustrated when Alice overhears an irritable interchange between Mrs Adams (Ann Shoemaker) and her husband Virgil (Fred Stone), who is an invalid. As Alice arrives home triumphantly holding her violets, Mrs Adams is heading upstairs with Virgil's lunch tray. An irritable exchange ensues; standing at the open bedroom door, Mrs Adams remarks sharply: 'Look at your daughter, she's going to a big party tonight, and she's got to wear a dress that's two years old!' Virgil, who is in bed, looks cowed, and mutters indistinctly, 'Oh dear ...'. Alice overhears the exchange, and tries to intervene (Figures 42 and 43).

Mrs Adams: (off-screen, dialogue bridges from previous shot) 'How do you expect her to get anyone...' over reaction shot of Alice listening on the landing

Interrupted by Alice, 'Mother!'

Figure 42   *Alice Adams.* Alice Adams (Katharine Hepburn) overhears her parents arguing

[Alice reacts to her mother's words, moving upscreen, she closes the bedroom door and places herself between Mrs Adams and the door]:

Alice: 'For heaven's sake Mom, can't you wait till Father's up and around before you start hammering at him?'

Figure 43   *Alice Adams.* Alice reproaches her mother for nagging at her father

The brief interchange between the three characters gains its resonance from the mode in which the narrative plays out both spatially and emotionally. An integration of *mise-en-scène*, dialogue performance, and sound and picture cutting emphasises the spatial and emotional dynamics of the domestic space. Mrs Adams' needling of Virgil from the doorway to his bedroom flows over the shot of him reacting from his position in bed, and over the shot of Alice overhearing her mother, from the landing (Figure 42). The flow of Mrs Adams' dialogue over the two reaction shots creates a soundscape in which overhearing forms a narrative device, and the sonic signature given to her dialogue marks two different positions of audition – one for Virgil and a lower, more muffled, position of audition for Alice.

Sources detailing decisions taken in the post-production stage of *Alice Adams* indicate that dialogue volume levels were deliberately manipulated to signal character audition and overhearing. The re-recording cue sheet specifies the processes required to achieve the desired balance of dialogue, score and sound effects for each reel of the film. It details cues where dialogue volume needed to be raised or lowered, cues for sound effects to mark action, and cues for the entrance and exiting of the score.[56] These decisions on the balance of soundtrack elements involved collaboration between different areas of creative labour on the film. While there were well-known and widely shared conventions governing the broad principles of soundtrack balance – the 'vococentric' practice of foregrounding clear dialogue over other sounds – in practice, the finer details of balance might be adapted and varied for different genres, or specific narrative situations.[57]

Cues for the final balances of sound were typically determined during review screening sessions. In the case of *Alice Adams*, the cue sheet was co-ordinated by RKO's Editorial Department, and it gave instructions to the personnel allocated to the re-recording process for the film. These were Editor, Jane Loring; Sound Cutter, Robert Wise; Musical Director, Roy Webb; Sound Effects Editor, Walter Elliott and the Unit Re-recording Supervisor Earl Mounce. The cue sheet was approved by Roy Webb (for the Music Department), Mr Maresca (for the Sound Department) and James Wilkinson (for the Editorial Department), and copies were sent to heads of department, the film's director, George Stevens, and the personnel allocated to re-recording.[58] For the sequence discussed above – of Alice overhearing her mother's veiled criticisms of her father – the cue sheet specified 'Lower Mrs. Adams' off-stage voiceover shot of Alice in hallway.'[59] This cue functions to introduce the narrative trope of overhearing, a trope which is developed, adapted and varied throughout the film. Three moments from different narrative junctures of the film serve to illustrate the multiple variants on this theme.

The first variation on the theme is at the party thrown by Mildred Palmer, a socialite whom Alice wishes to impress. At the party, Alice, so delighted and eager to be in society, is crushed to overhear unkind comments about her gown from two of her female contemporaries. In this instance the relative volume level of the dialogue is raised above the diegetic dance music and 'crowd babble' of the party's *mise-en-scène* so that it is distinctly heard by Alice, and a reaction shot foregrounds her discomfort and isolation in the social space. Here, overhearing exposes insincerity in the polite discourse of social conversation, and undermines Alice's hopes of fitting in with Mildred's crowd.

Hollywood Soundscapes

A second variation on the theme of overhearing occurs on Alice's return home from the party. She is filled with mixed emotions, having had the excitement of meeting and dancing with Arthur Russell (Fred MacMurray), but also having been shamed in front of Arthur when her brother Walter (Frank Albertson) is caught playing dice. The design and balance of the soundtrack serves to amplify and underline Alice's emotions. As she closes the front door, low non-diegetic theme music begins. The music is a variation of the song Alice and Arthur danced to.[60] We hear two bars of the melody as Alice makes her way upstairs; the music then dies away briefly as Mrs Adams eagerly calls out to ask about the party, after which the theme returns, with more development, and a wider range of instrumentation. Once in her bedroom, Alice moves to close the window, and the action cuts to the outside, from where, in a mobile shot, the frame moves in to a close-up on her face as she breaks down (Figure 44). For this close-up framing, the balance of the soundtrack elements are calibrated to foreground the paravocal sounds of Alice sobbing, against lower-volume diegetic background sounds of the rain. The non-diegetic score is arranged sparingly, and instrumented with strings, and it is heard at a slightly higher volume than the rain, offering highly empathetic scoring of this moment. The trope of overhearing is introduced as the action cuts away from Alice sobbing and to her father, in his bedroom across the landing, becoming aware of her distress. On this cut away to Virgil, the sound volume level for Alice's sobbing is lowered in order to structure the audience's sense of the spatial relationship of Virgil to his daughter, a levelling of volume that is specified in the re-recording notes.[61] On hearing Alice, Virgil sits up in bed (Figure 45), looking towards the source of the sound, and seems, momentarily, to deliberate about whether to go to her, but then his expression becomes more resigned, and he lies down again. In this instance of overhearing, there is an empathetic alignment of sound and image.[62] The proximity of father and daughter is marked by the sound flowing through the space of the house, and Virgil is evidently attuned to Alice's unhappiness, but it is their spatial separation – and Virgil's stasis in not going to comfort Alice – which amplifies the pathos of the moment.

A third variation on the theme of overhearing occurs at an important narrative juncture for Alice's developing romance with Arthur, and it marks a crescendo of

Figures 44–45 *Alice Adams.* Virgil overhears Alice crying

the tensions between Alice's parents. Alice has been waiting, and hoping, for Arthur to call on her, and when he does his appearance is underpinned by expectation. On the evening that Arthur calls, Alice sits on a swing out on the porch, and contemplatively listens to a gramophone record of the music she and Arthur danced to on the night they met. The diegetic music is interrupted partway through the song by Mrs Adams, who lifts the needle off the record to quieten the living room, where she settles down to read her newspaper. As Alice is about to go back inside, Arthur appears behind her, having arrived without her noticing him. Caught unawares, and seemingly ashamed of the scruffiness of the Adams' living room, Alice takes Arthur out onto the porch (Figure 46).

The dialogue scene that unfolds between Arthur and Alice has a number of functions in terms of the film narrative as a whole. It is important in deepening the connection between the characters and in giving the audience deeper insight into their character psychology, traits and inferred hopes and desires. The scene ostensibly foregrounds the nascent romance between Alice and Arthur, but it takes on additional connotations through the integration of the dialogue with the spatial arrangement of *mise-en-scène*, the editing of image, sound and character/actor performance and reaction. As Alice and Arthur sit down on the porch, their exchange is framed by a cutaway shot to Mrs Adams listening at the window, and thus their interaction becomes inflected by audience knowledge of a diegetic listener, in this case one invested in the progression of the romance (Figure 47).

The dialogue in the exchange between Alice and Arthur is notable for its style. As Sarah Kozloff argues, dialogue often functions in multiple ways in a film narrative. She outlines the main narrative functions that it fulfils in Hollywood cinema, such as: 'anchoring' the diegesis and its characters; 'communicating' narrative causality; 'enacting' narrative events; supplying exposition; revealing character; underlining codes of realism pertaining to the narrative world; and controlling 'viewer evaluation and emotions'.[63] But Kozloff also observes that dialogue can fulfil functions that 'go beyond narrative communication'.[64] These functions might include the 'aesthetic effects' garnered by 'exploitation of the resources of language'; 'thematic', 'authorial' and 'allegorical' commentary through dialogue; and 'opportunities for

Figures 46–47   *Alice Adams.* Alice and Arthur talk on the porch; Mrs Adams listens from the living room

"star turns"'.[65] The dialogue between Alice and Arthur serves a range of functions: it is narratively communicative, but simultaneously exploits stylistic resources of language, and provides a realm for star performances by Katharine Hepburn and Fred MacMurray.

For example, on Arthur's arrival at the Adams' house, Alice's delight at seeing him, evident in her expression, is balanced by her careful use of what she seems to believe is an appropriate social register. When he apologises that social engagements have prevented him from visiting sooner, she replies, as transcribed below:

> Well, you *have* been in a social whirl, Mr Russell. I envy you. Father's illness has simply tied me to the house, and everyone has to come here, that is, if they want to see me. You know the worst of it is that the poor thing must have peace and quiet and I must entertain on the porch as I'm doing tonight. Though of course now there's just the two of us.

As noted, the style of Alice's dialogue is light, polite, restrained; it is also revealing of character: Alice's social pretensions, and hope for Arthur's approval, are clearly evident. Her 'envy' for the 'social whirl' of Arthur's sphere is communicated, not just by her direct statement of it, but through her performative construction of herself as 'entertaining' on the porch, and a 'casting' of herself as hostess and dutiful daughter via the trope of self-commentary that weaves through her speech. However, the scene gains its import not only from the style of the dialogue, but, as Kozloff productively demonstrates, from the integration of dialogue with other elements – namely, 'performance, shot content and scale, editing and sound design'.[66] During Alice's speech, Hepburn and MacMurray are framed in a medium long shot, a frame scale that, partnered with the medium take, allows performance and gesture to be captured. Seated on the porch swing, Hepburn is the centre of interest. She matches Alice's slightly nervous vocal tone with a range of small movements and gestures suggesting the character's self-consciousness: she touches her hair, rearranges and plumps a cushion on the swing, shifts her seating position, plucks at her skirt and shuffles her feet. In contrast, MacMurray remains still throughout, and his eyeline, directed at Alice, channels the audience's attention to her. The composure that MacMurray gives to his performance of Arthur signals to the audience that, despite Alice's nervousness, he is happy to be there. The editing of the interchange confirms this. As Alice finishes speaking, Arthur takes the opportunity to break in with 'I'm glad it's just the two of us, Miss Adams,' and a cut shifts the shot scale to a close-up of Arthur, his facial performance underlining his sincerity. The cut to a close up begins a conventional shot-reverse shot exchange as dialogue moves to a more intimate register. Alice exclaims: 'Miss Adams – oh, how formal!', and directs him to call her 'Alice'. Now they are on first-name terms, the dialogue between Alice and Arthur becomes less constrained by formality, friendlier and more self-consciously exploratory. Alice asks, 'What shall we talk about, Arthur?', using his name for the first time and delivering it with a pause, and a deliberate quality. Her question doesn't move the conversation on, but halts it briefly, and retains some of the performative aspects of her character dialogue that are part of the larger pattern of the film's characterisation of Alice. The exchange of lines that follows is revelatory of both characters, and the dialogue style exploits linguistic resources:

ALICE: What shall we talk about, Arthur? (said lower, with deliberateness, as though trying out the name)

ARTHUR: About you?

ALICE: Oh no! don't let's talk about me, let's talk about you. [CUT TO ARTHUR] What kind of man *are* you?

ARTHUR: I've often wondered. What kind of a girl are you?

ALICE: Don't you remember? I told you, I'm just me.

ARTHUR: (off screen) But who is that?

ALICE: (looking down) I've often wondered (she laughs, nervously). Uh-huh no, but, no, err … You know the other day when you walked home with me, I got to wondering what I wanted you to think of me, in case I should ever happen to see you again.

ARTHUR: [OVER CUT-IN TO CLOSE-UP, OVER-THE-SHOULDER SHOT OF ALICE] And what did you decide?

ALICE: I decided I should probably never dare to be just myself with you. Not if I cared to have you want to see me again. And yet here I am, just being myself … after all.

ARTHUR: Alice, I'd like to see you pretty often if you'd let me. Will you?

ALICE: Well … (lower) lean toward me a little … (she cups her hands) [LOUDER] yes!

ARTHUR: [CUT TO ARTHUR, CLOSE-UP] Now when will it be? I mean, when will I see you again?

ALICE: [CUT TO ALICE, CLOSE-UP] (she gestures with her hands) Anytime.

ARTHUR: Well, look, you're going to Henrietta's dance aren't you?

The style of Alice's dialogue might be described as indeterminate, halting and hopeful, while Arthur's might be described as confident, direct and assuring, and the dialogue styles of the characters productively contrast. Alice's lines develop an intimacy of revealing what she feels about Arthur, and Arthur's lines confirm and stabilise her exploratory dialogue ('And what did you decide?'/'I'd like to see you pretty often'), until he mentions a party to which Alice has not been invited.

It is with this line that the dynamic of the scene between Alice and Arthur shifts. The mention of the party motivates movement, as Alice gets up from the swing and stands at the edge of the porch, concealing her disappointed expression. The frame and shot scale shift, so that the characters are shown in a medium two shot, with Arthur standing behind Alice and unable to see her face. When he presses her to come to the dance as his date, Alice declares that she is not going, because she is anxious about her father's illness. But the truth is, as the audience know, that she has not been invited, and Arthur has unwittingly touched upon their social difference.

As Alice continues to embellish her reasons for not attending the dance, the action cuts inside to a medium shot revealing Mrs Adams' reaction to Alice's words. This cut shifts the emphasis of the sequence; Mrs Adams' facial expression shifts from disappointment and fixes in determination. She folds her paper, gets up and heads upstairs to confront Virgil with Alice's predicament. The dialogue interaction between Mrs Adams and Virgil rapidly develops an acrimonious tone, with the two characters trading accusations. Characterisation in the

Figure 48 *Alice Adams.* Alice (on the porch) overhears her parents arguing (upstairs in the house)

dialogue is illustrated by the provocative hooks in Mrs Adams' dialogue; she repeatedly goads Virgil by using question tags at the end of her accusatory statements, suggesting a nagging aspect to her character. Virgil's dialogue style also characterises him; he moves from protecting what is unarticulated to a tone of the inarticulate. As the tone of the exchange with his wife becomes angrier, Virgil becomes less and less able to express himself, resorting to shouting 'Dang, dang, dang' in frustration as Mrs Adams loudly weeps.

As the exchange reaches a noisy emotional crescendo, the theme of overhearing is deployed again; the action cuts away from Virgil's bedroom to show Alice on the porch, and simultaneously the sounds of the argument are audible for Alice and Arthur. This is registered through Alice's anxious off-screen glance (Figure 48), and she draws Arthur away from the house and onto the street to bid him goodbye. The audibility of the argument was planned in Walter Elliott's effects list: for this scene he specifies, 'Loud, angry, indistinct voices (off scene).'[67] And the task of overlapping the noise of the argument over Alice's discussion with Arthur was part of the final re-recording process. The cue sheet specifies: 'Carry noise of off-stage fight over scenes on porch at low level.'[68] In addition to the carrying over of the sounds of Virgil and Mrs Adams from upstairs to the porch, when the argument is heard from Alice's point-of-audition the indistinct and angry voices have a reverberant quality. This suggests that the sounds of the argument were recorded separately, and treated for reverberation, and it also demonstrates a moment where the narrative demands a departure from the prevailing convention of intelligible dialogue to privilege emotional tone.

The action cuts back to Virgil and Mrs Adams, who continue to argue vociferously, and Alice enters to try to calm the situation, only to become drawn into the conflict as Virgil asks her whether not going to the dance is 'so hard to bear'. Alice bravely tries to suppress her feelings, but her emotions well up and she leaves the room in tears, taking her weeping mother with her. The final shot of the sequence shows Virgil, also misty-eyed, sitting down wearily in his armchair, and the action ends with a fade-out.

It is clear that sound plays a key role in structuring the narrative and emotional dynamics in *Alice Adams*, as is evident in all three of the sequences discussed; overhearing is a theme that is strongly emphasised and underlined throughout. It forms part of the film's thematic denouement and is central to the resolution of the romance narrative. The Adams host Arthur for a disastrous dinner, spoiled by their overeagerness to stage a socially appropriate meal. Tensions build further as Alice's wayward brother Walter comes home and admits that he has been caught stealing money from Mr Lamb, his boss, and the man who Virgil Adams worked for before his sickness. Mr Lamb arrives, and old resentments between him and Virgil surface, culminating in an argument overheard by Alice and Arthur, who are sitting on the porch. Alice manages to smooth over relations with Mr Lamb, even offering to take a secretarial job to repay Walter's debt. Her honest appeal to Lamb's good nature softens his mood, and he makes peace with Virgil.

Alice slowly and reflectively moves through the house, turning down lights ready for the night. She steps out onto the porch, and finds, to her dismay, that Arthur has been waiting for her and has overheard the whole drama of Lamb's confrontation and reconciliation with Virgil. When Alice begins to protest, Arthur declares he loves her, a move that cuts through all the petty gossip, all Alice's anxieties about social status, and all the troubles with her family. It also resolves the trope of overhearing by puncturing its power to harm Alice, and confirms Arthur as her ideal match.

The sound elements in the sequences discussed above are carefully balanced, and dialogue is integrated with performance, shot content and editing with subtlety and care. Decisions about this balance and integration, and decisions about the emphasis given to dialogue and to overhearing at various points in the sequence, were made during the final re-recording stage and are archived in the film's production files. Those decisions were flexible (made according to story contexts), shared (made by multiple creative personnel) and malleable (were reshaped by the contingencies of production). This is evident by tracing the changes made to the sound planning for *Alice Adams*. Cross-checking the list of sound effects planned by Elliott (from pre-production in May) against the re-recording cue sheet (from the final stages of post-production in July), and the textures of sound in the final film, a range of subtle modifications and adaptations are evident. Many of Elliott's suggestions for the most quotidian effects to evoke the small-town setting of South Renford, and the domesticity of the Adams' household, are reduced, but other aspects of his sound plans, particularly his suggestions for the creation of narrative sound space by overlapping sounds, and by placing sounds off screen, are retained, and in the final balancing and re-recording process these aspects are developed and emphasised in order to amplify the theme of 'overhearing'.

CHEYENNE (RAOUL WALSH, WARNER BROS., 1947): LOCATION SOUND AND SONIC MOBILITY

Warner Bros.' 1947 Western *Cheyenne*, directed by Raoul Wash and produced by Robert (Bob) Buckner, was an 'A' budget film made at a transitional moment in the fortunes of the Hollywood majors in the post-war period.[69] Economic histories of the film industry have established that the booming wartime American economy boosted profits for the motion picture industry. The Hollywood majors experienced a period of prosperity during the 1942–1946 seasons when Warner Bros.' earnings rose significantly, placing the studio on a competitive footing with the top-performing majors: Paramount, MGM and Twentieth Century-Fox.[70] During the wartime boom in cinema attendances, Warner Bros. calibrated its production strategy to prioritise the first-run market, making fewer films, but proportionately more 'A' features and 'super-specials', and investing them with higher production values.[71] The average costs for Warner Bros.' films rose during the war years: from $406,000 in 1940–1941 to $1,497,000 in 1945–1946.[72] As cinema attendances declined in the post-war period, Warner Bros.' average earnings per film fell in the period between 1946 and 1949. But during the 1946–1947, 1947–1948 and 1948–1949 seasons, Warner Bros. continued with its strategy of making around twenty films per season at higher costs.[73]

It was within this market context that the planning and development for *Cheyenne* was undertaken by producer Bob Buckner. The film provides a useful case study of production regimes and routines on an 'A' budget feature; the genre and production values of *Cheyenne* demanded location shooting of action and sound. By drawing on archival sources detailing the production and post-production processes behind the making of the film, and by examining selected sequences from the film, with contrasting audiovisual moods and style, I will examine in detail how the story was constructed, and the ways in which sound played into the film's larger 'story values'.

Early stages of development for *Cheyenne* began in 1945, and it went into production in the 1946–1947 season. The main development of the script was completed by early March 1946, and shooting began on 14 March. The production was allotted a sixty-day shooting schedule, and shooting took place on sound stages at the studio, at the Warner Bros.' Calabasas Ranch, and on location in and around Flagstaff, Arizona. The film had negative costs of $1,929,000, a little above the studio's average budgets for that season (of $1,541,000), but below the costliest films: *Possessed* (Curtis Bernhardt, 1947), with a cost of $2,592,000, and *Deception* (Irving Rapper, 1947), with the highest cost of the season, at $2,882,000.[74] *Cheyenne* performed well at the box office, earning $2,506,000 in the domestic market and $797,000 overseas.[75] These box-office figures place the film at seventh in Warner Bros.' top-earning titles of the 1946–1947 season.

The managerial cultures governing production at Warner Bros. had been reorganised in the mid-1940s. Following the departure of executive producer Hal B. Wallis at the end of 1944, Jack Warner himself took on the supervision of production, assisted by Steve Trilling as 'Executive Assistant in Charge of Production'. This change modified the lines of reporting that governed production. Thomas Schatz argues that this new arrangement brought the primary decision-making under Warner's control: 'Trilling was really nothing more than a glorified secretary, and Warner had no intention of letting him or anyone else have authority over production operations. Warner was the sole executive producer, and to supervise production he used a half-dozen producers, with Henry Blanke and Jerry Wald handling the more ambitious productions.'[76] These lines of reporting are evident in the archival sources that record the production process of *Cheyenne*.

The development of story ideas for *Cheyenne* began in early May 1945. The film was adapted from a story by Paul Wellman, and there were a number of writers involved in the drafting and refining of the script. Buckner worked with three screenwriters in the course of production. Emmet Lavery, uncredited, was involved in the early stages of development, and Alan Le May and Thames Williamson contributed to producing the main script drafts, and to the numerous refinements and revisions – revisions that continued right on into the shooting phase of production. Correspondence about *Cheyenne*'s script in the Warner Bros.' production files shows that, from the outset, Buckner identified two strong story and exploitation values for the production: the use of landscape as a backdrop to the action, and the creation of intrigue about character motivations. The screenwriters developed the intrigue in particular ways, specifically through the characterisation of Ann Kincaid, played by Jane Wyman.

Early in the script development phase, Buckner established the need for location shooting with the Front Office. In submitting his list of principal set and locations required for *Cheyenne*, Buckner underlined location as a priority:

> This is of great importance and value in CHEYENNE. We feature the Colorado–Wyoming border country, the Rocky Mountains and Black Hills of Wyoming. Much of the action is played against the location – straight plot action, run-throughs with stagecoaches ... and [it is] necessary [for] establishing of genuine atmosphere. These are the principal requirements as the script is now being written ... we plan no extraordinarily expensive element, but intend to stick to the standard sets as closely as possible. But this picture absolutely requires genuine location, wherein a great part of its plot and pictorial values rest.[77]

Buckner's wish to exploit location influenced the overall production planning of *Cheyenne*, and a key part of these plans included location sound recording. As I will go on to establish, this practice played a strong role in creating the film's dynamic action and the wider soundscape of its story.

Once location shooting was approved by the Warner Bros. Front Office, the evocation of setting was relatively simple for the screenwriters to plan. The aspect of the script that was more difficult for Buckner and his screenwriters to resolve was how to write the character of Ann. Between the early story ideas written in May 1945, and the production of the revised final script, dated 9 March 1946), Buckner negotiated numerous iterations of Ann's character and actions with the Breen Office, whilst also trying to integrate input from Jack Warner, who desired Ann to exhibit character traits of a 'typical' Western 'girl'.

The plot of *Cheyenne* is complex and it hinges on character subterfuge and double-crosses. The film is set in Wyoming Territory in 1867, where the Wells Fargo stagecoach routes have been disrupted by 'The Poet', a bandit of unknown identity. The Poet's trademark is to empty the Wells Fargo boxes, leaving a poem in place of the money. Gentleman gambler Jim Wylie (Dennis Morgan) is hired to foil 'The Poet', who turns out to be married to the mysterious Ann, and to be having an affair with showgirl Emily Carson (Janis Paige). Throughout the period of the drafting, and redrafting, of the script, the filmmakers tried to find ways of imbuing Ann Kincaid's character with a certain sense of moral ambivalence that would increase the plot's intrigue, but leave them with enough latitude under Production Code recommendations to resolve the film with a romantic ending between Jim and Ann.

ACTION, SENSATION, LOCATION

Cheyenne exploits its setting by situating key events of the 'bandit' storyline in the landscape representing Wyoming Territory. The film's title sequence showcases landscape as the backdrop to the credits, and action located in the landscape occurs early in the film as Jim, Ann and Emily take the stagecoach from Laramie to Cheyenne, and along the way are ambushed by the Sundance gang in a spectacular action sequence.

The stagecoach moves through the remote territory in a series of shots cutting between the incidental discussion between Jim, Emily and Ann inside the coach, and camera set-ups that frame the coach within the spectacular landscape. After establishing the remoteness and scale of the setting, the action cuts to Sundance (Arthur Kennedy) and his gang – Chalk Eye (John Ridgely), Pecos (Tom Tyler), Bucky (Bob Steele) and Limpy Bill (John Compton) – situated on a ridge looking down onto the stagecoach trail. The gang ride fast in pursuit of the coach (Figures 49–50); Sundance shoots to delay it, injuring the driver, and, overtaking the stage, brings it to a halt. The gang force Jim, Emily and Ann to disembark, robbing them of their valuables. They shoot the padlock off the strongbox, but on opening it find that it is empty, except for a short poem from 'The Poet'.

The sequence forms the first really dynamic action of the film and was the result of considered planning at the writing and production phases. Buckner thought carefully about the specific ways that landscape might be foregrounded and exploited, continuing to refine the script scenes for the first hold-up after principal shooting on *Cheyenne* had begun. Just three days before the company departed for location shooting in Arizona, Buckner wrote to Trilling requesting approval for a rewrite of the hold-up sequence. The changes added action and dialogue, and gave greater emphasis to the introduction of Sundance and his gang, changes which, Buckner wrote, 'Walsh and I feel [are] needed to punch up the excitement'.[78]

With the changes okayed by Jack Warner's office, the company left for Flagstaff on 27 April 1946. The company as a whole spent three weeks on location, with the main players returning to the studio earlier than technical crew and second unit crew.[79] During the three weeks of location shooting, a range of exterior shots were filmed, footage which featured in the opening credits, hold-up sequences and the film's denouement. Alongside this, a good deal of location sound and wild sound was recorded.[80]

Figures 49–50 *Cheyenne.* Location shots of the gang chasing and holding up the stagecoach

Analysis of the workflow in the Daily Production and Progress Reports reveals the organisation and division of labour. The exterior scenes featuring the key players were prioritised and shot first. The filming of dynamic action using character doubles, and the recording of wild sound used in the action sequences, were tasks completed later in the location shooting period. While the main players were on location, work continued at the studio on filming process shots, glass shots and other required effects.[81] This parallel organisation of workflow demonstrates how the studio deployed resources for an 'A' picture such as *Cheyenne*; alongside this production, the studio had five other pictures in production or post-production.[82] Indeed, *Variety* noted that the first quarter of 1946 involved a particularly ambitious production schedule for Warner Bros., with at least forty-six pictures planned to go into production.[83]

The production sound recording on *Cheyenne* involved a number of Warner Bros.' Sound Department employees. Information in the Daily Production and Progress Reports reveals that there was some variation in which personnel filled the established roles on production recording. As was common practice, there was a sound crew of four: a production mixer (the most senior member of the crew on the set or location), a boom operator and two sound recordists. On *Cheyenne* the experienced Production Mixer, Oliver Garretson, was the lynchpin of the sound crew – he was listed every day in the Daily Production and Progress reports, and was in place throughout the production recording, supervising the recording on the sound stages at the studio, at the Warner Bros. ranch and on location.[84] For most of the recording work on the film, Garretson had the same Boom Operator: D. H. (Dick) Williams. There was some variation in the sound recordists on the production – both J. E. (Joe) Brown and E. J. (Mac) McDonald worked on different days.[85] The role of Second Sound Recordist, and Cableman, was filled by Edwin Weixel.

Working through the Daily Production and Progress Reports and noting the sound work completed gives a picture of how sound was crafted for the hold-up, and other action sequences. The first hold-up sequence is composed of shots filmed at the studio and out on location, and consists of script scenes numbers 35–41. All the exterior shots were filmed on location, and the interiors of Jim, Ann and Emily inside the stagecoach were filmed at the studio, on Stage 2.[86]

The exterior scenes for the first hold-up were filmed, and sound recorded, over three days.[87] Director Walsh prioritised the script scenes with the key players, and, after a day of interruption when the weather prevented shooting, these were filmed and recorded on 4 May. In addition to completing script scenes 35–40 (comprising the scenes of Jim, Ann and Emily being held up next to the stagecoach), Walsh and his crew covered a number of alternative angles for script scene 39: the business with Bucky and Pecos opening the strongbox from the stagecoach to find that the money is gone, replaced by a poem from 'The Poet', with the key players in the background.[88] The completion of script scenes for the key players allowed them to return to the studio on 10 May.

Between 10 and 15 May 1946, the crew, secondary characters and doubles worked to shoot the balance of chase shots for the first hold-up (as well as the sequence of the stagecoach wreck, and location shots for exteriors for the final sequence). As we would expect, the chase shots were filmed without synchronised sound; and additional image coverage was gained by using a second unit, led by special effects expert Hans

Koenekamp, evidencing a judicious division of labour.[89] On 14 and 15 May, Oliver Garretson and his crew recorded a good deal of wild sound, as well as specific sound effects. For example, the Daily Production and Progress Report for 14 May details that the sound crew 'Recorded 4,000 Ft. Sound Track, wind and birds', equating to around 44 minutes 26 seconds of soundtrack.[90] The report for 15 May itemises the sounds recorded, and logged that the sound crew 'made Stock Sound Tracks of Stream rapids' and 'Stream quiet', as well as a specific sound effect: 'Sound Track ... Single horseman riding through stream.'[91]

This very specific effect was captured for use in the action that built towards the denouement of the film, which had been revised through script changes to include Jim's pursuit by a posse, led by sheriff Fred Durkin (Alan Hale), who assume that Jim is 'The Poet'. The revised script covered scenes 238a–238k, and conveyed action from the point at which Durkin observes Jim boarding the stagecoach in Cheyenne, including the posse's pursuit of Jim, Jim's escape and a dynamic night-time chase. The posse pursue Jim through open country, across a stream and into woods, where he hides and gives them the slip.

The script directions for the revised chase – script scene 238k – are succinct, but specific. The direction reads, 'INTERCUTS RUNNING CHASE POSSE AFTER JIM, NIGHT (ALREADY SHOT ON LOCATION)' and describes the action as follows: 'The exciting chase of Jim by Durkin's posse, as fully covered in Flagstaff location, ending with Jim's escape through the stream.'[92]

In the finished film this is an exciting sequence that builds in pace; it gains its momentum from the cross-cutting between Jim and the pursuing posse, and from Max Steiner's scoring. There is a careful balance between score and sound effects in the finished film; and the tempo of Steiner's score matches the beat of the galloping horses that move towards and past the camera in a series of shots. Up to the point that Jim reaches the stream, the score is uppermost in the sound mix, with a distinct motif of horns and brass (suggesting, perhaps, the 'hunting' of Jim by the posse). As Jim urges his horse forward through the stream (Figures 51–52), for the first time the instrumentation of the score includes percussive cymbals, suggestive of the water spraying around him. But as he reaches the far side of the stream, and hides among the trees, the score shifts from the heroic and onward movement for the chase, and changes mood

Figures 51–52 *Cheyenne.* Jim crosses the stream (script scene 238k, with wild sound especially recorded on location)

markedly, quietening and becoming more restrained. The posse move on past Jim, and he turns his horse back, to cross the stream again. This time, the sounds of the horse galloping through the water are uppermost in the mix, and signal his escape as he eludes the posse.

The action and excitement of the chase is rendered through very precise attention to detail. Buckner's script revisions refined the action to maintain the forward pace of events towards the film's denouement and to keep Jim at the centre of the plot. The production team, including the sound recordists in the second unit, were responsive to the script changes, ensuring that the appropriate wild sound was recorded to fully render the excitement of the night-time chase.

As is clear from the attention to the production decisions and location work, the sound crew worked to realise the action, sensation and setting that was emphasised so strongly in Buckner's early ideas and outline for the film. But the sound style in *Cheyenne* as a whole is far from 'one note'; rather, it is adapted to the needs of narrative and mood in specific sequences. A contrast to the spectacular dynamic chases, discussed above, is offered by a sequence where sound fosters an ambience of tension.

The sequence in question includes action on the first evening that Jim, Emily and Ann spend in Cheyenne.[93] It opens at the Bird Cage Saloon, where Emily performs 'Going Back to Old Cheyenne'. Jim enters the saloon (Figures 53–54), and during Emily's song observes two of the Sundance gang – Pecos and Chalk Eye – gambling. Eager to reclaim the money that the gang stole from him in the hold-up earlier in the day, Jim follows them as they leave from the back of the saloon, and trails them through secluded back streets. Pecos and Chalk Eye realise that Jim is following them, but he contrives to distract their attention, allowing him to get ahead of them, and hold them at gunpoint. At a disadvantage, Pecos and Chalk Eye take Jim through the back streets of Cheyenne to a dug-in shack, used by Sundance and the rest of the gang.

Sound is deployed in a range of ways in the finalised sequence, and the sound mix is carefully balanced at different narrative junctures to exploit dialogue, diegetic music, sound effects and mood scoring; the dominant function of sound in the sequence is to integrate the ambience of several settings with the narration of characters and events. As outlined above, it is Jim's actions that drive the narration in the sequence.

Figures 53–54   *Cheyenne.* Jim enters the Bird Cage Saloon from the main street; the soundscape shifts to feature Emily's song performance

Hollywood Soundscapes

In the opening shot of the sequence, ambient sounds cue the spatial and temporal setting, establishing the busy main street of Cheyenne where music flows from saloons into the street. The script directions for this shot specify the role of sound:

> The street is beginning to fill with people out for a night's entertainment. Music is HEARD from saloons and dance halls. Jim walks casually along the sidewalk, past the dance halls, cribs, gambling joints, towards BIRD-CAGE SALOON, a few doors away. He stops as he HEARS a woman singing inside; then enters.[94]

The soundscape of Cheyenne's night-time street is layered, the sound of men on horseback coming and going is laid over the ambient background music floating out from the saloon. On Jim's entrance to the Bird Cage Saloon, the sound and image cuts match to establish the new setting; the volume of Emily's song increases with Jim's proximity to her. Emily's performance of the song – 'Going Back to Old Cheyenne' – is foregrounded in the sound mix as Jim enters the saloon and looks around.[95] As was conventional for the rendering of song performance, the number was pre-scored – that is, pre-recorded separately and then re-played so that Janis Paige timed her performance in the scene to match the playback.[96] During the song's performance, the volume is maintained at a uniform level, and Paige's vocal delivery was pre-recorded throughout with close miking and with no reverberation. Paige's performance is foregrounded; this emphasis fulfilled early story ideas sent to Buckner from Jack Warner's office, communicating Warner's desire for Emily's character to be – 'a dancehall girl doing everything a dancehall girl does'.[97] Paige's performance in the finished film was expanded from the script to become more central to the scene; the original directions specify that Emily's song will be performed on a small stage at the far end of the saloon.[98] Instead, the finished film has Paige performing on the bar, and with close-up shots giving her performance more emphasis.

The song and its orchestral accompaniment dominates the sound mix for most of the performance; however, at the beginning of the final verse the sonic balance is recalibrated and the accompaniment is quietened down to a single guitar, giving Paige's vocal delivery more audibility and centrality. Within this balance, sound effects from the saloon (such as the hum of conversation, and the clinking of glasses) are layered into the sound mix, adding verisimilitude to the setting. Throughout Emily's song, Jim has been watching her performance and, at the same time, has been carefully casing the Bird Cage Saloon looking for the Sundance gang. He notices two of the gang, Pecos and Chalk Eye, and, as we have seen, follows them through to a back room of the saloon, and out to the street through a rear entrance.

The characters' passage from the busy saloon to the quieter street is also conveyed sonically. As they move away from the main room of the saloon to the back room, the auditory perspective of the action shifts, the diegetic music of the band and the incidental sound effects become lower in volume and establish the characters' distance from the band. The spatial proximity of the characters to each other becomes a salient narrative feature as Jim trails Pecos and Chalk Eye along the boardwalks of Cheyenne's back streets. As the characters move away from the back of the Bird Cage Saloon, the music of the band becomes fainter, underlining the quietness of the street. Pecos and Chalk Eye are aware of Jim following them, but wish to avoid a confrontation in a populated area of town (Figures 55–56).

Figures 55–56 *Cheyenne.* Jim follows Pecos and Chalk Eye through the back of the Bird Cage Saloon; the soundscape of the bar is heard at lower volume, indicating auditory perspective; Jim trails them through the back streets

Tension begins to build as the action cuts between the pair moving down the boardwalk, and Jim determinedly following. The trail sequence is structured around this intercutting, and offers moments where the action pauses – for example, at a street corner, where Pecos and Chalk Eye cast a look backward to determine how close Jim is to them. During the trail sequence the footsteps of Pecos and Chalk Eye are clearly audible on the boardwalk, but Jim's are not.

Audibility and audio interpretation within the story space are key features of the trail sequence. As the three characters move further away from the centre of Cheyenne, the

Figures 57–60 Audio-misdirection in *Cheyenne* – Jim cuts down a side street, Pecos and Chalk Eye are deceived by hearing the footsteps of a passer-by they take to be Jim. Jim cuts down an alley and comes around behind them

Hollywood Soundscapes

back streets darken and the setting is more remote. Jim gains on Pecos and Chalk Eye, but instead of challenging them on the boardwalk, he contrives to misdirect their attention by capitalising on the audible presence of a passer-by (Figures 57–60). As the man comes level with Jim on the boardwalk, Jim cuts down an alleyway, allowing him to come around behind Pecos and Chalk Eye. Thinking that the footsteps they hear mark Jim's approach, the pair arm themselves to ambush him, only to find that Jim has bettered their position, and he gains the advantage, forcing them to drop their guns (Figures 57–60).

The beginning of the trail sequence – the shots of the rear part of the saloon and the first shots of the boardwalk – were filmed on a stage on Warner Bros.' backlot. The later shots in the sequence, and the audio-misdirection of Pecos and Chalk Eye, were filmed on the Cheyenne set at the Warner Bros. ranch.[99] The directions for script scenes 60 and 61 cover the main section of the trail sequence, as tension builds, but the directions offered wide latitude for decisions to be made in shooting, and in the final editing of the sequence. Directions for script scene 60 specify the ambience of the sequence: 'Pecos and Chalk Eye are moving into a quieter part of town. The MUSIC from a honky-tonk is heard quietly over the shot. The two men turn into an alley and disappear in the darkness.'[100] But the intricacies of the action that misdirects Pecos and Chalk Eye, intricacies that are central to the narrative clarity and impact of the finalised sequence, are left open. Directions for this scene in the script read as follows:

> TWO OR THREE CUTS OF JIM FOLLOWING. He turns into the alley, then we work out the geography of the next moves on the set. The point is that Jim avoids a trap and cuts around to a spot ahead of them at the far end of the alley.[101]

As the film entered post-production and the first stages of editing, the sequence was covered in Jack Warner's Cutting Notes, from his viewing of the first rough cut of the film. Warner advises that the denouement of the trail sequence should be modified to draw out the tension; his note reads: 'Scene of Morgan overtaking two bandits too abrupt, and also his overpowering them too easy. Show Morgan going down alley.'[102] The extent to which the director and production crew were given latitude to work out this aspect of the sequence suggests how well-honed production regimes for sound were at Warner Bros. at this time.

CONCLUSION

The three case studies examined in this chapter offer insights into how sound work fitted within production and post-production regimes at a fine-grained level. By analysing archival sources that reveal sound work at the 'micro level' of sequence and scene construction, I have been able to construct a picture of how the craft-led decisions of sound work were integrated as part of a production, as well as the place of that production against the larger framing contexts of budget, studio production culture and genre. Attention to these archival sources makes it evident that sound work was fully integrated into the demands of production from early in the sound era. All three case studies evidence the adaptability of sound technicians to production needs and the malleability of their practices in context-dependent situations. In *I Am a Fugitive from a Chain Gang* different devices were used to render the rhythm and pace of the chase sequence, and the tension of the denouement was intensified by expanding the final section of cross-cutting, and the contrasts between silence and sound. In *Alice Adams* the planning and then modification of sound effects also demonstrates flexibility in the application and execution of sound work for story, and the methods by which pre-production plans became refined to enhance the film's soundscape – in this case to amplify the theme of overhearing. *Cheyenne* provides a case study of a larger-budget film, with 'wild sound' recorded on location to showcase spectacular action, but even within the demanding environment for capturing sound, it is evident that technicians were able to retain flexibility in practice and precision in their execution of recording exactly the effects needed. Together, these production case studies show that sound technicians had a repertoire of sound techniques at their command, the ability and insight to adapt their practices to best fit the story values of particular sequences, and that they tailored their work to fit the constraints of time and budget which characterised the controlled regimes of filmmaking within the studio system.

5

From Gadgeteers to Sound Experts: Defining and Recognising Sound Labour and Expertise

The dazzling spotlight which Hollywood turns upon its Personalities throws into shadow the thousands who work in the movie studios – technicians and craftsmen, musicians and sound engineers, painters, carpenters, laboratory workers. These, plus the thousands of extras whose faces are used in an agglomerate mass, are the anonymous people who swarm over the sound stages, the lots, and the offices wherever pictures are fabricated. They are movie workers, as distinguished from what we shall call movie makers.

Leo C. Rosten, *Hollywood: The Movie Colony and the Movie Makers*
(New York: Harcourt and Brace, 1941), p. 32

INTRODUCTION

Leo C. Rosten paints a vivid picture of the power relations inherent in the hierarchies of Hollywood's organisation, as it existed in the early 1940s, in his social analysis of the Hollywood film community quoted above. In *Hollywood: The Movie Colony and the Movie Makers*, Rosten devotes his attention and his social analysis to the elite figures in 'the dazzling spotlight' rather than those in the shadows. This chapter considers the structures and power relations that put those 'movie workers' in the shadows. It explores ways in which the labour of one group – Hollywood's studio era sound technicians – can be made visible by analysing how sound work was defined and organised within studio sound departments and by wider labour organisations in the period after the transition to sound.

Rosten conceives of the 'movie colony' of Hollywood as composed of a series of three 'concentric circles', with the groups inside them becoming increasingly elite towards the centre.[1] At the centre of Rosten's map, and at the heart of influence on the rest of the colony, are 'the movie elite', the studio heads and senior executives who ... earn[ed] $75,000 or more a year'; the middle circle contains roles such as 'the producers, actors, directors, and writers who participate in Hollywood's social and professional life'; and most remote from the centre of power is the outer circle, which 'embraces all of the thirty thousand movie workers and movie makers'.[2] Thus Rosten provides a relational map, on which different constituencies of workers were placed in the classical Hollywood era. The sound technicians, belonging to the rank of 'movie workers', were located within this outer circle. The value of Rosten's work is this clear mapping, his identification of the power dynamics in Hollywood's filmmaking community and his focus upon the importance of social groupings in the operation of these dynamics.

Rosten's work, alongside that of Hortense Powdermaker, has had a distinct influence upon studies of media industries, and on studies of production in particular. In the work of Rosten and Powdermaker, the working conditions, status and relations of workers to their work are central to the enquiry.[3] Their work constitutes a background tradition for analyses of motion picture industry and labour, and Rosten's and Powdermaker's focus on social relations underpins recent analyses of the cultures of industrial organisations and working groups.[4] Vicki Mayer underlines the importance of Rosten and Powdermaker in establishing a historical tradition to production studies. She sees their work as exemplifying a social approach to investigating production contexts, pinpointing the value of their emphasis on understanding the relational frameworks within which motion picture workers laboured. Mayer argues that a social approach provides a 'grounding' of studies of media production, an approach which permits case studies of production to be placed in relation to wider relations and contexts. She writes:

> Production studies ... 'ground' social theories by showing us how specific production sites, actors or activities tell us larger lessons about workers, their practices, and the role of their labors in relation to politics, economics and culture. It is this connection between the micro contexts and the macro forces, which illuminates the social implications in an otherwise narrow case study and modifies the grand claims that have become commonplace regarding the role of media in society.[5]

The connections between 'micro contexts and macro forces' had a distinct impact on the status and labour of Hollywood's sound technicians. These connections become visible once we analyse the different ways their activities were organised in the classical Hollywood era. As previous chapters of this book have demonstrated, sound technicians participated in different spheres of activity, and they were the 'nodes' connecting these activities at different levels of the industry; from the micro level of craft-oriented production tasks, through the middle level of studio sound departments, to the macro level of cross-studio networks of expertise, such as their participation in the Academy's Technical Branches, or wider networks and industry interest groups. These also included SMPE membership and committee work, and collaborative research projects with corporations in the research sector. Within each of these contexts the roles, and occupational identities, of sound technicians were defined in distinct ways. The purpose of this chapter is to examine how some of the role definitions arose from, and operated within, these different contexts and, further, how role definitions shifted according to the 'macro forces' in the period. It examines how sound work was defined in response to the shaping and organising influences of wider agendas, from the organisational structures prevailing at particular studios, to the labour relations movements and the economic climate of the industry during the period.

ORGANISING A NEW WORKFORCE: SOUND TECHNICIANS AND THE STUDIO SOUND DEPARTMENT

A snapshot of Hollywood's workforce in January 1930 clearly reveals how the composition of production crafts changed with the arrival of sound technicians. *Variety* estimated that there were 949 sound employees working for the studios; this group

Table 2 Employees in Hollywood's production crafts in 1930

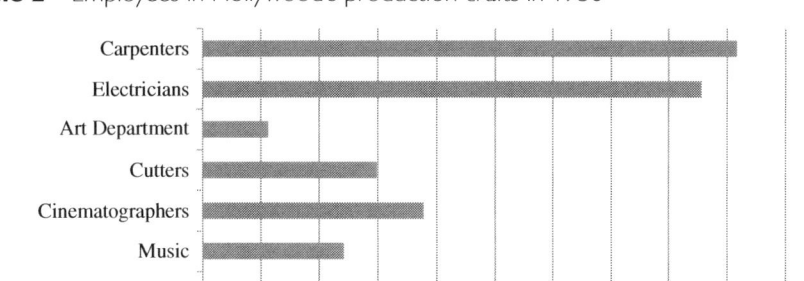

Source: 'Pictures', *Daily Variety*, 8 January 1930, p. 90.

was larger than cinematographers (numbered at 755), employees in music (at 484), art department staff (at 225) and film cutters (at 595). As a section of the production workforce, sound personnel were only outnumbered by studio electricians (at 1,711) and carpenters (1,834) (Table 2).[6]

At this census point, Warner Bros. was the company with the largest sound department, followed by MGM, Paramount and Universal. A further breakdown of the numbers of personnel in each studio sound department is shown in Table 3.

Table 3 Studio sound department employment in 1930

Company	Number of employees in sound	Company	Number of employees in sound
Warner Bros.	193	Columbia	22
Metro-Goldwyn-Mayer	147	Tiffany	15
Paramount	105	Tec-Art	12
Universal	100	Hal Roach	10
Fox	75	James Cruze	9
United Artists	44	Mack Sennett	4
Metropolitan	41	Educational	4
RKO	32	Larry Darmour	4
Pathé	32	Miscellaneous	21
First National	29	Freelance	50
		Total	**949**

Source: *Daily Variety*, Wednesday 8 January 1930, p. 90.

The labour of these sound personnel was organised, defined, structured and recognised by different agents and factors during the post-transitional period, and it would be impossible to account for the organisational differences of every studio. The archival sources that have survived from the classical Hollywood period are tantalisingly revealing of tendencies in the organisation and activity of sound personnel, but they are partial. In itself, this is revealing of the status relations that Rosten identifies; the hierarchies in the studios overall, and within the sites and contexts of particular productions, are evident in the organisation of archival collections. The labour of directors, producers and screenwriters is visible in the often plentiful documentation confirming their agency. Archival production sources, such as production memos, progress reports, budgets, story conference notes and cutting notes, all function to record not only the work that took place in a specific production site or context, but also record the relational dynamics of labour within that site. The 'address', the circulation and the destination of these documents reveals where decisions were made, at which level in the studio hierarchy, and by whom. Unsurprisingly, the documentation of the work of producers, directors and screenwriters 'above-the-line' is much more plentiful and elaborates their labour more fully than the sound technicians, working 'below-the-line.' As Miranda Banks demonstrates, the division of workers into 'above-the-line' and 'below-the-line' labour is a strong delineation and indicates how labour is defined and valued:

> 'Above-the-line' and 'below-the-line' are industry terms that distinguish between creative and craft professions in production. The distinction is derived from a particular worker's position in relation to a bold horizontal line on a standard production budget sheet between creative and technical costs, establishing a hierarchy that stratifies levels of creative and craft labour. ... The work of writers, directors, producers and celebrity actors is considered, and compensated, above the line. ... Below-the-line practitioners are considered ... industrially and socially – as craftspeople or technicians, people who work with their hands. These practitioners hold distinct trade knowledge, much of which they have learned through apprenticeships or on the job.[7]

As Banks argues, the distinction between above- and below-the-line work 'is crucial to understanding the nature of production, and ... to 'seeing the different possibilities' for production studies scholars to intervene, and to understand, the 'invisible labour' of production more fully.[8]

In the rest of the chapter I try to 'ground' some of the broad notions about the power relations and hierarchies in labour in the Hollywood studio system by looking at case studies of sound labour within four contexts that illustrate how the occupational identities and labour of Hollywood's sound personnel were defined, organised and recognised in the post-transitional period. I select case studies of 'specific production sites' by tracing the departmental organisation and the workflow of sound in production at Warner Bros., the largest sound department of the majors. I trace the influence of labour organisations on the delineation of the occupational roles for sound, and the jurisdictional tensions that arose in the early 1930s when different unions competed over the representation of Hollywood's new technical workforce. I discuss the recognition of 'good sound' by the Academy in its awards; and finally I contrast the careers of two influential technicians in the Hollywood studio era: Nathan Levinson, the Head of Sound at Warner Bros., and James G. Stewart, who worked for RKO studios in various sound roles from the early 1930s to 1945, and then for David O. Selznick's Vanguard Pictures from 1945 to 1949.[9] These case studies and contexts illustrate how the structures organising sound labour 'placed', or located, sound technicians within relational hierarchies. These structural hierarchies were underpinned by cultural and discursive definitions of labour: the languages and descriptions that constituted, constructed and defined technical work, and its value, within classical Hollywood's production cultures.

Research in the fields of organisational science, in the sociology and ethnography of work, and in labour history is valuable in analysing and interrogating the cultural discourses defining technical work. Stephen Barley's research on the construction of occupational identities for technicians, and the typical status they occupied within large organisations is particularly relevant.[10] Barley offers broad insights about the constitution of technicians' knowledge, their labour and their place in organisational cultures, insights which offer a framework for understanding the placement of sound technicians in classical Hollywood production cultures.

Cultural constructions of 'the technician', in a range of industries, have reinforced stereotypes of technical work as 'functional' and instrumental, stereotypes noted by Banks, cited above. In the period after the transition to sound, Hollywood's trade press reinforced a division between 'art' and 'science', a discursive tension that I pinpoint and discuss in earlier chapters. Personnel in technical roles were often labelled as, to use *Variety* parlance, 'gadgeteers'.[11]

The cultural construction of technical work as functional arose, as Barley notes, in early recorded uses of the term 'technician'. In the late nineteenth century, technical roles were equated with the 'practical arts'; by the mid-twentieth century, there was a strong association of the title 'technician' with 'work revolv[ing] around instruments' and 'training in a science or technology', and the term came to be strongly linked with work in media industries and electronics. It was also associated with military work; a 'technician' connoted 'a rating in the armed services including those qualified for technical work'.[12]

The task of locating technicians in the structures and cultures of large organisations in the early twentieth century raised challenges. Technical roles had characteristics that contested the common social divisions of work into 'professional' or 'white collar' – those performing administrative or management functions – from 'blue collar' workers, who performed routine, manual tasks.[13] Technicians frequently moved across the boundaries that typically defined and divided occupational roles: technicians were highly educated, often possessed specialist and complex scientific knowledge 'yet they use[d] tools and instruments, work[ed] with their hands, [made] objects, repaired equipment, and, from time to time, [got] dirty'.[14] Barley expands on how technicians often displace work divisions:

> Technicians resemble professionals in that their work is sufficiently esoteric that few outsiders can claim to possess their skills or knowledge. Their work is relatively analytical and often requires specialised education. Some technicians' occupations have even developed occupational societies and journals. Yet, in other ways, technician's work most closely resembles

the crafts. Apprenticeships and on-the-job training play a crucial role in the education of technicians, just as they do in the training of craftpersons ... and a significant number of technicians are trained solely through informal apprenticeships ... Moreover, like craftpersons, most technicians operate equipment, create artifacts, and possess valued manual skills.[15]

The alliance between 'technical' and 'craft' work, suggested by Barley above, is productive in understanding the textures of sound work. The execution of technical tasks in classical Hollywood sound production was underpinned by knowledge which became honed by repeated practice, or, in Richard Sennett's description of craft knowledge, by 'material consciousness'.[16] Cultural ideas about, and discursive constructions of, technical roles surface in the varying ways that Hollywood sound work was defined in the post-transitional period. I trace these different ways of defining, and recognising, sound work within studio, labour and institutional organisations in the rest of the chapter.

THE ARRIVAL OF SOUND TECHNICIANS IN HOLLYWOOD

An intricate and highly evolved business had to assimilate, in the space of a year or two, a large body of technicians from another field, train them in its methods, and in turn modify its own technique to meet new and exacting requirements.[17]

The organisation and the definition of roles for sound personnel within the studios was a topic addressed by Carl Dreher in the Academy's publication *Recording Sound for Motion Pictures*, and cited above.[18] Dreher maintained that the influx of sound technicians created 'some peculiar problems of employment and organization'.[19] The experiences, and backgrounds, possessed by the new sound technicians were quite diverse, and Dreher characterised three broad routes through which the new workforce entered Hollywood. The first route was from the radio industry; Dreher conceived of sound technicians, who possessed experience in the early days of the radio medium, as 'adventurous'. They had, he suggested, the capacity to deal with the 'instability and financial turbulence' typical of a new industry, and displayed an understanding of showmanship.[20]

The second career path to Hollywood for sound technicians was via the phonograph industry. With the advent of electrical sound recording processes, many sound technicians from the radio and telephone industries had been recruited to the phonograph industry in the 1920s; this experience was relevant for the new sound roles in Hollywood.[21]

The third route to Hollywood was from the research sectors of electrical and sound engineering: engineers who had worked in 'the laboratories of the electrical and telephone companies' were, wrote Dreher, 'more or less fitted for the special requirements of sound-picture production'.[22] As the following brief profiles of some of Hollywood's most senior sound experts attest, the path from the research sector to the studios was well established. John Livadary came from Bell Labs to take up the position of Director of Sound for Columbia Pictures in 1928, remaining in post until his retirement in 1959. Livadary had an advanced degree from the Massachusetts

Hollywood Soundscapes

Institute of Technology in electrical engineering and mathematics;[23] MGM's Head of Re-Recording, Kenneth Lambert, joined the studio in 1928. Lambert held professional qualifications in electrical engineering, and had been employed in apparatus development at Bell Labs, working on research projects for telephone transmission and sound recording technologies, and on filters and equalisers for sound.[24] Loren Ryder, Paramount's Head of Sound from 1928 to 1948, had been a student of telephony at the University of California, Berkeley, before joining the studio.

Warner Bros.' Sound Department comprised men with a range of experience and expertise. The studio's long-serving Head of Sound, Nathan Levinson, had an extensive background in related technical roles before joining Warner Bros.. He began his technical career in telegraphy, and worked as a radio engineer for Marconi, and in technical roles for the US Navy. During World War I he served as a major in the Signal Corps, supervising the Fort Monmouth Laboratories in New Jersey. After the war he entered radio as a commercial engineer for Western Electric in the Pacific Coast area. By 1925 he was Managing Director of KPO, San Francisco's radio station. Levinson is reported to have had a role in convincing Warner Bros. to invest in sound.[25] He was working for Western Electric when Warner Bros. acquired interests in radio, and he supervised installation of equipment at the Warner Radio stations (KFWB).[26] When Western Electric began to demonstrate and market their sound-on-disk system for sound pictures, Levinson prompted Sam Warner's interest in the new process. Warner Bros. created their subsidiary company, Vitaphone, in April 1926, to specialise in sound picture production, and Levinson started to work for Vitaphone in September of that year. He brought with him William Mueller, who had been his assistant at Western Electric. Levinson was contracted as Warner Bros.' Director of Sound from 1926 until his death in October 1952.[27] As well as heading up the Sound Department for Warner Bros., Levinson also acted as Technical Director for Warner's radio station KFWB, and was President of United Research Corporation – a company managing Warner Bros.' patents.

Mueller was Chief Engineer at Warner Bros., working mainly in a research role at the studio, and he was Head of the Sound Department in the 1950s, following the death of Levinson. George Groves, Warner Bros.' Head of Sound Recording, came to the studio from Bell Labs during Warner Bros.' transition to sound. The British-born Groves had a background in telephony, and through research networks he made contacts at Bell and moved to New York in 1922, joining the Bell Labs' team that was working on electrical recording on phonograph records, and its synchronisation with motion pictures. When Vitaphone was incorporated, Groves was transferred to Warner Bros..[28] Groves supervised recording of many of the Vitaphone shorts, as well as *The Jazz Singer*; he remained at Warner Bros. for the rest of his career working in a number of roles, including Head of Sound, until he retired in the early 1970s.

A large number of the Warner Bros.' Sound Department technicians had experience in radio engineering, sound transmission engineering and sound equipment installation, experience shared by the following names: Gerald Best (Chief Recorder, recruited 1928);[29] Everett Brown (Sound Mixer recruited 1931);[30] Oliver Garretson (Production Sound Mixer, recruited 1928);[31] Charles B. Lang (Production Sound Mixer, recruited to Warner's KFWB in 1928);[32] Clare Alfred Riggs (Production Sound Mixer, recruited 1929);[33] and Hal Shaw (Re-Recording Supervisor recruited to Warner's KFWB in 1925).[34]

THE SOUND PRODUCTION WORKFLOW, OCCUPATIONAL ROLES AND THE ORGANISATION OF THE SOUND DEPARTMENT

The integration of sound engineers into the production cultures of the Hollywood studios, the organisation of their roles, and the workflow of sound recording and post production evolved during the post-transition period. In a lecture given in the Academy's Schools of Sound training sessions, and published in 1931, Carl Dreher outlined a schematic overview of the roles and the organisation of work in the early sound period. At the top of the department structure was the Director of Sound. Dreher defined the essential aspects of this role as combining technical and administrative skills. The Director of Sound, he opined, needed to be able to 'translate technical verbiage into concise English', to have 'a critical appreciation of quality in speech and music', to understand other craft roles, to 'merit the confidence' of his department and to network with the technical and research sector.[35]

The sound production workflow and the organisation of sound roles in the developing departments of the early sound era were influenced by the technological infrastructures in place within different studios. Dreher outlined two broad schemas of workflow; these varied depending on whether studios, or specific productions, were recording with portable equipment, such as a recording booth or a recording truck, or with a central installation, involving transmission of the recorded sound from the sound stage to a recording building located elsewhere on the studio lot (Figure 61).

Portable and centralised recording methods each required different staffing. Dreher's essay described the usual roles and practices needed for portable recording, represented diagrammatically in Figure 62 overleaf:

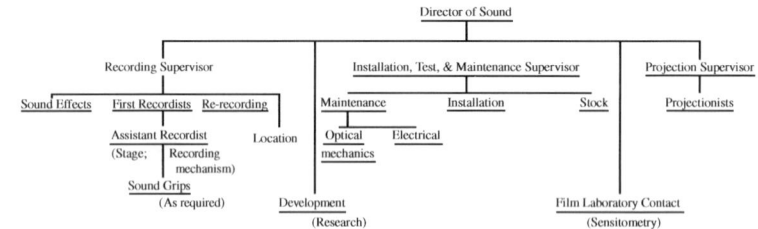

STUDIO USING PORTABLE EQUIPMENT; FILM RECORDING ONLY

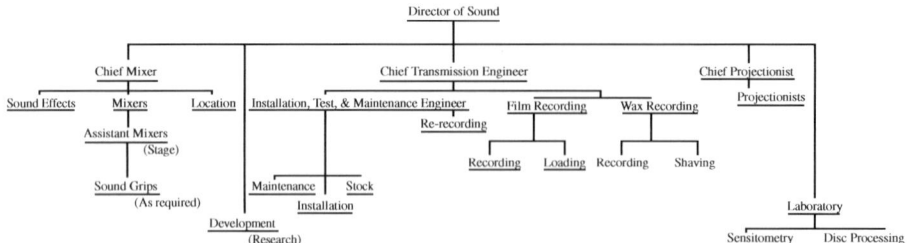

STUDIO USING CENTRALIZED INSTALLATION; FILM AND DISK RECORDING

Figure 61 Two charts representing organisation of sound departments: above, with portable equipment and sound on film; below, with centralised installation and film and disk recording. From Carl Dreher, 'Sound Personnel and Organization', in *Recording Sound for Motion Pictures*, ed. Lester Cowan (New York and London: McGraw-Hill, 1931), p. 343. Reprinted with permission from McGraw-Hill Education

Hollywood Soundscapes

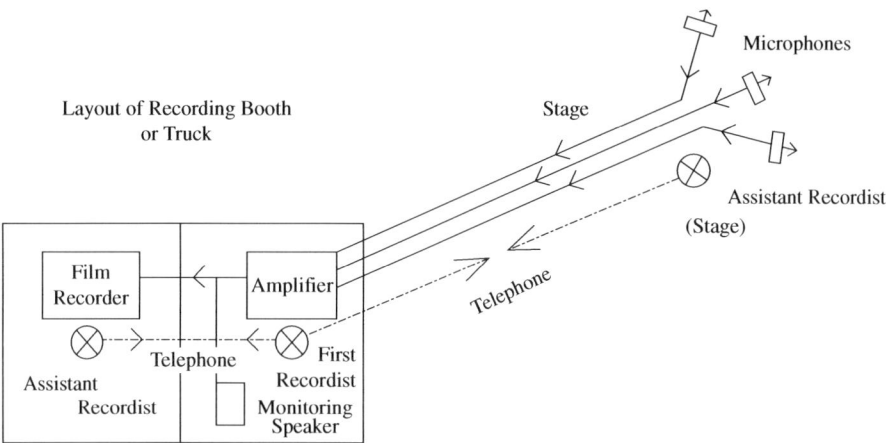

Figure 62 'Typical layout of recording booth or truck in studio using portable equipment for sound on film recording', in Carl Dreher, 'Sound Personnel and Organization', in *Recording Sound for Motion Pictures*, ed. Lester Cowan (New York and London: McGraw-Hill, 1931), p. 345. Reprinted with permission from McGraw-Hill Education

In his essay Dreher outlined the typical responsibilities and workflow hierarchies in a portable recording set-up in the early sound era. Recording was under the overall 'superintendence' of a 'Recording Supervisor', who assigned personnel to specific productions, with a view to the best fit in terms of personalities.[36] Typically, the crew comprised a 'First Recordist', also referred to by Dreher as 'the Mixer,' and two 'Assistant Recordists'.[37] The term 'Mixer' for the Head of the Production Sound Crew gained wider currency as it became common practice for more than one microphone to be used for recording. Dreher noted that 'the term *First Recordist* is intended to correspond to *First Cinematographer*', and that the term '*Recordist* ... [was] used to differentiate the man from the machine, which is called a *recorder*'.[38] This illustrates how the emergence of these roles was modelled on the existent organisation of production craft personnel and their hierarchies. Dreher's distinction between 'man' and 'machine' is also significant, indicating the cultural tie between technology, apparatus and worker in the emerging technical craft roles of the early sound period. Typically, one of the assistant recordists was on the sound stage overseeing the microphones, the other was in the recording booth, or truck, and 'operate[d] the recording machine'.[39] The first recordist was in charge of the crew, and was 'stationed' in the recording booth or truck. He monitored the sound through a speaker, and adjusted the gain of the amplifier. When more than one microphone was used, the first recordist mixed the outputs, and carried final responsibility for microphone placement.

The plan, shown in Figure 62, represents where the members of the crew would typically be located, with lines of communication by telephone allowing them to confer on the quality of the recording, and about any problems. Dreher noted, 'When communication through intermediaries is unsatisfactory, the first recordist goes on the stage and contacts directly with the director or his assistants.'[40]

Testimony in oral histories, and accounts in craft commentaries about common practice in sound production methods, frequently discussed how sound recordists dealt with communications with director and stars on the sound stage, or location, in the course of their daily tasks. Sketching out the production process at MGM, Douglas

Shearer, the studio's Director of Sound, described the role and responsibilities of the mixer, located in a sound monitoring booth:

> During the rehearsal of a scene, interruptions from the 'mixer' are frequent. He presses a button and speaks into a microphone from which his voice is amplified onto the set. 'Mr Blank will have to be a little louder on that last sentence,' he may call to the director. 'He moves away from the microphone and fades a bit.' The actor hears the comment and nods to indicate he will attend to the matter in the next rehearsal.[41]

Shearer's account of on-set practice emphasises the role and influence of the mixer, and his description of the actor meekly nodding to accept performance notes from the technician was not a situation universally experienced by Hollywood's sound men. Craft-lore and anecdotes abound about the sensitivities of talent to the 'disruptions' to the flow of shooting and performance by below-the-line sound technicians. The ability to deal with the tensions on set, and to communicate clearly about problems in production, was, in Dreher's opinion, an essential characteristic:

> Of all the elements of character required for the job, coolness in difficult situations is the *sine qua non*. Agitation, except on the part of actors and a few directors, cannot be tolerated on a stage ... Furthermore, a show of apprehension or uncertainty results in a loss of confidence which, in the atmosphere of a picture production, is extremely harmful ... Closely connected with this quality of calmness under tension is the power to make decisions quickly and without elaborate explanations. When the first recordist is asked whether a take is good for sound or not, he should be able to answer 'yes' or 'no'. If he is uncertain, the proper answer is 'no', with a compact statement of what he believes will improve the take from the viewpoint of sound. In this way production is accelerated and the best mental and emotional attitude maintained among the members of the company.[42]

Innovations and improvements in sound equipment brought changes to sound practices and roles. The advent of the microphone boom, for example, shaped sound recording practices, as well as sound production recording and support roles. The boom enabled sound recording to be mobile, and to allow dialogue to be recorded along with fluid action on the sound stage, and introduced extra sound men to co-ordinate its movement.

In the early years of his employment at RKO, James G. Stewart worked as a Boom Operator, and in his Oral History he recalled that the pragmatic needs of particular production situations often influenced how communication flowed on the set. In terms of organisational hierarchy, the mixer headed up the sound crew, but in the early sound era, because the mixer was often located in a recording booth to monitor sound, he 'was isolated from the actual stage production', whereas the boom man was on set, in close proximity to director and producer, and consequently often communicated directly with them.[43] Stewart recalled the process and tasks necessary for the preparation for a shot. Between set-ups the director, cameraman and boom man would discuss and plan for their next shot:

> the cameraman dictated where his camera was going to be. As a boom man you looked that over, and then you directed your crew where the microphone boom would go to give you the maximum reach and accessibility to the performers.[44]

Hollywood Soundscapes

For complicated mobile shots, three, or even four, rehearsals of the movement for the actors, camera, and sound crew were not unusual.[45] Stewart described watching the rehearsal to allow him to see 'the mechanics of the shot', and to assess the positions of the principals and of the camera to determine where the boom might be placed. Following that, a process of discussion and negotiation between camera, lighting and sound would take place to come to the best arrangement for all crafts.

As Stewart recalled, co-ordinating the boom movement with camera, lights and action required precise organisation and timing, and a combination of physical strength and dexterity. The boom permitted mobility, but the microphones used with them were heavy, and even with the improvements in microphone recording range in the early 1930s, microphones had to be kept within five feet of the actor.[46]

Occasionally you got into a shot [where you had to move the boom]. You had two or three men who could move the boom, but it was not made to be moved. ... On the big booms you stood on a platform ... anywhere from two to five feet off the ground. And there was the physical effort involved in moving it. The mass of the microphone ... weighed 20 pounds in some cases, and the boom when extended ... was 15 feet from the pedestal out to the boom.[47]

Stewart described co-ordinating the microphone, the extension arm of the boom, and a counterbalancing weight stabilising the boom:

So you had three things to do ... under your arm you had the full weight of the ... boom. In your left hand, you had [a device] which changed the position of the microphone. And in your right arm you had a crank [to drive] the boom arm in and out ... So you had to become very expert at moving the microphone with the actor, keeping your feet on the [boom] plat-form ... and keeping the microphone out of the picture.[48]

Stewart also had experience as a mixer at RKO. Mixing practices using portable equipment evolved as sound mixers moved to monitoring the recording through headphones rather than using a loudspeaker. This afforded mixers the freedom to be located on the sound stage, much closer to the action, and to mix the microphone inputs on a portable panel. Stewart recalled mixing the inputs from up to six microphones at once, guided by dialogue cues from the script.[49]

Centralised sound recording required a different organisation of workflow and roles, and technical support and maintenance roles were essential to keep the complex electrical machinery and planting in good working order. Accounts of centralised recording processes at Warner Bros. offer a case study of how workflow was organised, and indicate how personnel and resources were allocated to different areas of work in the sound recording and post-production chain.

The typical routines of work in centralised recording at Warner Bros. were outlined by Sam Goode of the Sound Department in the studio's house magazine *Warner Club News* in October 1939. In his article Goode related the steps in recording and re-recording from the boom man on the sound stage, through to the final release print. He described the involvement of the Warner Bros. sound men at each step. The workflow began with the boom operator on the sound stage, who 'anticipat[ed]' the moves of the actors from the dialogue cues he had memorised; the Sound Department had six boom men in its employ at the time of Goode's article.[50] The next step in the sound recording chain was the mixer, located at a mixing console on the sound stage and listening, through earphones, to the inputs from 'as many as three microphones', and keeping 'each one at the proper volume, according to its relative value in the picture'; Goode names nine mixers in the department.[51] In the course of monitoring the production sound, the mixer communicated by telephone with the boom man on the sound stage, and with the sound recordist in the central recording building.

The sound stages were connected with the main amplifier room of the recording building by sound transmission circuits. The amplifier room had apparatus that was assigned to the different companies filming simultaneously on different sound stages. Sid Ryan, a sound engineer with expertise in transmission, managed the allocation of apparatus. George Groves, Warner Bros.' Chief Mixer, oversaw the recording and communicated with the stage mixers, and William 'Bill' Mueller (Chief Engineer) and Dr Burton 'Burt' Miller (Senior Transmission Engineer), both senior sound experts for the studio, provided further supervision and expertise.[52]

From the main amplifier room, the sound for each company was transmitted to one of the recording rooms, located on a lower floor of the same building. Goode explained, 'these rooms are assigned each day to various companies working on the stages, and may be switched from stage to stage at the Patch Panel'.[53] Each room was equipped with sound recorders, operated by a team of sound recordists; Goode named nine recordists, and an additional four men who undertook relief recording or specialised work.[54] The recorder rooms were maintained by Ryan, Miller and other transmission engineers. From the recording rooms, the optically recorded sound film was sent to the laboratory for processing, and the 'dailies' checked.

The next tasks that Goode outlined are of the editorial assembly, the addition of music and sound effects by dubbing, and the final re-recording of the release print. These tasks were common to both portable and centralised recording at Warner Bros., and I have described these practices in more detail in Chapter 3. Goode outlined the steps for dubbing of music and sound effects, which were undertaken in one of four re-recording rooms in Warner Bros.' Dupe Building.[55] Each re-recording room was operated by a separate crew, of three to four re-recording mixers, supervised by a head of crew. Evidently, Warner Bros. had four such crews in the Sound Department in 1939, and this sector of the department also included one re-recording mixer who specialised in sound editing and effects for cartoons, and one sound man responsible for the film vaults – in total, this comprised eighteen personnel.[56] The final phases of re-recording were undertaken in the Machine Room, located in the Dupe Building. The music, sound effects and dialogue tracks were run 'to be combined by the Mixer'; Goode names a staff of six mixers.[57] He wrote that the Machine Room 'concentrates' the machines necessary 'to supply four Dupe rooms' (i.e. the multiple tracks were combined into one final track): 'it is not uncommon to see as many as twelve sound tracks being duped into one track for the final recording'.[58] Goode related that the final recording was supervised by just three staff.[59]

In addition to covering the workflow of sound from recording to release, Goode's article detailed the roles and personnel assigned to maintenance, servicing and administration in the Sound Department. The Machine Shop housed the three mechanical maintenance staff, the Sound Department Storeroom was supervised by one member of staff, and the Workshop had two staff who performed maintenance on cables, moviolas 'and miscellaneous electrical equipment'.[60] The administrative roles for the department were filled by Nathan Levinson, William Mueller and George Groves. These senior sound technicians assigned all the mixers, recordists and stage men to the companies in production; they also organised the allocation of equipment and ensured that necessary maintenance was undertaken.[61]

Goode's account is obviously just a snapshot of typical practices at Warner Bros. in the late 1930s, but it offers useful insights into the scale of personnel employed by the department, and the numbers of staff in particular roles. It makes visible the allocation of resource to particular areas of activity, revealing that the most labour-intensive area of employment was re-recording, followed by centralised recording. These were areas where there was evident group-working of crews on a single task. Goode's account also points up the importance of expert supervision by senior sound experts – such as George Groves, William Mueller and Burton Miller – at specific points of the sound chain; and the presence of specialised sound experts in transmission, as well as a tier of supporting and maintenance staff who did not have roles in direct production tasks, but in the day-to-day, albeit essential, routine jobs of keeping plant and apparatus functioning. By comparing the range of roles, and the tasks completed by these roles, described in Goode's account with those outlined by Dreher, it is evident that between 1931 and 1939 sound roles became much more distinctly demarcated, specialised and stratified into hierarchies of responsibility.

The definition of what sound work entailed was part of the wider division and demarcation of roles for the Hollywood labour force. Janet Staiger pinpoints the divisions that separated 'talent' from 'craft' roles, and the ways that these divisions governed the ability of workers to negotiate for the value of their labour as the Hollywood industry matured and production became more stratified and corporatised. 'Talent', such as screenwriters, directors and stars, had what employers considered 'desired knowledge' and their 'special abilities' were not substitutable. In contrast, to a large extent craft roles, and less skilled labour roles, had 'a ready supply of willing and able replacements'.[62] Labour organisations, in the form of guilds and unions, sought to organise Hollywood's workforce, to negotiate between workers and employers on pay and conditions, and to shape how labour was defined and recognised. The role demarcations of the sound craft emerged as a consequence of the organisational forces, and struggles, beyond individual studio departments, forces exerted as different labour unions sought to organise, represent and mobilise the new workforce of sound personnel.

UNIONS, ROLES AND LABOUR RELATIONS IN THE 1930s

The new sound personnel and the technological changes of Hollywood's transition to sound production profoundly and rapidly shifted the labour relations agenda; Murray Ross describes what the sound technician meant to labour organisations:

> The sound technician arrived on the Hollywood scene. He was a desirable asset and both stagehands and electricians claimed him. Everyone was convinced that the future of the industry centered on sound. The union that controlled the sound men, therefore, would hold a strategic bargaining ace; these well-paid technicians could also help materially in lining union coffers.[63]

The battle to hold the 'strategic bargaining ace' of Hollywood's new technical workforce was bitter, and it extended throughout the 1930s. The struggle for the jurisdiction of sound labour was affected by a range of factors. It was constrained by the labour relations agreements in place before the transition to sound production, and it was framed by the wider economic conditions of the Depression. Labour relations between Hollywood workers and management were also shaped by the US government's establishment of an industrial code of fair competition for the motion picture industry as part of the National Industrial Recovery Act (NIRA), passed in June 1933; the reputational standing of unions were also affected by the extortion scandal that involved the leadership of the International Alliance of Theatrical Stage Employees (IATSE) at its highest level.[64]

In the period that the Hollywood majors began the transition to sound production in earnest, the relations between management and labour were framed by the Studio Basic Agreement (SBA), which had been signed in November 1926. The signatories to the agreement were the nine major producing companies that formed the membership of the Association of Motion Picture Producers (AMPP) and five large unions that, between them, represented a large body of motion picture production workers: stagehands (represented by IATSE), carpenters (represented by the United Brotherhood of Carpenters and Joiners), electricians (represented by the International Brotherhood of Electrical Workers [IBEW]), painters (represented by the International Brotherhood of Painters, Decorators and Paperhangers) and musicians (represented by the American Federation of Musicians). The 1926 SBA was Hollywood's first labour agreement, and it was periodically renegotiated and renewed during the 1930s. Before it came into effect, the industry was 'open shop', meaning that producers could employ union or non-union workers. But during the 1920s, as the production workforce became more unionised, union leaders were able to begin to pressure management on labour relations, and the studios sought to 'regularize [their] relations with labor' through a central agreement mechanism.[65] As Denise Hartsough observes, 'the SBA centralized the power to negotiate', enabling labour negotiations to be managed and limited through a committee comprising five union and five management representatives dealing with all discussions on wages, hours and working conditions. As Hartsough points out, centralising negotiations in this manner suited both parties, and she argues that 'high union officials tend to share with management an interest in stability' even if it required them to 'hold the rank and file' to SBA agreements on hours and pay.[66]

Sound engineers arriving in Hollywood before 1930 did not have a dedicated union to serve their interests. The IBEW and IATSE pitched strongly to sign up the sound technicians as members. Many of the engineers with backgrounds in the radio, telephone and electrical engineering industries, and sound engineers with sound equipment installation experience, had existing affiliations with the IBEW, the union that had strong membership among these areas of labour. IATSE also courted the sound technicians to join its Local 37 branch, which represented the Hollywood mechanics. Membership of either the IBEW or IATSE Local 37 put sound work under a broad umbrella definition of 'mechanical' or 'electrical' work, and sound technicians began to try to organise for union representation more tailored to their skills and craft.

Throughout 1930 the IBEW and IATSE competed to represent Hollywood's sound engineers. In April 1930 *Variety* reported on talks between IATSE and the IBEW over the jurisdiction of sound technicians and installation engineers, noting: 'The talker mechanics are comparatively a new labor group with recognized status in the union but no direct connections.'[67] Later that year *Variety* acknowledged the importance of Hollywood's sound workers:

> Of all technicians in pictures considered most important from a standpoint of knowledge and training are the sound engineers, cameramen and lab workers. These men belong ... to the only group who could not be replaced on short notice.[68]

Variety had pinpointed that technical labour gained a specific hold in the motion picture industry; there was, as Stephen Barley conceives, a 'tightly coupling' of technical work and its specialised knowledge with complex technological processes. This tight coupling gave technicians a particular status as workers positioned at 'the cut point' of production processes; and their absence could bring the process to a standstill.[69]

In September 1930 a group of sound men, all of whom were already members of Local 37, organised to form a new IATSE Local specifically for sound technicians; this was the origin of Local 695, which was chartered on 29 September 1930.[70] By April 1931 Local 695 had a membership of 625 sound workers, and had ambitions to represent all sound-related work in Hollywood. They also aimed to gain jurisdiction of sound installation and testing of sound systems, an area of labour represented by IBEW Local 40. The dispute over jurisdiction was an issue taken up by the IATSE executive nationally, with talks taking place between IATSE and the IBEW in Washington in May 1931.[71]

Underpinning these jurisdictional issues were wider struggles for the unions to obtain recognition for the sound craft from Hollywood's producers. It was not possible for IATSE Local 695 to gain recognition under the terms of the 1926 SBA, because these terms had been drawn up before the transition to sound, and hence did not cater for Hollywood's sound workers. The SBA specified that 'no new group could enter the agreement' unless it obtained the unanimous consent of the signatory unions'.[72] With the IBEW and IATSE at loggerheads over the jurisdiction of sound work, it was impossible to get the agreement necessary for sound to be recognised under the SBA.

Consequently, Local 695 had little bargaining power with the majors on wages or working conditions. Local 695 tried to gain recognition by setting up agreements with some independent producers, which were not members of the AMPP, and hence were not signatories to the SBA. This strategy aimed at 'giving the local implicit recognition as the proper bargaining agent for sound men'.[73] At meetings to renew the SBA in 1931, IATSE lobbied for the revised SBA to cover IATSE Locals for lab workers and sound technicians, but industry executives objected to an increase in membership. In response, IATSE Local 695 threatened to strike over the lack of recognition under the SBA.[74]

In a bid to secure recognition, Local 695 approached Columbia Pictures in March 1932 and tried to induce the company to sign its wage-scale contract for sound technicians. Columbia had not been a member of the AMPP at the point of the SBA renewal in 1931 and, Local 695 argued, this meant the company was free to sign the 695 contract. Columbia refused, and Local 695 rested their request for the rest of 1932.[75]

Wider contexts also affected labour relations, and amplified these issues of recognition and representation for sound workers. The strong economic downturn of the Depression resulted in the studios introducing deep cuts in wages in the spring of 1933. Initially, the studios planned to cut the wages of all workers, but after uproar from the unions the plan was modified so that lower-paid workers sacrificed only a small percentage of their pay.[76] IATSE lost control of its Locals for camera, lab work and sound technicians over the wage cuts, and during July 1933 these Locals went out on strike, determined to hold the majors to the terms of the SBA.

Hartsough notes that studios found these specialised workers most difficult to replace, and their absence 'hindered production'.[77] Under a headline 'Strike Ties up Hollywood', *Variety* reported that: 'Production at 11 studios was considered at a standstill by the walkout of IATSE union crafts ... This mandate throws 5,000 union men out of employment, and affects 27,000 people working in all departments of the studios', and went on to describe how the studios were temporarily mitigating the absence of striking sound technicians:

> Paramount started early this morning at sound speed with dead mikes, rehearsing casts and training new sound men. United Artists got its replacements from ERPI, Metro transferred men from recording department to sets, replacing them with radio and telephone men to handle inside technical work. [The] studio, however, had no idea the kind of sound it will get.[78]

Some producers also replaced IATSE sound technicians with members of the IBEW, and the studios advertised widely for replacement sound technicians; IATSE's ability to represent sound workers was further eroded when the studios recognised the IBEW as the representative for sound technicians from August 1933.[79] This had a distinct impact on Local 695 membership and, as Hartsough argues, the studios were able to use the changing economic circumstances to put pressure on IATSE as a whole, and to radically reduce its negotiating power. The gains that the IBEW had made in membership allowed it to negotiate wage scales and conditions for sound roles with the major studios. These scales are detailed in Tables 4 and 5:

Table 4   Wage scale for sound roles for studio work, February 1934

Studio rates 1934	
Position	**Rate**
Mixers	$2.00/hr for 1st 6 hours, $3.00/hr after 6
Recordists	$1.50/hr for 1st 6 hours, $2.25/hr after 6
Stage Men, Stage Engineers, Boom Men, Microphone and Cablemen	$1.16/hr for 1st 6 hours, $1.75/hr after 6 hours
Construction, Maintenance, Repair and Installation Technicians	$1.16/hr for 1st 6 hours, $1.75/hr after 6 hours

Source: Scott D. Smith, 'Beginnings of Local 695: Part 2', *695 Quarterly*, vol. 3, no. 1, 2011, p. 30. Reprinted with permission from Scott Smith and Local 695.

Hollywood Soundscapes

Table 5 Wage scale for sound roles for location work, February 1934

Location rates 1934		
Position	**Daily**	**Weekly**
Mixer	$24.50	$145.00
Recordists	$18.25	$109.25
Class C (Boom, Utility, Cable)	$11.75	$41.25

Source: Scott D. Smith, 'Beginnings of Local 695: Part 2', *695 Quarterly*, vol. 3, no. 1, 2011, p. 30. Reprinted with permission from Scott Smith and Local 695.

Although the IBEW made gains during and after the 1933 strikes, the balance between labour organisations shifted again when the National Labor Relations Act (or Wagner Act) came into effect in 1935.[80] The Act recognised the rights of employees to organise and bargain collectively with employers on wages and working conditions. As Hartsough argues, within this context the majors returned to the strategy of centralising their labour negotiations, and looked to IATSE as the union that was best placed to represent a large body of workers and to streamline negotiations about labour relations. By December 1935 IATSE was once again the union representing studio workers for most crafts, although the history of labour relations in the film industry in the 1930s was clouded by the deals made between IATSE and organised crime, particularly the racketeering of George Browne and William Bioff.[81]

Due to the fact that Hollywood's rank-and-file craft workers and technicians worked on an on-call basis, rather than being contracted for regular and long-term employment, their income depended on the cumulative time they worked as well as their rates of pay.[82] Studio production executives rigidly managed production schedules and workflow as a way of controlling costs, and during the economic downturn of the Depression, efficiencies were sought in all areas of work. In this environment, technicians writing for professional Journals and trade press were at pains to underline how their work processes deployed technologies to form expedient and efficient work regimes.[83] But the working conditions of on-call employment often created a demanding and insecure experience for sound technicians. In his Oral History, Milo Lory

Table 6 Sound department studio wage scale, April 1937

Position	Hourly	Weekly (54 hours)	Weekly (3 week guarantee)
Class 1	$2.42	$116.15	$79.20
Class 2	$1.82	$87.10	$66.00
Class 3	$1.41	$67.75	$52.20
Class 4	$1.01	–	–

Source: Scott D. Smith, 'Beginnings of Local 695: Part 3', *695 Quarterly* vol. 3, no. 2, Spring 2011, p. 29. Reprinted with permission from Scott Smith and Local 695.

Table 7 Work classifications as defined by National Labor Relations Board, September 1939

Y-1 – Music Mixer	Y-8 – Microphone Boom Operator
Y-2 – Re-Recording Mixer	Y-9 – Recording Machine Operator
Y-3 – Unit Mixer	Y-10 – Journeyman Soundman
Y-4 – Operative Supervisor and/or Engineer	Y-11 – Cableman
Y-5 – Amplifier Room Operator	Y-12 – Playback Operator
Y-6 – Technical Testing Engineer and/or Gang Boss	Y-13 – Public Address Operator
Y-7 – Service Recorder and/or Location Engineer	Y-14 – Dubbing Machine Operator
	Y-15 – Film Loader

(Sound Editor at Columbia, at MGM and an IATSE member) recalled that it was during the Depression that the studios ceased to employ technical personnel between pictures: 'there was a change in the tendency to carry you between pictures; they eased off that. They laid you off.'[84] In the context of on-call employment, the negotiation of guaranteed periods of work in the 1937 wage scale and conditions, shown in Table 6, represented some progress by the unions in addressing the periodic nature of employment for technicians.

During the mid-1930s Local 695 expanded its membership numbers; its membership had always included sound technicians in sound recording, and re-recording roles, but it began to sign up members in maintenance, installation and laboratory roles for sound as well, campaigning for jurisdiction of all sound roles. In September 1939 the National Labor Relations Board (NRLB) certified that Local 695 was responsible for all sound-related work, and it codified sound roles into a set of classifications, labelled 'Y'. These are listed in Table 7. The NLRB ruling read: "'This certification by its terms includes all 'Y' classifications and the installation, construction, operation, maintenance and repair of all sound equipment.'"[85]

A comparison of the roles defined in the early sound period with the detailed classifications laid out in 1939 reveals the manner in which sound labour became more demarcated and tasks were organised and allocated according to areas of specialisation.

RECOGNISING SOUND WORK: THE ACADEMY AWARDS OF MERIT FOR SOUND

Outside of studio departments and labour unions, the work of sound technicians was defined and recognised through other organisations and networks, a key example being recognition through the Academy Awards. The Academy Awards of Merit were, from the foundation of the Academy in 1927, an opportunity to publicise the institution and wider industry, and the awards have always been a high-profile index of the Academy's institutional presence. The Awards of Merit programme was originally conceived by a small committee, comprising members from different fields of the industry. During the history of the Academy, the range of award categories, numbers of nominees and other aspects of the awards has changed periodically, but as Pierre Norman Sands notes, the awards programme 'always adhered to the basic concept of awards given for achievement of outstanding creativity as evaluated by a group of proven ability in the same field'.[86]

The Academy set up an award category for Best Sound Recording for the 1929/1930 (3rd) Academy Awards round. Sound departments were invited by the Academy to put forward the films they considered to represent their best work. From this selection, the general Academy membership nominated a list of films. The nominated films were reviewed by a Board of Judges, comprised of personnel that represented the five Academy branches (actors, directors, producers, writers and technicians) and decided by a vote from the general membership.[87]

The judging procedure and criteria for the Best Sound Recording award were as follows. Samples of all the nominated films were screened twice for an audience composed of the Board of Judges and Academy members. For the first running of samples, members were instructed to vote (on a scale of one to ten) on the most 'effective' film, defined as the picture they preferred 'purely from an entertainment standpoint, without reference to any technical quality'.[88] The samples were then run for a second time, and members were asked to score each one on the following technical criteria: 'uniformity of level, frequency characteristic, freedom from bad overloads, acoustic fidelity, freedom from ground noise'.[89] The involvement of representatives from the Technicians Branch in the judging of awards brought the technical culture into dialogue with other crafts to reach a judgment of what constituted 'good sound' both in terms of the quality of its recording and its entertainment values. In specifying both entertainment and technical 'values', the criteria for the award echoes the dual values of 'art' and 'science' that are threaded through technical discourses on Hollywood sound, and the dual values against which 'good sound' were commonly measured in the period.

As noted, award categories were added to the programme periodically, and according to the perceived need for recognition of different areas of endeavour. By the time the 1938/1939 (11th) Awards of Merit were up for selection, Academy members were more attuned to the contribution that special effects processes made to entertainment values. Archival sources detailing the awards process are revealing of how different aspects of special process work were considered for recognition.

Nathan Levinson was Chairman of the Academy's Technicians Branch in 1938 and he was asked by the Awards Committee to review the year's releases and determine if any warranted a special award for outstanding effects. Levinson wrote to the Awards Committee asserting that both pictorial and sound effects should be considered in the criteria for the award. The effects should, he wrote, have both a 'dramatic necessity' and an 'economic necessity to the picture' but 'should be accomplished with such skill that the mechanism by which the effect is achieved is not apparent in the final result'.[90]

Six films from the 1938/1939 release period were nominated for the award, and a committee reviewed special effects sequences from them. Out of the nominations, Paramount's *Spawn of the North*, discussed in more detail in Chapter 3, was granted the special award.[91] The Technical Committee recommended that both photographic and sound effects should be mentioned in the citation of *Spawn of the North* for the award. They also argued that the 'importance and value' of special effects should be recognised in a new annual award category of Best Special Effects, and that the award should be marked with a statuette, rather than any other kind of recognition, such as a certificate or an honourable mention. A statuette clearly signalled the mark of prestige in film achievement. In their correspondence they argued that if the Awards Committee were unwilling to award a statuette, then 'no recognition should be extended until such time as, in the opinion of the Awards Committee, Special Effects Achievements merit recognition in this major classification'.[92] This negotiation for the terms of the recognition, status and visibility of technical work is revealing. It is clear that the Technicians Branch were determined to make the work of technical crafts visible within the industry. After being inaugurated by *Spawn of the North*, the award for Special Effects became a competitive category, and was awarded every year between 1939 and 1962. From the 1963 Academy Awards, it ceased, and was replaced by categories for Sound Editing and Visual Effects.[93]

THE POSITION OF TECHNICIANS AND SOUND WORK CULTURES IN DIFFERENT COMPANIES

I want to conclude this chapter by drawing some brief comparisons between how sound worked in two contrasting companies and production cultures in Hollywood in the studio era. Warner Bros., a vertically integrated major studio with a large sound department, represents a culture of relative stability for sound work; a contrasting case study is provided by the organisation of sound work and technical personnel on a picture-by-picture basis by the independent producer David O. Selznick at his company Vanguard Pictures in the mid-1940s.

I have described the sound workflow at Warner Bros. earlier in the chapter. From available sources it is evident that there was a high degree of stability in the department; many of its personnel had long service records. A column in *Warner Club News* in December 1940 maintained that of the seventy-one staff employed, 64 per cent had been with the department for over ten years, and 25 per cent for more than five years.[94]

George Groves (Chief Mixer) was, at this point, the longest-serving member of the department. Warner Bros. had the same Head of Sound for twenty-six years; Nathan Levinson was appointed in October 1926 and served in the role until his death in 1952.[95] Other senior Warner Bros. sound personnel, such as William Mueller, were also long serving; Mueller took on the role of Head of Sound for the studio after Levinson's death, and subsequently the role was taken by Groves from 1957 until 1967, following Warner Bros.' reorganisation as Warner-Seven Arts.

Nathan Levinson was initially appointed to Warner Bros. on a three-year contract, starting on a salary of $300 per week (in 1926), with six-monthly incremental increases to $500 per week at the end of the contract.[96] In 1933 the studio renewed Levinson's employment, with a seven-year contract, starting at $300 per week, and with annual incremental increases. As noted in the discussion of labour relations above, during the early 1930s studios made cuts to wage scales for on-call workers, and seemingly also did so with contracted staff such as Levinson. However, from March 1934 Levinson received a regular 'bonus payment' of $100 per week, which mitigated some of the effects of the wage reduction.[97] Levinson's contract was renewed in 1937 (at $500 per week, plus a $100 weekly bonus and periodic increments), and again in 1941 (at $750 per week, and with periodic increments rising to $1,250 per week). In 1949 Levinson's contract was adapted towards his retirement; the two-part contract was for a total of seven years: Period A, for three years, in his role as Director of Sound at $1,250 per week, followed by Period B, a period of four years' 'consultancy' for the studio, with a salary of $200 per week in addition to his studio pension.[98] Levinson died in 1952, partway into Period A of his contract.

The terms of Levinson's contract give an insight into how the duties of a senior sound technician were defined. Paragraph 1 of the contract specified his duties loosely; the wording reads that the studio expected him 'to perform such duties in connection with the sound reproducing department ... consistent with the standing and experience of the employee, as Producer may designate'.[99] The contract outlined terms and conditions relating to issues such as sickness, absence and exclusivity, as might be expected. The stature of his technical expertise is also indicated; in Paragraph 10 the contract defined the character of his work as follows:

> It is understood and agreed by and between parties that the services to be rendered by the Employee ... are of a special, unique, extraordinary and intellectual character, which give them a peculiar value, the loss of which cannot be reasonably or adequately compensated in damages in any action at law.[100]

Levinson's salary was obviously significantly higher than the wage scales of the rank-and-file sound men (detailed above in Tables 4, 5 and 6), but to understand more broadly how sound roles were rewarded, it is instructive to draw a comparison with remuneration for other technical roles at the studio, particularly in senior positions with responsibility for a department's administration and direction. A useful comparator is Fred Jackman, who worked as the 'supervisor of all technical effects, trick camera and mechanical scenes' for Warner Bros. between 1929 and 1937. In 1930 Jackman was earning $750 per week, and his contract was for one year, with an option to extend; this rose to $1,000 per week in 1931, with a reduction to $800 per week in December 1931, and his salary seemingly stayed at this level until he left the studio to go freelance in 1937.[101] Jackman's salary was higher than Levinson's, and he had a smaller department to administrate, but overall it is evident that Warner Bros. valued their technical staff, and salaries and terms were commensurate with this.

The organisational culture was quite different at the independent Vanguard Pictures. Archival sources in the David O. Selznick Collection at the Harry Ransom Centre allow insights into David O. Selznick's management of technical tasks and his interaction with his technicians in the course of production. From these sources it is evident that his mode of management and the production culture of his organisation provide a contrast with the stable routines and the scale of personnel and facilities at Warner Bros.[102] When Selznick set up Selznick International Pictures (SIP) in 1935, he did not have an in-house sound department; production sound personnel, and re-recording facilities were provided by contract arrangements with RKO-Pathé, Goldwyn Sound Services or Sound Services Inc.[103] At SIP, and at Vanguard Pictures – the company Selznick set up in 1945 – the overall supervision of finalising the soundtrack for Selznick's pictures rested with Hal Kern, Head of Editorial.

From correspondence in production files, it is evident that the quality, expressiveness and reliability of sound was a recurrent source of concern for Selznick; it seems that sound work did not match the 'tradition of quality' that was the SIP trademark. Sound quality was a topic on which he expressed dissatisfaction at several points during the SIP years. For example, after he had attended the preview screening of *The Young in Heart* (Richard Wallace, 1938), Selznick wrote to Kern expressing his concerns about sound quality and intelligibility:

> I am simply in a quandary as to what to do about our sound. There is no point in arguing any longer that it is as good as the sound of other studios, because it is not, as is clearly demonstrated every time one of our pictures is run on the same program and in the same theatre as a picture of another studio. Subtle shadings in sound values perhaps are of no consequence, and I would not be worried about these – but what I am worried about is that our sound, on occasion, is so bad that the audience does not understand our dialogue ... Perhaps the trouble is not in the recording but in the dubbing, because certainly sound that seems all right in our projection rooms becomes simply ghastly by the time we get our pictures dubbed.[104]

In response to Selznick's concerns, Kern, and Ray Klune (one of Selznick's production managers), looked into technical problems, and worked to isolate and solve them. By 1945 Selznick began to focus on the need for greater expertise in technical matters at the studio. In March of that year he wrote to Hal Kern, again reiterating his dissatisfaction with sound quality:

> On several occasions I have expressed my concern to you about my feeling that we are kidding ourselves with the extreme amount of work we do to get our sound effects and sound levels exactly the way we want them because in the final printing ... this work is disregarded.[105]

He wrote to members of his senior executive team conveying his opinion that 'in all of our technical work we are in the horse and buggy age, way behind the industry'.[106] It seems that Charles Glett (Production Executive) suggested appointing a specialist to take care of technical issues, and in October 1945 James G. Stewart was appointed as Director of Sound. Stewart moved to Vanguard from RKO, where he had been Head of Re-Recording. He found out about the opening at Vanguard from Glett, with whom Stewart had worked when they were both employed by RKO.[107]

Stewart was appointed on a one-year contract, with an option for Vanguard to renew for a further year. His salary was $300 per week. The wording of Stewart's contract illustrates that his role was quite widely conceived. Paragraph 1 of the contract outlined a range of responsibilities:

> we hereby employ you to render your exclusive serves to us as a Sound Director and/or as a Sound Engineer, and/or as a Sound Supervisor, and/or as an Executive, Supervisor and/

or Engineer in our Sound Department, it being understood that we may assign you to render any services in any way connected with the application of sound to the production of motion pictures or in any capacity relating to or involving research in the field of sound engineering.[108]

The qualities of Stewart's work role were defined in the same terms as those in Levinson's contract: 'your services are special, unique, unusual, extraordinary and of an intellectual character giving them a peculiar value'; these terms are also used in Hal Kern's contract with the Selznick organisation, suggesting that this was a standard phrasing for describing senior technical roles.[109] Hal Kern's salary, as specified in his 1944 contract, was $325 per week.

Soon after starting in his role at Vanguard, Stewart prepared a report for Selznick on how arrangements for sound could be improved. He costed out, and recommended, the purchase of portable sound recording equipment, and suggested ways that Vanguard might ensure better sound quality in dubbing and the looping of lines of dialogue, by installing telephone lines to facilitate the transmission of sound from the production stages that the company were using at the RKO-Pathé studio with the recording and dubbing facilities installed in the Goldwyn Sound Department.[110]

Stewart began work for Vanguard while Selznick's prestige budget Western, *Duel in the Sun* (King Vidor, 1946), was in production.[111] From correspondence in the production and sound files, it is evident that even before the shooting was completed, Selznick was anxious to have technical arrangements in place that would facilitate manipulation of all aspects of *Duel in the Sun*'s soundtrack in post-production. In mid-October 1945 Selznick wrote to Glett and Kern:

> We were among the first, if not the very first, to use loops and to dub lines for improved readings, but steadily we have gone backwards in this work so that now we have the greatest difficulty in getting accurate synchronization, and even more difficulty in getting proper sound tones and qualities so that lines can be used, with the result that more often than not we have to throw away lines we make because they simply won't fit in.[112]

Selznick's cause for concern sprang from problems with the dubbing and looping of lines on *Spellbound* (Alfred Hitchcock, 1945), a film produced by Selznick at Vanguard. Evidently, Gregory Peck, who co-starred in *Spellbound*, had commented to Selznick that his usual experience of dubbing and looping dialogue at MGM Studios had been a much easier process than at Vanguard, an observation that had stung Selznick into trying to tackle this technical issue.[113]

Only two days after sharing his concerns about dubbing, Selznick wrote to Glett and Kern on the subject of sound again. This time he indicated two particular sequences in *Duel in the Sun* which required special sound treatment. He identified the closing sequence of the film, in which the two lovers, Pearl Chavez (Jennifer Jones) and Lewt McCanles (Gregory Peck), lie fatally injured, and their calls reverberate across a wild and open space; he also pinpointed a sensational action sequence in which a posse of men rapidly ride to defend open territory from railway builders encroaching at the edge of ranch land. The posse are halted by the arrival of the US cavalry to protect the

Figures 63–64 *Duel in the Sun.* The 'ride to the fence' sequence begins with the ringing of the bell at the McCanles' ranch

railroaders. Selznick wanted Stewart's input as a sound expert to realise the entertainment values of the sequence:

> I am counting on him [Stewart] to do something extraordinary with the ride of the clan and with the cavalry. As to the ride of the clan, I am counting on a really stunning sound effect starting with one horse, two, five, fifty, hundreds, et cetera, in accordance with the film. The test of this will be whether the track played by itself has the thrilling effect we are after of a start from one rider up through a huge array of riders.[114]

The 'ride of the clan' derives its effectiveness from a balance between distinct audiovisual techniques.

The sequence opens at Spanish Bit, a ranch owned by the ageing but indomitable Senator McCanles (Lionel Barrymore). McCanles' ranch foreman, Sid (Scott McKay), rides up to the ranch bringing the news that the railroaders will be progressing onto Spanish Bit land later that day. The Senator orders him to 'sound every bell on Spanish Bit!' to summon men to gather in numbers and ride to the boundary fence to arrest the railroaders' progress (Figures 63–64).

The action moves, in a series of shots, between the bells being sounded and the men congregating to come to Senator McCanles' aid. This part of the sequence is not scored in a conventional way; it privileges the sound effects of the bells over the score, and exploits different bell tones, combining these with the sound of galloping horses steadily increasing in number. This section of the sequence comes to a rest with an audiovisual cut from an extreme long shot of horsemen galloping along a ridge, accompanied by a chorus of bells, to the train bell tolling and the train moving diagonally through the frame.

The middle part of the sequence presents brief plot exposition: the railroaders discuss the imminent arrival of the US cavalry to defend them; Senator McCanles addresses his posse to get their blood up. As the posse start their ride to the fence, the insistent onward motion of the horses and riders is accompanied by Dimitri Tiomkin's score, instrumented with brass and horns, and it rises to a crescendo as the action shows the posse at maximum strength.

Hollywood Soundscapes

Figures 65–66 *Duel in the Sun.* Dynamic cross-cutting and sound effects create the sensation of the 'ride to the fence'

The 'ride of the clan' to the fence concludes the sequence; in this section there is no score, the soundtrack is given entirely to galloping horses, cross-cut with the opposing movement of the train, and sound effects of clanking machinery and its bell (Figures 65–66).

With each cross-cut the shot framing tightens, intensifying a sense of two different and opposing bodies of motion on a collision course.

An extreme long shot establishes the approach of the posse in relation to the railroad worksite, and as the ranchmen come to a halt at the wire fence, the sense

Figure 67 *Duel in the Sun.* The onward motion of the posse is halted at the fence

of arrested action is palpable (Figure 67). A brief confrontation ensues between Senator McCanles and the railroaders, in which it transpires that, legally, the Senator cannot prevent the progress of the railroad, and at the end of the sequence the cavalry arrive as reinforcement for the railroad workers.

In his Oral History testimony, Stewart recalls the methods that he used to create the patterning of sound effects in the ride to the fence sequence, and addresses the decisions made about the balance of sound effects and film score:

> I decided that it would be interesting to try to build the score for this ride to the fence using bells. So Tiomkin wrote for us a version of the theme which could be played on single notes of the bells. We had a very good ... sound effects cutter, but he was also a musician. And he built these tracks. I think we had something like 18 or 20 tracks eventually. Unfortunately, due to the nature of the music, this had to be done over and over again. It was very hard, at that time with photographic track, to achieve a low enough [ground] noise level. But we did quite well with it, and it was in the picture. The theme is played on the bells, in the ride to the fence.[115]

Archival materials from the production of *Duel in the Sun* include a set of handwritten notes, most likely by Stewart, demonstrating the processes of planning for the sounds to be used; the sounds are all library effects. The notes read:

> Ride to the fence: all the horse effects are from the sound library; both body and presence being gained by using ... tracks compositely. The railroad train effect is a composite of library track rerecorded separately to match the action ... due to the magnitude of this scene the use of library tracks has saved the producer thousands of dollars on men, horses and machinery that would be required to record this effect.[116]

From his Oral History recollections of his time at Vanguard, it is evident that initially Stewart appreciated the freedom and resources that working for Selznick afforded him. Stewart was able to execute plans for purchasing new equipment, and he was given scope to bring creative ideas to the crafting of particular aspects of the sound for *Duel in the Sun*. However, other aspects of the production were more demanding for Stewart to deliver to Selznick's satisfaction. As established earlier, Selznick prized the ability to dub and loop lines of dialogue in the post-production phase. This was a practice that allowed the producer latitude to reshape, or refine, aspects of performance should he wish to do so. Dubbing and looping were widely used practices, as discussed in previous chapters, but the extent to which Selznick intervened in reworking line readings, or demanded retakes, was unusual. *Duel in the Sun* exemplifies Selznick's tendency to an extreme extent. The cutting notes for *Duel in the Sun* record more than fifty reviews of footage and associated notes instructing modifications he desired. Not every review was of the whole print of the film, but nevertheless, the cutting and review stage involved intense activity for a period from June 1946 to the preview of the film in January 1947.[117] Many of the notes given by Selznick pinpoint very specific changes he desired to the dialogue, even to the extent of mixing fragments of dialogue from different takes into the finalised soundtrack. Having Stewart, an expert in sound post-production, on his staff meant that Selznick was able to transform, or even create, the dialogue, treating it as a découpage of vocal elements rather than as an integral recording of a performance. Selznick's request for his sound man to deploy his skills in this way ran counter to the conventions of dialogue recording held by the sound craft, conventions that prized the integrity of performance, and that preserved star charisma, intonation and synchronisation. Stewart recalled:

> [*Duel in the Sun*] ... was a good sound job, it would have been a very good sound job, but I was faced with a very serious problem with Selznick. When he discovered what I could do with a sound track, then he started to do a number of things that were really not practical, from a standpoint of good sound. For instance, it was particularly true of Jennifer Jones' performance, which he was very careful to make as good as possible. He would want one word from take 3, two words from take 4, and three words from take 5, all in the same sentence. You can't do this, and of course it was doubly difficult with optical track. So I had splices in the middle of sentences. So it did not come out to my full satisfaction.[118]

Alongside Selznick's exacting management style and mode of working, Stewart's responsibilities for Vanguard gradually extended beyond the role of Director of Sound.

Stewart took on technical supervision of Vanguard's release prints, and became involved in the complex administrative co-ordination of these release prints with Vanguard's distribution arm – the Selznick Releasing Organisation (SRO). These extra administrative duties became particularly demanding during the release of *Duel in the Sun* in 1946. The film was released in multiple versions, each version cut to meet the stipulations of local censorship boards. Stewart also took on responsibility for co-ordinating the release of *Portrait of Jennie* (William Dieterle, 1948); the film featured a 'special' final reel, which required bespoke arrangements in exhibition. From correspondence in the film's production and sound files on *Portrait of Jennie*, it is evident that organising and administering the release of the special prints created problems in exhibition that were beyond Stewart's control. These problems, inevitably, led to tensions with Selznick, and subsequently Stewart's departure from the company in February 1949.

CONCLUSION

This chapter has explored the different ways that the work of technicians – workers in the 'outer circle' of Rosten's map of Hollywood labour – was defined, contested, recognised and valued by different forms of organisation in Hollywood's studio era. Sound technicians were 'valuable' to the industry, working at the 'cut point' of production, but rank-and-file workers were easily replaced by casual hires during times of labour unrest. In comparison, Hollywood's senior technicians, whose work was defined by contract as 'unique and individual', had roles where value was mapped to their professional qualifications or experience. In the case of Levinson's career at Warner Bros., it seems that he enjoyed stability and salary rewards commensurate with his experience. In the case of Stewart, working for Selznick offered latitude for innovation, but his responsibilities and duties for the organisation far exceeded the supposed limits of his role.

6

Conclusion

This book has tried to restore classical Hollywood's sound technicians to the historical picture by undertaking a multi-level approach. By tracing sound technicians across the axes of their activities, and by highlighting their influence and agency at different levels, and in distinct contexts, of the industry, the remarkable diversity and range of their activity becomes evident. My analysis of this activity puts the technicians who undertook sound work on the map, but I also have tried to understand the frameworks of their labour: how they worked, and why they worked in the way they did. In taking this approach, I have tried to make the labour of a particular craft visible, but also attempted to offer some broader methods for tracing the complex networks of creative practice that underlie histories of the classical Hollywood period.

The chapters of the book have set out four frames within which the dynamic changes of the period can be studied. Chapter 2 showed the participation of sound technicians in a technical culture that fostered and shaped technological change, and which connected the Hollywood studios to the wider research sector. The balance between stability and change is an ongoing feature of the period, and that balance was negotiated and mediated by sound technicians, who fully recognised the interplay between the requirements for sound quality and the need for entertainment values.

The third chapter illustrated how sound technicians developed subtle and flexible ways of working with sound. By understanding how sound craft interlocked with other film elements, we can overcome the clichéd notion of the awkward sound technician disrupting production values by holding to the technically perfect recording. In fact, as Chapter 3 reveals, the refinement of techniques in manipulating sound in post-production, and the development of work with sound effects and sound libraries, demonstrates how fluently and fully technical processes were put to the service of aesthetic needs.

The fourth chapter detailed how sound worked within production cultures at a fine-grained level. It traced how sound work was organised on a production, and the ways that subtle decisions were made about techniques to be deployed, from an array of possible options, revealing the 'variations' that sound craftsmen were able to draw upon from a repertoire honed by experience.[1] These decisions were always shaped by constraints – for example, co-ordination between different crafts, the needs of the story and the limits of budget.

The fifth and final chapter examined the different definitions of sound work that circulated in Hollywood's studio era. The emergence of sound roles in the studio departments of the early sound era, and the gradual multiplication, differentiation and demarcation of roles, evidences how technical roles came into sharper focus, and became more fully embedded within the organisational structures of work. The labour struggles of the 1930s illustrate contestations over work, identity and value. Finally, a comparison of two production cultures and how they valued and deployed their technicians suggests that work roles might have been experienced very differently by specific figures.

Across the four main chapters that comprise the book, it was important to try to cover activities outside of, or in addition to, production and post-production roles, to give a sense of the involvement of technicians in the ongoing agendas for improvement that lay alongside, and influenced and intersected with, film style but did not always directly, or immediately, determine it.

The legacy of sound technicians' work lies in the many innovative, exciting and engaging soundscapes of studio era Hollywood films, films which still have vibrant 'story values' and strong 'ear appeal', even for us as contemporary audio-viewers accustomed to the clarity of digital sound and immersion in an enveloping sound field of multi-channel formats such as Dolby Atmos.

There are other long-lasting outcomes from the period; though this book ends its examination in 1948, many of the work roles, regimes and technical cultures formed during the 1930s and 1940s had enduring influence long after the organisations structure of the studio system shifted and changed.

Hollywood's sound technicians adjusted to the organisational changes that came with the end of the studio system in various ways, as these brief examples illustrate. Technicians adapted to working for smaller, independent producers, or independent sound houses. In 1948 Loren Ryder, Head of Sound at Paramount, exploited his technical expertise and set up Ryder Sound Services alongside his studio role. The company handled the rental of equipment, and was at the forefront of the new magnetic recording practices in the late 1940s. Ryder retained his role at Paramount until 1956, when he retired to focus full time on Ryder Sound Services. He also continued in research and development activities, and was a senior figure in technical networks, serving as President of the SMPE between 1947 and 1949.[2]

Technicians also adapted to changing entertainment media, taking on sound work for television. After leaving Vanguard Pictures, James G. Stewart worked for Glenn Glenn Sound, an independent sound post-production house, undertaking sound work on the *I Love Lucy* (1951–1957) television show, recorded at Desilu Studios, which were located on the site of the RKO studio where he had worked in the 1930s and 1940s. He had come full circle, though he was working with a new entertainment form, and he observed: 'the [recording] console that was in there [for Desilu] was the one that I had designed in 1937'.[3]

Finally, Hollywood's sound technicians participated in the next new wave of innovations in stereophonic sound, trialled in the 1950s alongside widescreen and 3-D film. A range of multi-channel, stereo magnetic sound formats emerged: Cinerama, CinemaScope, Todd AO were all marketed on an 'aesthetic of participation'.[4] The stereo and 3-D experimentations included an 'expedient' format developed and branded by Warner Bros. as WarnerPhonic Sound and used with the studio's 3-D film *House of Wax* (André de Toth, 1953). The strategy of working on expedient novelty in the 1950s has strong similarities to their work on Vitasound in the 1930s.[5]

There are many more strands to the story of Hollywood's sound craft in the studio era, as well as different ways of plotting it, but ultimately it is not a story that can be told through a focus on single technologies, on single films or on single figures. It is is an ensemble narrative: a story of networks, of interconnections, and of shared agendas. It is only by tracing these interconnections that we can begin to glimpse a different version of Hollywood's creative history, one that is driven, and enriched, by group dynamics.

Notes

CHAPTER 1

1. See William Whittington, *Sound Design and Science Fiction* (Austin: University of Texas Press, 2007), 17–37; Stephen Adriano Moore, *The Professional Culture of Hollywood Film Sound: Understanding Labor Politics and Culture through Practitioner Discourse* (Unpublished PhD thesis, University of Nottingham, 2012); and Jay Beck, *Designing Sound: Audiovisual Aesthetics in 1970s American Cinema* (New York: Rutgers University Press, 2016).
2. R. Murray Schafer, *The Soundscape: Our Sonic Environment and the Tuning of the World* (Rochester, VT: Destiny Books, 1977; 1994), 274.
3. David Sonnenschein draws on Schafer's concept of soundscape in his book on the practices of sound design. He writes: 'Stories happen in a time and place, and these parameters are characterized by their acoustic environments or soundscapes.' *Sound Design: The Expressive Power of Music, Voice and Sound Effects in Cinema* (Saline, MI: Michael Wiese Productions, 2001), 182. In her book *The Soundscape of Modernity: Architectural Acoustics and the Cultures of Listening in America: 1900–1933* (Cambridge, MA, and London: MIT, 2002), Emily Thompson offers a rich cultural history of noise in early twentieth-century America. She builds on the work of Alan Corbin on historical soundscapes, and defines her soundscape 'as an auditory or aural landscape. Like a landscape, a soundscape is simultaneously a physical environment and a way of perceiving that environment' (1). Drawing on the work of Schafer, Randolph Jordan productively advocates for the relationships between the elements of image and sound in sound cinema to be considered as an 'ecosystem', in which the elements are separate, but related. 'Acoustic Ecology and the Cinema', *Cinephile* 6:1 (2010): 26. Jonathan Sterne notes that 'no concept has proven more fertile or ubiquitous in the academic study of sound' than 'soundscape'. He attributes this to the seemingly wide explanatory power of the term, and its applicability to different media forms, but argues for cultural critics to be precise in their invocation of 'soundscape' by recognising that both the production and understanding of a soundscape is always interwoven with the cultural practices of how space is produced and inhabited. 'The Stereophonic Spaces of Soundscape', in *Living Stereo: Histories and Cultures of Multichannel Sound*, ed. Paul Theberge, Kyle Devine and Tom Everett (New York and London: Bloomsbury, 2015), 65, 68.
4. Schafer, *The Soundscape*, 272–275.
5. Ibid., 272.
6. Ibid., 10.
7. Ibid.
8. Helen Hanson, 'Sound Affects: Post-Production Sound, Soundscapes and Sound Design in Hollywood's Studio Era', *Music, Sound and the Moving Image* 1:1 (2007): 27–50; Helen Hanson and Steve Neale, 'Commanding the Sounds of the Universe: Classical Hollywood Sound in the 1930s and Early 1940s', in *The Classical Hollywood Reader*, ed. Steve Neale (London and New York: Routledge, 2012), 246–261; Helen Hanson, 'The Ambience of Film Noir: Soundscapes, Design and Mood', in *A Companion to Film Noir*, ed. Andrew Spicer and Helen Hanson (Boston, MA: Wiley-Blackwell, 2013), 284–301.
9. Donald Crafton, *The Talkies: American Cinema's Transition to Sound, 1926–1931* (Berkeley: University of California Press, 1997), 1.

10. It would be impossible to list all the works covering the transition to sound; arguably histories of the period began within the timespan of transition itself, with books such as Fitzhugh Green, *The Film Finds Its Tongue* (New York and London: Putnam, 1929). Key critical histories include: David Bordwell, Janet Staiger and Kristin Thompson, *The Classical Hollywood Cinema: Film Style and Mode of Production to 1960* (London: Routledge, 1985), 298–308; Douglas Gomery, 'Writing the History of the American Film Industry: Warner Bros. and Sound', in *Movies and Methods: Volume II*, ed. Bill Nichols (Berkeley: University of California Press, 1985); Douglas Gomery, 'The Coming of Sound: Technological Change in the American Film Industry', in *The American Film Industry*, ed. Tino Balio (Madison: University of Wisconsin Press, 1985); Scott Eyman, *The Speed of Sound: Hollywood and the Talkie Revolution, 1926–1930* (Baltimore, MD, and London: Johns Hopkins University Press, 1997); Crafton, *The Talkies*; James Lastra, *Sound Technology and the American Cinema: Perception, Representation and Modernity* (New York: Columbia University Press, 2000); Douglas Gomery, *The Coming of Sound: A History* (New York and London: Routledge, 2005); James Buhler, David Neumeyer and Rob Deemer, *Hearing the Movies: Music and Sound in Film History* (New York and Oxford: Oxford University Press, 2010).
11. Crafton, *The Talkies*, 1.
12. Rick Altman, *Silent Film Sound* (New York: Columbia University Press, 2004).
13. Lastra, *Sound Technology and the American Cinema*; Lea Jacobs, *Film Rhythm after Sound: Technology, Music and Performance* (Berkeley: University of California Press, 2015).
14. Michael Slowik, *After the Silents: Hollywood Film Music in the Early Sound Era 1926–1934* (New York: Columbia University Press, 2014).
15. Katherine Spring, *Saying It with Songs: Popular Music and the Coming of Sound to Hollywood Cinema* (Oxford: Oxford University Press, 2013).
16. Amanda Lotz, 'Industry-Level Studies and Gitlin's Prime Time', in *Production Studies: Cultural Studies of Media Industries*, ed. Vicki Mayer, Miranda Banks and John Caldwell (London and New York: Routledge, 2009), 26.
17. Ibid., 26–7.
18. Ibid., 27.
19. Lotz cites David Hesmondhalgh, *The Cultural Industries: 2nd Edition* (London: Sage, 2007), 3; in Lotz, 'Industry-Level Studies', 27.
20. Stephen R. Barley, 'Technicians in the Workplace: Ethnographic Evidence for Bringing Work into Organizational Studies', *Administrative Science Quarterly* 41:3 (1996): 404–441, 409–410.
21. Ibid., 412; Stephen R. Barley and Julian E. Orr (eds), *Between Craft and Science: Technical Work in U.S. Settings* (Ithaca, NY, and London: Cornell University Press, 1997). See also Richard Sennett, *The Craftsman* (London and New York: Allen Lane/Penguin, 2008).
22. Barley, 'Technicians in the Workplace', 418–19.
23. Ibid., 429.
24. Ibid.

CHAPTER 2

1. Richard A. Peterson, 'Five Constraints on the Production of Culture: Law, Technology, Market, Organizational Structure and Occupational Careers', *Journal of Popular Culture* 16:2 (1982): 143–153; Paul M. Hirsch, 'Cultural Industries Revisited', *Organization Science* 11:3 (2000): 356–361; Vicki Mayer, 'Bringing the Social Back In: Studies of Production Cultures and Social Theory', in *Production Studies: Cultural Studies of Media Industries*, ed. Vicki Mayer, Miranda Banks and John Caldwell (London and New York: Routledge, 2009), 15–24; John Thornton Caldwell, *Production Culture: Industrial Reflexivity and Critical Practice in Film and Television* (Durham, NC, and London: Duke University Press, 2008); John L. Sullivan, 'Leo C. Rosten's Hollywood: Power, Status, and the Primacy of Economic and Social Networks in Cultural Production', in Mayer, Banks and Caldwell (eds), *Production Studies*, 39–53.

Hollywood Soundscapes

2. Peterson, 'Five Constraints on the Production of Culture'; David Bordwell, Janet Staiger and Kristin Thompson, *The Classical Hollywood Cinema: Film Style and Mode of Production to 1960* (London: Routledge, 1985); Janet Staiger (ed.), *The Studio System* (New York: Rutgers University Press, 1995); Donald Crafton, *The Talkies: American Cinema's Transition to Sound, 1926–1931* (Berkeley: University of California Press, 1997); Thomas Schatz, *Boom and Bust: American Cinema in the 1940s* (Berkeley: University of California Press, 1999); Thomas Schatz, 'Film Studies, Cultural Studies, and Media Industries Studies', *Media Industries Journal* 1:1 (2014): 39–43; Douglas Gomery, 'The Coming of Sound: Technological Change in the American Film Industry', in *The American Film Industry*, ed. Tino Balio (Madison: University of Wisconsin Press, 1985).

3. Janet Staiger, 'Standardization and Differentiation: The Reinforcement and Dispersion of Hollywood's Practices', in Bordwell, Staiger and Thompson, *The Classical Hollywood Cinema*, 97.

4. On Hollywood's transition to magnetic recording, and gradual integration of magnetic tape into existing editing practices, see Stephen Handzo, 'A Narrative Glossary of Film Sound Technology', in *Film Sound Theory and Practice*, ed. Elisabeth Weis and John Belton (New York: Columbia University Press, 1985), 391–392. Magnetic recording was being widely discussed within the technical cultures of the Society of Motion Picture Engineers from 1945 onwards, and progress on the topic was reviewed by both SMPE and AMPAS committees. See M. Camras, 'Magnetic Sound for Motion Pictures', *Journal of the Society of Motion Picture Engineers* [hereafter *JSMPE*] January 1947: 14–28; R. J. Tinkham and J. S. Boyers, 'A Magnetic Sound Recorder of Advanced Design', *JSMPE* January 1947: 29–35; AMPAS Research Council, 'Research Council Basic Sound Commitee: Discussion of Magnetic Recording', *JSMPE* January 1947: 50–56; Wesley C. Miller, 'Magnetic Recording for Motion Picture Studios', *JSMPE* January 1947: 57–62; S. J. Begun, 'Recent Developments in the Field of Magnetic Recording', *JSMPE* January 1947: 1–13; Dorothy O'Dea, 'Magnetic Recording for the Technician', *JSMPE* November 1948: 468–480; Earl Masterson, '35-mm Magnetic Recording System', *JSMPE* November 1948: 481–489; *JSMPE*, 'Report of the SMPE Progress Committee', *JSMPE* May 1949: 580–596; William A. Mueller and George R. Groves, 'Magnetic Recording in the Motion Picture Studio', *JSMPE* June 1949: 605–612; O. B. Gunby, 'Portable Magnetic-Recording System', *JSMPE* June 1949: 613–618; John G. Frayne and Halley Wolfe, 'Magnetic Recording in Motion Picture Techniques', *JSMPE* September 1949: 217–235.

5. See W. F. Kelley, 'Motion Picture Research Council', *JSMPE* October 1948: 418–423, and Pierre Norman Sands, *A Historical Study of the Academy of Motion Picture Arts and Sciences: 1927–1947* (New York: Arno Press, 1973), 84–90.

6. I follow James Lastra in using the term 'technical culture' for the network of sound engineers that emerges from the transition to sound. Lastra also covers the technical culture up to 1934 in *Sound Technology and the American Cinema: Perception, Representation and Modernity* (New York: Columbia University Press, 2000). My book seeks to extend an examination of the ongoing influences and activities of the technical culture through the 1930s and into the 1940s.

7. Stephen R. Barley, 'Technicians in the Workplace: Ethnographic Evidence for Bringing Work into Organizational Studies', *Administrative Science Quarterly* 41:3 (1996): 418.

8. See Trevor J. Pinch and Wiebe E. Bijker, 'The Social Construction of Facts and Artefacts: or How the Sociology of Science and the Sociology of Technology Might Benefit Each Other', *Social Studies of Science* 14:3 (1984): 399–441; and Donald MacKenzie and Judy Wajcman, *The Social Shaping of Technology* (Maidenhead: Open University Press, 1999).

9. See, for example: Carolyn Marvin, *When Old Technologies Were New: Thinking about Electric Communication in the Late Nineteenth Century* (New York and Oxford: Oxford University Press, 1988); Stephen R. Barley, 'What Can We Learn from the History of Technology?', *Journal of Engineering and Technology Management* 15:4 (1998): 237–255; Susan J. Douglas, 'Some Thoughts on the Question "How Do New Things Happen?"', *Technology and Culture* 51:2 (2010): 293–304.

10. Rick Altman, *Silent Film Sound* (New York: Columbia University Press, 2004); Jay Shields Beck, *A Quiet Revolution: Changes in American Film Sound Practices, 1967–1979* (Unpublished PhD thesis, University of Iowa, 2003).

11. Pinch and Bijker, 'The Social Construction of Facts and Artefacts', 404.

12. Ibid., 405–406.

13 Ibid.

14. Ibid., 411.

15. Carl Dreher, 'Sound Personnel and Organization', in *Recording Sound for Motion Pictures*, ed. Lester Cowan (New York and London: McGraw-Hill, 1931), 352.

16. Edward W. Kellogg, 'History of Sound Motion Pictures: First Intallment', in *A Technological History of Motion Pictures and Television*, ed. Raymond Fielding (Berkeley: University of California Press, 1955; 1967), 184.

17. Harry M. Geduld, *The Birth of the Talkies: From Edison to Jolson* (Bloomington: Indiana University Press, 1975); Bordwell, Staiger and Thompson, *The Classical Hollywood Cinema*, 298–308; Barry Salt, *Film Style and Technology: History and Analysis – 2nd Expanded Edition* (London: Starword, 1992), 148–194; David Bordwell and Kristin Thompson, *Film History: An Introduction* (New York: McGraw-Hill, 1994), 211–219; Crafton, *The Talkies*; Scott Eyman, *The Speed of Sound: Hollywood and the Talkie Revolution, 1926–1930* (Baltimore, MD, and London: Johns Hopkins University Press, 1997); Lastra, *Sound Technology and the American Cinema*.

18. Edward Bernds, *Mr Bernds Goes to Hollywood: My Early Life and Career in Sound Recording at Columbia with Frank Capra and Others* (Lanham, MD, and London: The Scarecrow Press, 1999).

19. David Bordwell and Kristin Thompson, 'Technological Change and Classical Film Style', in *Grand Design: Hollywood as a Modern Business Enterprise 1930–1939*, ed. Tino Balio (Berkeley and London: University of California Press, 1993), 116.

20. Ibid., 117.

21. Ibid.

22. Sands, *Historical Study of AMPAS*, 82.

23. Ibid., 83.

24. Ibid., 84–85.

25. Minutes of Meeting of Technicians Branch together with Pacific Coast Section of Society of Motion Picture Engineers, Wednesday 23 January 1929, 1: Academy Archives, Box 19, Margaret Herrick Library.

26. Ibid., 15.

27. Ibid., 12.

28. Frank Woods, Academy Secretary, Memorandum 'Academy Sound Production Problem Survey', 21 June 1929: Academy Archives, Box 19, Margaret Herrick Library.

29. Ibid.

30. Minutes of Conference of Academy Members and Sound Engineers, Saturday 27 July 1929: Academy Archives, Box 19, Margaret Herrick Library.

31. The Producers-Technicians Joint Committee held its first meeting on 12 November 1929. The members were: Irving Thalberg, M. C. Levee, Fred W. Beetson, J. A. Ball, Fred Pelton, J. T. Reed, Sol Wurtzel, William Sistrom, Walter Stern, H. Keith Weeks and Nugent H. Slaughter; Sands, *Historical Study of AMPAS*, 85.

32. Academy of Motion Picture Arts and Sciences [hereafter AMPAS], *Technical Bureau Bulletin*, 15 July 1930, cited in Sands, *Historical Study of AMPAS*, 87.

33. The following studios were included in the Academy Survey: First National, Fox Film Company, MGM, Paramount, Pathé, RKO, United Artists and Warner Bros.

34. In the latter part of 1929 the Academy organised events open to all members on acoustic control, dubbing and volume control in movie theatres.

35. AMPAS, Progress Report, 20 August 1929, n.p.

36. Ibid., my emphasis.

37. Ibid.

38. Ibid.

39. Irving Thalberg, 'Technical Activities of the Academy of Motion Picture Arts and Sciences', *JSMPE* July 1930: 3–19, 4.

40. Ibid., 3.
41. Ibid., 4.
42. Lastra, *Sound Technology and the American Cinema*, 167–170.
43. Cowan (ed.), *Recording Sound for Motion Pictures*.
44. Bordwell and Thompson, 'Technological Change and Classical Film Style', 123.
45. Ibid.
46. See International Photographer, 'Micks and Mikes', *International Photographer*, January 1930: 30, and Elmer Richardson, 'A Microphone Boom', *JSMPE* 15:1 (1930): 41–45.
47. Handzo, 'A Narrative Glossary of Film Sound Technology', 390–391.
48. Rick Altman, McGraw Jones and Sonia Tratoe, 'Inventing the Cinema Soundtrack: Hollywood's Multiplane Sound System', in *Music and Cinema*, ed. James Buhler, Caryl Flinn and David Neumeyer (Middletown, CT: Wesleyan University Press, 2000), 339–359.
49. Crafton, *The Talkies*, 355.
50. Ibid., 12.
51. Ibid., 16–17.
52. Kellogg, 'History of Sound Motion Pictures'; Rick Altman, 'Evolution of Sound Technologies', in *Film Sound: Theory and Practice*, ed. Elisabeth Weis and John Belton (New York: Columbia University Press, 1985).
53. Barrett C. Kiesling, *Talking Pictures: How They Are Made and How to Appreciate Them* (Richmond, VA: Johnson Publishing Company, 1937), 205.
54. AMPAS, *Motion Picture Sound Engineering* (New York: D. Van Nostrand Company, 1938).
55. Lastra, *Sound Technology and the American Cinema*, 138–139.
56. Ibid.
57. Ibid., 207.
58. Balio (ed.), *Grand Design*, 223–224; John Kobal, *Gotta Sing, Gotta Dance: A History of Movie Musicals* (Twickenham: Spring Books, 1983), 148–154.
59. Balio (ed.), *Grand Design*, 211.
60. Mordaunt Hall, Review of *A Lady's Morals*, *New York Times*, 8 November 1930, n.p.
61. J. P. Maxfield, 'Some of the Latest Developments in Sound Recording and Reproduction', *Academy Technical Bulletin* 9, 20 April 1935: 1–8; 5. Paper presented at meeting of the Academy Technical Branch, 13 February 1935.
62. For discussion of forms of integration in the musical, see Steve Neale, *Genre and Hollywood* (London and New York: Routledge, 2000), 106–107.
63. Composed by Alberto Pestalozza, with lyrics by Carlo Tiochet.
64. Michel Chion, *The Voice in the Cinema* (New York: Columbia University Press, 1999), 5–6.
65. Victor Schertzinger, 'Psychological and Dramatic Possibilities of High Volume Recordings for Musical Pictures', *JSMPE* June 1936: 661–665; 661–662.
66. Ibid., 662.
67. Ibid.
68. Ibid., 664.
69. Ibid., 662.
70. R. H. Townsend, 'Some Technical Aspects of Recording Music', *JSMPE* September 1935: 259–268.
71. Homer G. Tasker, 'Current Developments in Production Methods in Hollywood', *JSMPE* January 1935: 3–11.
72. Ibid., 6.
73. Ibid.
74. John Livadary, 'Recording "One Night of Love"', *American Cinematographer* April 1935: 140, 152; 140.
75. Ibid., 140.
76. Tasker, 'Current Developments in Production Methods', 7.
77. Ibid.

78. Tasker reported a demonstration of 'popless' disk recording by ERPI. He also reported the rapidly grow-ing use of recording on cellulose disks for pre-scoring musicals at Warner Bros., noting that this practice was used for Busby Berkeley numbers. See Tasker, 'Current Developments in Production Methods', 7.

79. Ibid., 7–8.

80. J. W. McNair, cited in Alex E. Alden, 'The Commitment of SMPTE to Standardization', SMPTE Journal 110:10 (2001): 736–739.

81. Kobal, A History of Movie Musicals, 149.

82. Nathan Levinson, 'A New Method of Increasing Volume Range of Talking Motion Pictures', JSMPE February 1936: 111–116; 111.

83. The preparation of fader cue sheets for projection are detailed as part of the sound editing process in I. James Wilkinson and Earl W. Reis, 'Editing and Assembling the Sound Picture', in Cowan (ed.), Recording Sound for Motion Pictures.

84. Levinson, 'A New Method of Increasing Volume Range', 113.

85. Ibid.

86. Source: http://www.oscars.org, accessed 28 March 2012.

87. Levinson, 'A New Method of Increasing Volume Range', 113–114.

88. Discussion in ibid., 115.

89. JSMPE, 'Report of the SMPE Sound Committee, April 1935', JSMPE April 1935: 353–357.

90. Ibid., 355.

91. Ibid., 355–356.

92. Ibid., 356.

93. Ibid.

94. Otto Sandvik, Committee Member, discussion in ibid., 357.

95. Ibid.

96. AMPAS, 'The Work of the Committee on Standardization of Theatre Sound Projection Equipment Characteristics: Standard Electrical Characteristics for Two Way Reproducing Systems in Theatres', Academy Technical Bulletin, 31 March 1937: 1–5, and AMPAS, 'Revised Specifications: Research Council Standard Electrical Characteristic for Two Way Reproducing Systems in Theatres', Academy Technical Bulletin, 8 June 1937: 1–3.

97. Ioan Allen, 'The X-Curve: Its Origins and History: Electro-Acoustic Characteristics in the Cinema and the MixRoom, the Large Room and the Small', Society of Motion Picture and Television Engineers Motion Imaging Journal 115: 7–8 (2006): 264–275.

98. AMPAS, 'Standard Electrical Characteristics for Two Way Reproducing Systems in Theatres', 1.

99. Variety, 'Films' Technical Advances of 1938', Weekly Variety, 4 January 1939: 44.

100. Jack Durst, 'An Outline of the Work of the Academy Research Council Sub-Committee on Acoustical Characteristics', JSMPE March 1941: 283–293; 284.

101. These dual values were threaded through criteria for the Academy's awards for sound. From the 1929/1930 (3rd) Oscars, the Academy gave an Award of Merit for Best Sound Recording. In 1938 a new Award of Merit category was created for Best Special Effects, for a combination of photographic and sound effects. Members of the Technicians Branch for Sound, and heads of studio sound departments played a role in nominating and judging for these awards. This topic will be discussed further in Chapter 5.

102. International Projectionist, 'Notes on ERPI's Stereophonic Sound Picture System', International Projectionist, 11 November 1937: 22–23; J. P. Maxfield, 'Demonstration of Stereophonic Recording with Motion Pictures', JSMPE February 1938: 131–135; Franklin L. Hunt, 'Sound Pictures in Auditory Perspective', JSMPE October 1938: 351–357.

103. James J. Finn, '"Fantasia" Technical Data', International Projectionist October 1940: 21; W. Garity and J. N. A. Hawkins, 'Fantasound', JSMPE August 1941: 127–146. The Fantasound system used a minimum of three speakers, but was trialled with more as the process went through a number of ver-sions; see Garity and Hawkins, 'Fantasound', 140–143. The number of speakers used to exhibit the Fantasound system with Fantasia during its roadshow release also depended upon the power capacity

and space available in the roadshow theatres; see William E. Garity and Watson Jones, 'Experiences in Road-Showing Walt Disney's *Fantasia*', *JSMPE* July 1942: 6–15. On the roadshow release of *Fantasia*, see Sheldon Hall and Steve Neale, *Epics, Spectacles and Blockbusters: A Hollywood History* (Detroit, MI: Wayne State University Press, 2010).

104. Nathan Levinson and L. T. Goldsmith, 'Vitasound', *JSMPE* August 1941: 147–153; H. I. Reiskind, 'Multiple-Speaker Reproducing Systems for Motion Pictures', *JSMPE* August 1941: 154–163.
105. Joel Finler, *The Hollywood Story* (London: Octopus, 1988), 286–287.
106. Walter Greene, 'Year's Sound Development', *Anniversary Variety*, 6 January 1937: 4.
107. Ibid.
108. Ibid.
109. Ibid.
110. Greene reports RCA's introduction of recording with ultraviolet light, an improvement to optical (sound-on-film) recording processes; ibid., 4.
111. Edwin Hartley, 'Sound Pictures in 1937', *International Projectionist* January 1937: 16.
112. C. W. Bunn, 'Sound Pictures in 1937', *International Projectionist* January 1937: 16.
113. Ibid.
114. Susan J. Douglas, *Inventing American Broadcasting 1899–1922* (Baltimore, MD, and London: Johns Hopkins University Press, 1987), xvi–xvii.
115. Ibid., xvii.
116. On early experiments with binaural and stereophonic sound, from the work of Alexander Graham Bell in the 1870s to innovations in the 1950s, see Beck, *Quiet Revolution*, 60–72.
117. Douglas, 'Some Thoughts on the Question "How Do New Things Happen?"'.
118. Douglas Gomery, 'Failure and Success: Vocafilm and RCA Photophone Innovate Sound', *Film Reader* 2 (1977): 213–221; Pinch and Bijker, 'The Social Construction of Facts and Artefacts', 404–405.
119. Gomery, 'Failure and Success', 213.
120. Cited in Oxford English Dictionary online, http://www.oed.com/view/Entry/189937?redirectedFrom=stereophonic#eid, accessed 16 August 2012.
121. Ibid.
122. Beck, *Quiet Revolution*, 60.
123. Robert E. McGinn, 'Stokowski and the Bell Telephone Laboratories: Collaboration in the Development of High-Fidelity Sound Reproduction', *Technology and Culture* 24:1 (1983): 38–75.
124. Beck, *Quiet Revolution*, 67.
125. Franklin Hunt describes a series of listening tests in stereophonic recording and reproduction for film undertaken at Bell Labs after their 1933 wire transmission demonstration; see Hunt, 'Sound Pictures in Auditory Perspective', 351–357.
126. Variety, 'Erpi Spikes Its Sound Track over Bowl', *Daily Variety*, Saturday 15 August 1936: 3.
127. Variety, '25,000 Jam Bowl for Stokowski's Magic', *Daily Variety*, Tuesday 18 August 1936: 3.
128. Variety, 'New ERPI Bowl Equip Ups Stokowski Ork', *Daily Variety*, Friday 14 August 1936: 3, 6; 3.
129. Variety, 'Techs Case Robots', *Daily Variety*, Friday 14 August 1936: 6.
130. Variety, '25,000 Jam Bowl for Stokowski's Magic', 3.
131. See for example: ERPI, 'Mirrophonic: A True Reproduction of the Original', Advertisement, *Daily Variety*, Monday 24 August 1936: 10–11; ERPI, 'A True Reproduction of the Original', Advertisement, *Weekly Variety*, Wednesday 26 August 1936: 44; ERPI, 'Thrills for Your Ears', Advertisement, *Motion Picture Herald*, Saturday 5 September 1936: 73–74. The feature of the system was its so-called 'Diphonic' speakers, comprised of two units, one of which transmitted all sound frequencies below 300 cycles, whilst the other unit carried all frequencies above 300 cycles; see R. C. Miner, 'More Data on the W. E. Mirrophonic Speaker System', *International Projectionist* October 1937: 20, 22.
132. The October 1937 demonstration was written up and published in the *JSMPE* in Maxfield, 'Demonstration of Stereophonic Recording with Motion Pictures'; also cited and discussed by Beck, *Quiet Revolution*, 67–69.

133. Maxfield, 'Demonstration of Stereophonic Recording with Motion Pictures', 132–133.

134. Ibid., 132.

135. Variety, 'The Ultimate in Sound', *Weekly Variety*, 3 May 1939: 22.

136. Ibid.

137. Film Daily, 'Studio Sound Directors Coming East as Erpi Guests', *Film Daily*, 22 March 1940: 1. The following studio heads of sound were invited: Douglas Shearer (MGM), Elmer Raguse (Hal Roach Studios), E. H. Hansen (Twentieth Century-Fox), Loren Ryder (Paramount), John Livadary (Columbia), Thomas Moulton (Goldwyn), Bernard Brown (Universal) and Jack Whitney (General Service Studios).

138. Motion Picture Herald, 'New Sound Race Is On; Millions Are at Stake', *Motion Picture Herald*, 13 April 1940: 12–13; see also the commentary article: Motion Picture Herald, 'This Week in the News – Sound Revolution', *Motion Picture Herald*, 13 April 1940: 8.

139. Herald, 'This Week in the News – Sound Revolution', 8.

140. Herald, 'New Sound Race Is On', 12–13.

141. Quigley quoted in ibid., 12.

142. Ibid.

143. Film Daily, 'Stereophonic Sound Use Put to Film Biz', *Film Daily*, 10 April 1940: 1, 3.

144. Variety, 'Stereophonic Sound Demonstration at Pantages Thurs.', *Daily Variety*, 11 June 1940: 6; Variety, 'Stereophonic Show Draws Capacity Audience', *Daily Variety*, 20 June 1940: 8.

145. Variety, 'Spectators Awed by Stereophonic Sound Demonstration', *Daily Variety*, 21 June 1940: 3; Variety, 'Pix Not Ready for New Sound, Execs Report', *Daily Variety*, 25 June 1940: 7.

146. Variety, 'Pix Not Ready for New Sound', 7.

147. Ibid.

148. American Cinematographer, 'Hollywood Hears Stereophonic Reproduction: It Is Good', *American Cinematographer* July 1940: 325–326; 326.

149. Film Daily, 'Stereophonic Sound for 1940–41 Films?', *Film Daily*, 24 June 1940: 4.

150. Motion Picture Herald, 'Hollywood Considers 3-Dimensional Sound', *Motion Picture Herald*, 29 June 1940: 18.

151. Ibid.; see also John K. Hilliard, 'The Theater Standardization Activities of the Academy Research Council', *Academy Technical Bulletin* 22 May 1940: 1–12.

152. Motion Picture Herald, 'Hollywood Considers 3-Dimensional Sound', 18.

153. Ibid.

154. *Variety* reported that ERPI were hosting a 'huddle' of the sound directors of studios with Western Electric licences to discuss sound improvements, 'including results of the recent stereophonic recording demonstration'; Variety, 'Sound Directors Sesh on Improvements', *Daily Variety*, Thursday 11 July 1940: 4.

155. Finn, '"Fantasia" Technical Data', 21. See also R. J. Kowalski, 'RCA's "Fantasound" System as Used for Disney's "Fantasia"', *International Projectionist* November 1940: 20–21; 24.

156. Finn, '"Fantasia" Technical Data', 21.

157. Ibid.

158. Sam Robins, 'Disney Again Tries Trailblazing', *New York Times*, 3 November 1940: 7.

159. Ibid.

160. Film Daily, 'Reviews of New Film "Fantasia"', *Film Daily*, 14 November 1940: 7; see also Film Daily, 'N.Y. Dailies See "Fantasia"', *Film Daily*, 14 November 1940: 7.

161. Motion Picture Herald, 'Showmen's Reviews – Fantasia', *Motion Picture Herald*, 16 November 1940: 40.

162. George Schutz, 'Showmen's Reviews – Fantasound', *Motion Picture Herald*, 16 November 1940: 40.

163. Motion Picture Herald, '"Fantasia" Sound: Its Processes and Their Portents', *Motion Picture Herald*, *Better Theatres* section, 16 November 1940: 7–8, 21.

164. Ibid.

165. Ibid., 21.

166. Film Daily, 'Only 76 Theaters to Get "Fantasia"', *Film Daily*, 11 November 1940: 1, 2.

167. See, for example, the following articles by R. J. Kowalski (of RCA's Service Division): 'RCA's "Fantasound" System as Used for Disney's "Fantasia"'; and 'Fantasound Soundheads and Amplifiers', *International Projectionist* December 1940: 7–8.

168. Film Daily, 'Warners Show Vitasound at "Santa Fe" Debut', *Film Daily*, 14 November 1940: 7.

169. Ibid.

170. Motion Picture Herald, 'This Week in the News – "Fantasound" and "Vitasound"', *Motion Picture Herald*, 16 November 1940: 8.

171. Ibid.

172. Variety, 'Vitasound Will Get Press Preem at Warners Today', *Daily Variety*, 19 November 1940: 5. See also Showmen's Trade Review, 'Vitasound Demonstrated at Warner Bros. Studio', *Showmen's Trade Review*, 30 November 1940: 23.

173. Variety, 'WB–RCA Vitasound Termed Revolutionary', *Daily Variety*, 20 November 1940: 3.

174. Ibid.

175. Ibid.

176. Thomas Pryor, 'By Way of Report', *New York Times*, 24 November 1940; Douglas W. Churchill, 'Hollywood Eyes Recent Technical Advances', *New York Times*, 1 December 1940.

177. Film Daily, 'Strand One of First Two Theaters to Get Vitasound', *Film Daily*, 20 November 1940: 1, 6; Film Daily, 'Vitasound Goes in All Warner Houses, First Installations Going into N.Y. Strand and Two Theaters on West Coast', *Film Daily – Equipment News*, 22 November 1940: 1, 4; Showmen's Trade Review, 'WB Develop Sound System', *Showmen's Trade Review*, 23 November 1940: 6; Pryor, 'By Way of Report'; Motion Picture Herald, 'This Week in the News – "Vitasound"', *Motion Picture Herald*, 30 November 1940: 8; American Cinematographer, 'Warner's "Vitasound" Praised at Showing', *American Cinematographer* December 1940: 547.

178. American Cinematographer, 'Warner's "Vitasound" Praised at Showing', 547.

179. American Cinematographer, 'Disney's "Fantasia" Is Really Revolutionary', *American Cinematographer* December 1940: 558.

180. Ibid.

181. Ibid.

182. Terry Ramsaye, 'Furore on "Fantasia"', *Motion Picture Herald*, 7 December 1940: 1.

183. Motion Picture Herald, 'This Week in the News – New Sound Coming', *Motion Picture Herald*, 14 December 1940: 8.

184. Ibid.

185. Motion Picture Herald, 'Preparing Another Advance in the Art', *Motion Picture Herald*, Better Theatres section, 14 December 1940: 7.

186. Motion Picture Herald, 'Preparation for a New Advance in Motion Picture Sound', *Motion Picture Herald*, Better Theatres section, 14 December 1940: 30, 32–33; 30.

187. Ibid., 32.

188. Motion Picture Herald, 'This Week in the News – New Sound for All', *Motion Picture Herald*, 12 December 1940: 8.

189. Motion Picture Daily, 'Photophone Has New Sound Development', *Motion Picture Daily*, 18 December 1940: 6.

190. RCA., 'RCA Panoramic Sound System Used by Warner Brothers for the "Vitasound" Presentation of Santa Fe Trail', Advertisement, *Daily Variety*, 2 January 1941: 10.

191. Film Daily, 'Small Houses May Get Realism of Fantasound', *Film Daily*, 18 December 1940: 6.

192. Ibid.; see also Film Daily, 'Nabes May Get Latest Sound, Small Houses Eyed for RCA Panoramic', *Film Daily Equipment News*, 20 December 1940: 1, 5.

193. Motion Picture Herald, 'This Week in the News – New Sound for All', 8.

194. Film Daily, ''41 Film Equipment Outlook Brighter', *Film Daily Equipment News*, 3 January 1941: 1, 5, 8; 1.

195. Ibid., 1.

196. Ibid., 5.

197. Ibid.

198. Showmen's Trade Review, 'To Standardize New Type Sound Recording', *Showmen's Trade Review*, 4 January 1941: 25.

199. Ibid.

200. Showmen's Trade Review, 'Cahill Sees New Sound a Factor for Big Year', *Showmen's Trade Review*, 4 January 1941: 38.

201. Film Daily, 'Motiograph Assures Exhibs. Company Will Meet All Sound Changes', *Film Daily Equipment News*, 31 January 1941: 1, 5; 1.

202. Variety, 'Films' Technical Advances in '40', *Variety Anniversary Edition*, 8 January 1941: 36.

203. Ibid.

204. Ibid.

205. See, for example: Variety, 'SMPE Speakers Stress Aid of Films in National Defence', *Daily Variety*, 6 May 1941: 4; Motion Picture Herald, 'Engineers Consider New Sound, Study Industry's Role in Defense', *Motion Picture Herald*, 10 May 1941: 37; and Motion Picture Herald, 'Industry Mobilizes for Defense', *Motion Picture Herald*, 21 June 1941: 56.

206. Pinch and Bijker, 'The Social Construction of Facts and Artefacts'.

207. H. I. Reiskind, 'Sound Reproduction', United States Patent number: 2,299,410, filed 30 April 1941, issued 20 October 1942.

208. Reiskind, 'Multiple-Speaker Reproducing Systems', 154–155.

209. Ibid., 158–159.

210. Levinson and Goldsmith, 'Vitasound', 147–152.

211. Reiskind, 'Multiple-Speaker Reproducing Systems', 155.

212. Reiskind quoted in discussion at end of Levinson and Goldsmith, 'Vitasound', 153.

213. Showmen's Trade Review, '"New Sound" Stalled by Studio Indecision', *Showmen's Trade Review*, 19 July 1941: 36.

CHAPTER 3

1. Anon., 'Actions Speak Louder ...', *Motion Picture News*, 1 March 1930: 1.

2. Donald Crafton, *The Talkies: American Cinema's Transition to Sound, 1926–1931* (Berkeley: University of California Press, 1997), 226.

3. Motion Picture Herald, 'Review of Flirtation Walk', *Motion Picture Herald*, 30 June 1934: 39.

4. Screenland, 'Tagging the Talkies – Review of "Follow Your Heart"', *Screenland*, November 1936: 12.

5. MGM, 'Advertisement for "Broadway Serenade"', *Motion Picture Herald*, 29 March 1939: 5.

6. Scott Higgins, *Harnessing the Technicolor Rainbow: Color Design in the 1930s* (Austin: University of Texas Press, 2007); Patrick Keating, *Hollywood Lighting: From the Silent Era to Film Noir* (New York: Columbia University Press, 2010); Patrick Keating, 'Shooting for Selznick: Craft and Collaboration in Hollywood Cinematography', in *The Classical Hollywood Reader*, ed. Steve Neale (London and New York: Routledge, 2012); Scott Higgins, 'Order and Plenitude: Technicolor Aesthetics in the Classical Era', in Neale (ed.), *The Classical Hollywood Reader*.

7. David Bordwell, *On the History of Film Style* (Cambridge, MA, and London: Harvard University Press, 1997), 156.

8. David Bordwell, 'The Classical Hollywood Style', in David Bordwell, Janet Staiger and Kristin Thompson, *The Classical Hollywood Cinema: Film Style and Mode of Production to 1960* (London: Routledge, 1985), 5.

9. Keating, *Hollywood Lighting*, 4–7.

10. Harold Lewis, sound recordist at Paramount, defined good sound practices as 'flexible' and responsive to story and genre contexts in his article 'Getting Good Sound Is an Art', *American Cinematographer* June 1934: 65, 73–74; 65; Wesley Miller, of MGM, described the necessity for the 'sound man' to understand

'the interlocking requirement of several crafts'; Wesley C. Miller, 'Basis of Motion Picture Sound', in *Motion Picture Sound Engineering*, ed. AMPAS (New York: D. Van Nostrand, 1938), 5.

11. Carl Dreher, 'Sound Personnel and Organization', in *Recording Sound for Motion Pictures*, ed. Lester Cowan (New York and London: McGraw-Hill, 1931), 345.

12. Ibid., 346.

13. Lewis, 'Getting Good Sound Is an Art', 65, 73–74; 65.

14. Miller, 'Basis of Motion Picture Sound', 5.

15. Groves, 'The Soundman', 220.

16. Wesley C. Miller and G. R. Crane, 'Modern Film Re-Recording Equipment', *JSMPE* October 1948: 400.

17. Lane, *New Technique of Screen Writing*, 3.

18. See Janet Staiger, 'The Producer-Unit System: Management by Specialization after 1931,' in Bordwell, Staiger and Thompson, *The Classical Hollywood Cinema*, 320–329.

19. The term 'draggy' was widely used. Sound Film Editor H. J. McCord (Warner Bros.) coached a meeting of the Academy's Technicians Branch in how to use editing to maintain story tempo: 'The film editor … [must] know the best dramatic, comedy, melodramatic or farce tempo of the scene – slow tempo may make the scene draggy and uninteresting, while some other tempo may on the contrary be too racy or fast.' Quoted in 'The Sound Film Editor', *American Cinematographer* April 1932: 41.

20. Cinematographer Lindsley Lane strongly criticises the constraints that early sound technologies and the influence of theatrically staged sound content put on cinematographers in the early sound period. See Lindsley Lane, 'Cinematographer Plays Leading Part in Group of Creative Minds', *American Cinematographer* February 1935, 48–49; 58.

21. Nancy Wood, 'Towards a Semiotics of the Transition to Sound: Spatial and Temporal Codes', *Screen* 25:3 (1984): 16–24; 16.

22. Lane, 'Cinematographer Plays Leading Part', 58, cited by Bordwell in *The Classical Hollywood Cinema*, 306.

23. Lea Jacobs, *Film Rhythm after Sound: Technology, Music and Performance* (Berkeley: University of California Press, 2015).

24. Stephen R. Barley, 'Technicians in the Workplace: Ethnographic Evidence for Bringing Work into Organizational Studies', *Administrative Science Quarterly* 41:3 (1996): 420–422.

25. Walter B. Pitkin and William M. Marston, *The Art of Sound Pictures* (New York and London: D. Appleton and Company, 1930), 98.

26. Ibid., 120.

27. In addition to Lane, discussed in some detail in the chapter, see the glossary of Nancy Naumberg, *We Make the Movies* (New York: W. W. Norton & Company, 1937), which defines a sequence as 'a series of scenes showing related action', 284.

28. Lane, *New Technique of Screen Writing*, 13.

29. Ibid.

30. Wilkinson and Reis, 'Editing and Assembling the Sound Picture'; McCord, 'The Sound Film Editor'; and Maurice Pivar, 'Sound Film Editing', *American Cinematographer* May 1932: 11–12, 46. See also Donald Fairservice, *Film Editing: History, Theory and Practice* (Manchester: Manchester University Press, 2001).

31. Pitkin and Marston, *The Art of Sound Pictures*, 194.

32. Ibid.

33. Ibid., 197, 200.

34. Lane, *New Technique of Screen Writing*, 47–48.

35. Ibid., 36.

36. Ibid., 36–37.

37. Lewis, 'Getting Good Sound is an Art', 65.

38. Ibid.

39. Ibid.

40. Ibid.

41. Ibid.

42. Ibid.

43. Dreher, 'Sound Personnel and Organization', 345.

44. Tino Balio (ed.), *Grand Design: Hollywood as a Modern Business Enterprise 1930–1939* (Berkeley and London: University of California Press, 1993), 245.

45. Lewis, 'Getting Good Sound Is an Art', 65.

46. Michel Chion discusses the ways in which film music (both source music and score) might be 'empathetic' or 'anempathetic' to a film scene; clearly, sound effects can also take on this role, as they do in this scene. See Michael Chion, *Audio-Vision: Sound on Screen* (New York: Columbia University Press, 1994), 8, 221–222.

47. Sequence Plan for 'The Retreat' (undated and uncredited), 'A Farewell to Arms', Paramount Pictures Script Collection, Box 297, Folder 99, Margaret Herrick Library.

48. Lane, *New Technique of Screen Writing*, 77.

49. Wood, 'Towards a Semiotics of the Transition to Sound', 17–18.

50. On 27 September 1934 the Academy Technicians Branch held a meeting on the topic of 'Transitions and Time Lapses, Fades, Wipes and Dissolves: Their Use and Value to Production'. The meeting was chaired by Cecil B. DeMille and papers were presented on the topic from different crafts. Fred Jackman (Warner Bros. Head of Special Effects Department) presented 'Organization of a Special Effects Department'; Rolla Flora presented 'Fades, Wipes and Dissolves'; Anne Bauchens (Editor, Paramount Pictures) 'How We Use These Devices to Increase Production Value'; Slavko Vorkapich presented 'The Psychological Basis of Effective Cinematography'; and Loren Ryder (Paramount Pictures) 'Sound Recording Treatment of the Transition Shot', a paper prepared jointly by Ryder and the following studio sound representatives: Lawrence Aicholtz (Universal), Roger Heman (United Artists), K. B. Lambert (MGM), Harry Leonard (Twentieth Century-Fox), Chester North (Warner Bros.), Nugent H. Slaughter (Columbia) and James G. Stewart (RKO). The papers were collected in: AMPAS, 'Transitions and Time Lapses, Fades, Wipes and Dissolves: Their Use and Value to the Production', *Academy Technical Bulletin*, 28 September 1934: 1–15.

51. Anne Bauchens, 'How We Use These Devices to Increase Production Value', *Academy Technical Bulletin*, 28 September 1934: 6–8.

52. Ibid., 6.

53. Loren Ryder, 'Transitions and Time Lapses: Sound Recording Treatment of the Transiton Shot', *Academy Technical Bulletin*, 28 September 1934: 11–15; 11.

54. Ibid., 11–12.

55. Barrett C. Kiesling, *Talking Pictures: How They Are Made and How to Appreciate Them* (Richmond, VA: Johnson Publishing Company, 1937), 207–208; Lane, *New Technique of Screen Writing*, 75–78; Ed Gibbons, 'Montage Marches In', *International Photographer* October 1937: 25–29; Herb Lightman, 'The Magic of Montage', *American Cinematographer* October 1949: 361, 381–382.

56. Gérard Genette, *Narrative Discourse: An Essay in Method* (Ithaca, NY: Cornell University Press, 1980), 161–162; Brian Henderson, 'Tense, Mood, and Voice in Film (Notes after Genette)', *Film Quarterly* 36:4 (1983): 4–17, 12–13.

57. Murray Smith, *Engaging Characters: Fiction, Emotion and the Cinema* (Oxford: Clarendon Press, 1995).

58. Murray Smith, 'Altered States: Character and Emotional Response in the Cinema', *Cinema Journal* 33:4 (1994): 34–56; 35.

59. The role that voices play as expressive elements in *Random Harvest* is analysed very productively in Susan Smith's work on the film. She persuasively discusses the 'nurturing' role of Greer Garson's voice in providing a bedrock for the film's rejuvenation of a male trauma victim, and hence for the romance that motivates the narrative. My focus is distinct in analysing the role that sounds (and sound effects particularly) play in the narrational modality and proximity to Smithy's character. Susan Smith, 'Voices in Film', in *Close-Up 02*, ed. John Gibbs and Douglas Pye (London: Wallflower Press, 2007), 196–224.

60. Chion, *Audio-Vision*, 129.

61. In her work on narration and film scoring, Claudia Gorbman argues that in moments where film music motifs connect with, or infer, a character's psychology or interiority, the narrational proximity of the score is 'metadiegetic' rather than 'non-diegetic'. She notes that motifs can gain these associations

through the processes of narration: for example, repetitions of musical leitmotifs previously heard, and which function expressively for the film's audio-viewer; hence, the music moves from a non-diegetic narrational location to one closer to character. Gorbman, *Unheard Melodies: Narrative Film Music* (Bloomington: Indiana University Press, 1987), 22–24. The concept of 'metadiegetic' music and sound has been taken up and developed by Robynn Stilwell, 'The Fantastical Gap between Diegetic and Non-Diegetic', in *Beyond the Soundtrack* ed. Daniel Goldmark, Lawrence Kramer and Richard Leppert (Berkeley: University of California Press, 2007), and by Ben Winters, 'The Non-Diegetic Fallacy: Film, Music and Narrative Space', *Music and Letters* 91:2 (2010): 224–244.

62. Chion, *Audio-Vision*, 91.

63. The AMPAS Technical Bureau defined 'dubbing' as follows: 'Re-recording of all or part of a sound record, for the preparation of a new master record, for editorial purposes, for changing volume levels or frequency characteristics, or for changing the recording medium (from film to disc, or disc to film.) Dubbing may or may not involve scoring, partial or complete.' 'A Glossary of Motion Picture Terms', in Cowan (ed.), *Recording Sound for Motion Pictures*, 366.

64. Minutes of AMPAS General Meeting on 'Dubbing, the Significance and Possibilities of Re-Recording in the Production of Sound Pictures', Wednesday 23 October 1929. Academy Archive, Box 19, Margaret Herrick Library. See also Bell Labs' engineer J. J. Kuhn, 'A Sound Film Re-Recording Machine', *JSMPE* September 1931: 326–342.

65. Staiger, 'The Producer-Unit System', 320–329.

66. The account of typical production processes outlined in Chapter 3 is drawn from a range of sources, and from my observations of different production regimes in a range of archival collections. There were variations in practice according to the needs of specific productions, and within different studio cultures. It would be impossible to include all variations, thus my account is not intended to be taken as totalising, simply as a broad map of the key stages involving sound technicians. The sources include: W. C. Harcus, 'Making a Motion Picture', *JSMPE* November 1931: 802–811; Nathan Levinson, B. F. Miller and Lloyd Goldsmith, 'Recording and Re-recording', in *We Make the Movies*, ed. Nancy Naumberg (New York: W. W. Norton & Company, 1937), 173–198; Kiesling, *Talking Pictures*; Sam Goode, 'How We Put Talk in "Talkies"', *Warner Club News*, October 1939: 1, 7; L. T. Goldsmith, 'Re-Recording Sound Motion Pictures', *JSMPE* November 1942: 277–283; and Oral History sources with Walter Elliot (RKO), George Groves (Warner Bros.), Milo Lory (MGM), Evelyn Rutledge (Columbia, RKO and Warner Bros.), James G. Stewart (RKO and Vanguard Pictures) and Murray Spivack (RKO).

67. On 'soundmarks', R. Murray Schafer writes: 'The term is derived from *landmark* to refer to a community sound which is unique or possesses qualities which make it specially regarded or noticed by the people in that community.' R. Murray Schafer, *The Soundscape: Our Sonic Environment and the Tuning of the World* (Rochester, VT: Destiny Books, 1977; 1994), 274.

68. Bordwell, in Bordwell, Staiger and Thompson, *The Classical Hollywood Cinema*, 303.

69. Kenneth Morgan, 'Dubbing', in Cowan (ed.), *Recording Sound for Motion Pictures*, 145–146.

70. Ibid., 150.

71. Ibid., 154.

72. George Lewin, 'Dubbing and Its Relation to Sound Picture Production', *JSMPE* January 1931: 38–48, 41–42.

73. Carl Dreher, 'Recording, Re-Recording and Editing of Sound', *JSMPE* June 1931: 756–765; 759, emphasis in original.

74. Ibid., 759.

75. See, for example, E. D. Cook, 'A Consideration of Some Special Methods for Re-Recording', *JSMPE* December 1935: 523–540. Cook's article covers how re-recording techniques were adapted for new recording formats, such as push-pull recording. Levinson, Miller and Goldsmith, 'Recording and Re-recording', 196; Nathan Levinson, 'Sound in Motion Pictures', *JSMPE* May 1942: 468–482.

76. Homer Tasker, 'A Dubbing Rehearsal Channel', *JSMPE* September 1937: 286–292; 286.

77. Ibid., 286.

78. Edwin Wetzel, 'Assembling a Final Sound-Track', *Journal of the Society of Motion Picture and Television Engineers* [hereafter *JSMPTE*]October 1937: 374–375; 374.

79. J. N. A. Hawkins, 'Slyfield's New Mixers Gallows', *International Photographer* June 1938: 18; 18.

80. This was sound mixing apparatus used to control the input of different soundtracks by using variable resistance. K. B. Lambert, 'An Improved Mixer Potentiometer', *JSMPE* September 1941: 326–342.

81. Wesley C. Miller and H. R. Kimball, 'A Rerecording Console, Associated Circuits, and Constant B Equalizers', *JSMPE* September 1944: 187–205; 187–88.

82. Wesley C. Miller and G. R. Crane, 'Modern Film Re-Recording Equipment', *JSMPE* October 1948: 399–417.

83. Ibid., 399–400.

84. Dreher, 'Recording, Re-Recording and Editing of Sound', 759.

85. David Lewis Yewdall, *Practical Art of Motion Picture Sound: Third Edition* (London and New York: Focal Press, 2007), 402–439; Vanessa Theme Ament, *The Foley Grail: The Art of Performing Sound for Film, Games and Animation* (London and New York: Focal Press, 2009), 3–10; Benjamin Wright, 'Footsteps with Character: The Art and Craft of Foley', *Screen* 55:2 (2014): 204–220; Lucy Fife Donaldson, 'The Work of an Invisible Body: The Contribution of Foley Artists to On-Screen Effort', *Alphaville: Journal of Film and Screen Media* 7 (2014) n.p.

86. Stephen Bottomore, 'An International Study of Sound Effects in Early Cinema', *Film History* 11:4 (1999): 485–498; Stephen Bottomore, 'The Story of Percy Peashaker: Debates about Sound Effects in the Early Cinema', in *The Sounds of Early Cinema*, ed. Richard Abel and Rick Altman (Bloomington: Indiana University Press, 2001), 129–142; Rick Altman, *Silent Film Sound* (New York: Columbia University Press, 2004), 133–156.

87. Robert L. Mott, *Sound Effects: Radio, TV and Film* (Stoneham, MA: Focal Press, 1990); Richard J. Hand, *Terror on the Air: Horror Radio in America 1931–1952* (Jefferson, NC, and London: McFarland, 2006); Neil Verma, 'Honeymoon Shocker: Lucille Fletcher's "Psychological" Sound Effects and Wartime Radio Drama', *Journal of American Studies* 44:1 (2010): 137–153; Frank Krutnik, 'Theatre of Thrills: The Culture of Suspense', *New Review of Film and Television Studies* 11:1 (2013): 6–33; Jesse Schlotterbeck, 'Radio Noir in the USA', in *A Companion to Film Noir*, ed. Andrew Spicer and Helen Hanson (Boston: Wiley-Blackwell, 2013), 423–439.

88. Oral History Interview with Walter G. Elliot, interviewed by Irene Kahn Atkins for 'Oral History with Early Sound and Music Editors', Part 2, 9 September 1974–17 April 1975. American Film Institute, Louis B. Mayer Library, OH 27, 151.

89. See Leo Murray, *Sound Design: Theory from Practice* (London and New York: Routledge, forthcoming).

90. Oral History Interview with Murray Spivack, interviewed by Charles Degelman for Academy of Motion Picture Arts and Sciences Oral History Program. Margaret Herrick Library, OH 118, 54.

91. Ibid., 55.

92. Ibid., 56.

93. H. G. Knox for AMPAS, 'A Paper from the Technical Digest Service – Sound in Motion Pictures by H. G. Knox, Vice-President Electrical Research Products. Inc', *Academy Technical Digest* Reprint no. 16 (1930): 1–27; Hand, *Terror on the Air: Horror Radio in America 1931–1952*, 26.

94. Goldsmith, 'Re-Recording Sound Motion Pictures'.

95. Oral History Interview with Milo Lory, interviewed by Irene Kahn Atkins for 'Oral History with Early Sound and Music Editors', Part 2, 9 September 1974–17 April 1975. American Film Institute, Louis B. Mayer Library, OH 27, 50.

96. Ibid.

97. Ibid.

98. Carl M. Effinger, 'The Filing and Cataloguing of Motion Picture Film', *JSMPE* February 1946: 103–110; Effinger's library is also covered in Lowell E. Redelings, 'The Hollywood Scene', *Hollywood Citizen News*, 19 December 1949, n.p.

99. Arnie Semler, 'The Question Box', *Warner Club News*, December 1939: 12.

100. Goldsmith, 'Re-Recording Sound Motion Pictures', 282.

101. R. H. Townsend, 'Some Technical Aspects of Recording Music', *JSMPE* September 1935: 259–268; P. C. Goldmark and P. S. Henricks, 'Synthetic Reverberation', *JSMPE* December 1939: 635–649; M. Rettinger, 'Reverberation Chambers for Rerecording', *JSMPE* November 1945: 350–357.

102. Rick Altman, 'Sound Space', in *Sound Theory Sound Practice*, ed. Rick Altman (New York and London: Routledge, 1992), 60. See also J. P. Maxfield, 'Technique of Recording Control for Sound Pictures', in Cowan (ed.), *Recording Sound for Motion Pictures*; J. P. Maxfield, 'Some of the Latest Developments in Sound Recording and Reproduction', *Academy Technical Bulletin* 9, 20 April 1935: 1–8; J. P. Maxfield, A. W. Colledge and R. T. Friebus, 'Pick-Up for Sound Motion Pictures (Including Stereophonic)', *JSMPE* June 1938: 666–679.

103. Altman, 'Sound Space', 60.

104. The screenplay for the film was adapted from Florence Barrett Willoughby's 1932 novel by Jules Furthman and Talbot Jennings. The film was produced by Albert Lewin, directed by Henry Hathaway, with associate director Richard Talmadge heading up a second unit for some of the location shooting. Cinematography was done by Charles Lang and the film was scored by Dimitri Tiomkin, with musical direction by Boris Morros. The sound was recorded by Harry Mills and Walter Oberst, with sound effects by Loren Ryder, assisted by Louis Mesenkop. Special visual effects were done by Gordon Jennings, with process photography by Farciot Edouart, assisted by Jan Domela, Dev Jennings, Irmin Roberts and Art Smith.

105. Sheldon Hall and Steve Neale, *Epics, Spectacles and Blockbusters: A Hollywood History* (Detroit, MI: Wayne State University Press, 2010), 100–101.

106. Variety, 'Studios Speed Pix', *Daily Variety*, 21 March 1938: 1, 7.

107. Paramount Pictures Production Files, Folder 1174, Paramount Pictures Collection, Margaret Herrick Library.

108. Homer G. Tasker, 'Current Developments in Production Methods in Hollywood', *JSMPE* January 1935: 3–11; 4–6.

109. Lyrics by Rida Johnson Young, music by Chauncey Olcott.

110. Variety, 'Preview: Spawn of the North', *Daily Variety*, Tuesday 16 August 1938: 3, 6; 3.

111. *Variety* reported that in its first week of release, *Spawn* was outperforming other releases in a range of territories. See: Variety, '"Spawn" Sets Par Record for Yr', *Daily Variety*, Thursday 1 September 1938: 1, 2; and Variety, 'First Run Grosses Here Near Half Million', *Daily Variety*, 30 October 1939: 12, 159.

112. Variety, 'Ryder Rides Projection', *Daily Variety*, 17 August 1938: 6.

113. As noted and discussed by Balio (ed.), *Grand Design*, 199, and Hall and Neale, *Epics, Spectacles and Blockbusters*, 100.

114. Loren Ryder, 'The Importance of Co-operation between Story Construction and Sound to Achieve a New Personality in Pictures', *JSMPE* January 1940: 98–102.

CHAPTER 4

1. Clive Hirschorn, *The Warner Bros. Story* (London: Octopus, 1979), 82; and Thomas Schatz, *The Genius of the System: Hollywood Film-Making in the Studio Era* (London: Faber and Faber, 1989; 1996), 142–148.

2. For an analysis of Warner Bros.' business strategy during the transition, see Douglas Gomery's 'Writing the History of the American Film Industry: Warner Bros. and Sound', in *Movies and Methods: Volume II*, ed. Bill Nichols (Berkeley: University of California Press, 1985).

3. For economic data and commentary on Warner Bros.' productions during the studio era, see H. Mark Glancy, 'Warner Bros Film Grosses, 1921–1951: The William Schaefer Ledger', *Historical Journal of Film, Radio and Television* 15:1 (1995): 55–73; and John Sedgwick and Michael Pokorny, 'The Risk Environment of Film Making: Warner Bros in the Inter-War Years', *Explorations in Economic History* 35:2 (1998): 196–220; 198

4. Sedgwick and Pokorny, 'Warner Bros. in the Inter-War Years', 199. Sedgwick and Pokorny outline Warner Bros.' growth activities such as the takeover of Vitagraph Studios and associated US and foreign distribution exchanges in 1925; its early partnership and agreements with Western Electric that allowed it to benefit from its commercially successful early sound films *Don Juan* (Alan Crosland, 1926) and *The Jazz Singer* (Alan Crosland, 1927); the studio's acquisition of the Stanley cinema circuit in 1929 and the acquisition of First National in 1928–1929.

5. Sedgwick and Pokorny, 'Warner Bros. in the Inter-War Years', 199–200. Warner Bros.' profits swung down from $14,514,628 in 1929 to a loss of over $14 million in 1932 (ibid., 200; Joel Finler, *The Hollywood Story* [London: Octopus, 1988], 238).

6. Tino Balio (ed.), *Grand Design: Hollywood as a Modern Business Enterprise 1930–1939* (Berkeley and London: University of California Press, 1993), 8–9.

7. Sedgwick and Pokorny, 'Warner Bros in the Inter-War Years', 200; Nick Roddick, *A New Deal in Entertainment: Warner Brothers in the 1930s* (London: BFI, 1983), 10.

8. Russell Campbell, 'I Am a Fugitive from a Chain Gang', *Velvet Light Trap* June 1971: 17–19; John E. O'Connor, *I Am a Fugitive from a Chain Gang* (Madison: University of Wisconsin Press, 1981), 9–13. Roddick, *A New Deal in Entertainment*, 73–98.

9. O'Connor, *I Am a Fugitive from a Chain Gang*, 10; Balio (ed.), *Grand Design*, 285–286.

10. Schatz, *The Genius of the System*, 142–148; O'Connor, *I Am a Fugitive from a Chain Gang*, 32–44.

11. Unable to resettle into home or job after returning from the war, Burns drifted into crime, and in 1922 was sentenced to six to ten years' hard labour on a Georgia chain gang for involvement in an armed robbery. Finding the conditions of the chain gang to be unbearable, Burns escaped and made his way to Chicago where, over a period of seven years, he gained respectability, built a career in magazine publishing and made a marriage of convenience. Burns' relations with his wife soured when she discovered he was having an affair, and she wrote to the Georgia authorities exposing his real identity. Burns was arrested and his story was played out in the headlines. Burns himself decided to return to Georgia voluntarily, but on the condition that he would not be forced to work on a chain gang and would be eligible for parole within ninety days. On returning to Georgia, Burns found he could not dictate the terms that he'd hoped for. Stung by the bad publicity that his case had created, the prison authorities were not inclined to be lenient. Burns was again interred in a prison camp with grim conditions, and his appeals for parole were met with numerous legal delays, despite vocal support from his family and others in the Northeast and Midwest. Burns contrived to escape a second time, and was at large during the production and release of *Fugitive*. He remained so until 1945 when he voluntarily returned to Georgia for a commutation of his sentence. See O'Connor, *I Am a Fugitive from a Chain Gang*, 16–17, and 'Burns En Route to Georgia to end "Fugitive's" Career', *The Atlanta Constitution*, 1 November 1945: 1, 11.

12. Robert Burns, *I Am a Fugitive from a Georgia Chain Gang!* (New York: Vanguard, 1932).

13. The studio paid Burns $12,500 for the rights; Contract between Warner Bros. and Robert Burns, 27 February 1932, *I Am a Fugitive from a Chain Gang*, Story Files, Folder 792, Warner Bros. Archives, University of Southern California School of Cinematic Arts Library (hereafter WBA).

14. Gerald Prince, *A Dictionary of Narratology* (Aldershot: Scholar Press, 1988), 86–87.

15. Oral History Interview with Milo Lory, interviewed by Irene Kahn Atkins for 'Oral History with Early Sound and Music Editors', Part 2, 9 September 1974–17 April 1975. American Film Institute, Louis B. Mayer Library, OH 27, 21.

16. Michael Chion, *Audio-Vision: Sound on Screen* (New York: Columbia University Press, 1994), 13–14.

17. Glancy, 'Warner Bros Film Grosses, 1921–1951', 60.

18. *I Am a Fugitive from a Chain Gang*, Production Files, Box 18, Folder 1994, Budget, n.d., WBA.

19. Glancy, 'Warner Bros Film Grosses, 1921–1951', Appendix 2: n.p.

20. Brown Holmes produced an eighty-page treatment of the story, dated 25 April 1932, and Sheridan Gibney produced a screenplay of 132 pages (undated). *I Am a Fugitive from a Chain Gang*, Story Files, Folder 792, WBA.

21. Ibid.

22. Story Conference Notes, 7 June 1932, *I Am a Fugitive from a Chain Gang*, Story Files, Folder 792, WBA.

23. Final Shooting Script, 23 July (additions 28 July) 1932: 64. *I Am a Fugitive from a Chain Gang*, Story Files, Folder 792, WBA.

24. Further details of these salaries are as follows: Director of Photography Sol Polito's salary ($400 per week for six weeks: $2,400), a second cameraman ($90 per week for five weeks: $450), two assistants ($48 per week for five weeks: $480), plus a stills man ($85 per week for five weeks: $425). We can compare Sol Polito's salary of $400 per week with Nathan Levinson's. In 1932 Levinson was on $500 per week (Source: Letter to Sam Warner, New York, from Warner Bros. Legal Dept, 13 October 1926, Warner Bros. Sound Department Legal Files, Folder 2818B, WBA).

25. Final Shooting Script, 23 July (with additions on 28 July) 1932. *I Am a Fugitive from a Chain Gang*, Story Files, Folder 792, WBA.

26. These are script scenes 143–154 and contain the action from the opening shots of the chain gang working; Allen getting permission from the guard to go to the bushes; whispered goodbyes to Bomber; the guard getting suspicious; and the beginning of Allen running and being chased by guards. All these scenes were shot on 10 August. In addition to these, scenes 156 (guards follow Allen through bushes), 157 (second guard unleashes dogs, which start yelping and running) and 159 (the dogs coming on, yelping) were also taken that day; Daily Production and Progress Report, 10 August 1932, *I Am a Fugitive from a Chain Gang* Production Files, Box 18, Folder 1448, WBA.

27. Muni's chase scenes were numbers 155, 158 (making his way away from the chain gang), 161 (coming across a shack in the woods and grabbing a shirt and overalls), 163 (taking off his prison uniform), 165 (dressing in the clothes) and 166, 168, 170 (fighting his way across the muddy ground). These scenes were shot on 11 August; Daily Production and Progress Report, 11 August 1932, *I Am a Fugitive from a Chain Gang* Production Files, Box 18, Folder 1448, WBA. The Production Report noted that 'Jackman to shoot balance of chase shots with guards and dogs. Scenes 162-167-169-171-172'; ibid.

28. Scenes 174 and 175; Daily Production and Progress Report, 12 August 1932, *I Am a Fugitive from a Chain Gang* Production Files, Box 18, Folder 1448, WBA.

29. Scenes 176 (guard and dogs seeking Allen) and 178 (guards puzzled as Allen seems to have disappeared); ibid.

30. Scenes 179–184, O'Connor, *I Am a Fugitive from a Chain Gang*, 119–120.

31. O'Connor, *I Am a Fugitive from a Chain Gang*, 33; Schatz, *The Genius of the System*, 145.

32. For example, three different set-ups of a close shot of Muni and Ellis just before the escape were filmed: scenes 144A, 144B and 144C; Daily Production and Progress Report, 10 August 1932, *I Am a Fugitive from a Chain Gang* Production Files, Box 18, Folder 1448, WBA; five different set-ups of the scene at the shack in the woods were filmed: scenes 161A, 161B, 161C, 161D and 161E; Daily Production and Progress Report, 11 August 1932, *I Am a Fugitive from a Chain Gang* Production Files, Box 18, Folder 1448, WBA.

33. For an outline of the Sound Department at Warner Bros., see Goode, 'How We Put Talk in "Talkies"', *Warner Club News* October 1939: 1, 7; and on C. A. Riggs, see Dolph Thomas, 'Soundings', *Warner Club News* October 1942: 10. Warner Bros.' sound department is discussed further in Chapter 5.

34. The picture of shooting and sound recording practices in the transitional sound period and up to around 1932 has been well established in historical work by historians such as David Bordwell, Janet Staiger and Kristin Thompson, *The Classical Hollywood Cinema: Film Style and Mode of Production to 1960* (London: Routledge, 1985), 298–308; Donald Crafton, *The Talkies: American Cinema's Transition to Sound, 1926–1931* (Berkeley: University of California Press, 1997), 225–249; and James Buhler, David Neumeyer and Rob Deemer, *Hearing the Movies: Music and Sound in Film History* (New York and Oxford: Oxford University Press, 2010), 278–307.

Typically, shooting and sound recording regimes were adapted to solve problems of managing unwanted noise on the set from cameras, which were housed in soundproof 'ice boxes'. A variety of angles on the action were obtained through the practice of multiple camera shooting, and the emphasis in sound work was on 'getting a good recording'; Buhler, Neumeyer and Deemer, *Hearing the Movies*, 304.

More detail on sound recording roles and practices can be found in numerous contemporaneous sources; the following are particularly pertinent in their coverage of practice: Elmer Richardson, 'A Microphone Boom', *JSMPE* 15:1 (1930): 41–45; American Cinematographer, 'Microphone Boom Great Aid in Making Talking Pictures', *American Cinematographer* August 1930: 26; Carl Dreher, 'Sound Personnel and Organization', in *Recording Sound for Motion Pictures*, ed. Lester Cowan (New York and London: McGraw-Hill, 1931), 344–345; Albert W. DeSart, 'Sound Recording Practice', in Cowan (ed.), *Recording Sound for Motion Pictures*, 268–285; Carl Dreher, 'Recording, Re-Recording and Editing of Sound', *JSMPE* June 1931: 756–765; Nathan Levinson, B. F. Miller and Lloyd Goldsmith, 'Recording and Re-recording', in *We Make the Movies*, ed. Nancy Naumberg (New York: W. W. Norton & Company, 1937); AMPAS, *Motion Picture Sound Engineering*; L. T. Goldsmith and B. F. Ryan, 'A Mobile Sound Recording Channel', *JSMPE* February 1938: 219–225; Homer Tasker, 'The Technique of Production Sound Recording', *JSMPE* October 1942: 213–227; L. T. Goldsmith, 'Re-Recording Sound Motion Pictures', *JSMPE* November 1942: 277–283; W. A. Mueller and M. Rettinger, 'Anecdotal History of Sound Recording Technique', *JSMPE* July 1945: 48–53; George Groves, 'The Soundman', *JSMPE* March 1947: 220–230; Oral History Interview with George. R Groves, interviewed by Irene Kahn Atkins for Oral History on 'Motion Picture Sound Recording', 4 August–24 October 1973. American Film Institute, Louis B. Mayer Library, OH 28; Oral History Interview with James G. Stewart, interviewed by Irene Kahn Atkins for Oral History on 'Developments in Sound Techniques', 11 April–20 June 1976. American Film Institute, Louis B. Mayer Library, OH 29.

35. The Daily Production and Progress Reports for the 10 and 11 August 1932 detail both 'wild shots' (camera) and 'wild record' (sound), with the log on the back of the report indicating which of the wild takes were to be printed for review of the dailies. *I Am a Fugitive from a Chain Gang* Production Files, Box 18, Folder 1448, WBA.

36. See Daily Production and Progress Reports for location shooting on *Santa Fe Trail* (Michael Curtiz, 1940), *Santa Fe Trail* Production Files, Folder 332; and Daily Production and Progress Reports for location shooting on *Cheyenne* (Raoul Walsh, 1947), *Cheyenne* Production Files, Folder 1488A, WBA.

37. Levinson, Miller and Goldsmith, 'Recording and Re-Recording', 192.

38. Arnie Semler, 'The Question Box', *Warner Club News*, December 1939: 12.

39. Oral History Interview with Evelyn Rutledge, interviewed by Irene Kahn Atkins for 'Oral Histories with Early Sound and Music Editors', Part 2, September 1974–17 April 1975. American Film Institute, Louis B. Mayer Library, OH 27, 294.

40. Daily Production and Progress Report, 3 September 1932, *I Am a Fugitive from a Chain Gang* Production Files, Box 18, Folder 1448, WBA.

41. Story conference notes, 7 June 1932, *I Am a Fugitive from a Chain Gang* Story Files, Folder 792, WBA.

42. *Alice Adams* had total negative costs of $324,000, and grossed $770,000. This comprised $574,000 in the domestic market and $196,000 in foreign markets, it made a profit of $164,000, putting it at no. 9 in RKO's most profitable films of the year. Source: Richard B. Jewell, 'RKO Film Grosses, 1929–1951: The C. J. Tevlin Ledger', *Historical Journal of Film, Radio and Television*, 14:1 (1994), Appendix 1: 3. RKO made a profit of $684,733 in 1935. Source: Richard B. Jewell and Vernon Harbin, *The RKO Story* (London: Octopus Books, 1982), 80. Except MGM, all the other major and minor studios suffered losses during the Depression, due to falling cinema attendances and the financial extension that many had made to refit their plant and movie theatres for sound production and exhibition. See Finler, *The Hollywood Story*, 32, and Balio (ed.), *Grand Design*, 31–32.

43. Balio (ed.), *Grand Design*, 179.

44. Walter Elliott, 'Alice Adams: Sound Effects List for Final Script', 16 May 1935. *Alice Adams* Production Files, Folder 17, George Stevens' Papers, Margaret Herrick Library.

45. Tamar Lane, *The New Technique of Screen Writing: A Practical Guide to the Writing and Marketing of Photoplays* (New York: McGraw-Hill, 1937), vii.

Hollywood Soundscapes

46. Elliott, 'Alice Adams: Sound Effects List for Final Script', 1.

47. Chion defines 'Elements of auditory setting' as 'Distinct, intermittent, localized sounds that flesh out and give individuality to a scene's setting', and 'Territory sounds' as 'ambient sound whose pervasive presence gives definition to a space, e.g., bird songs, church bells'. Chion, *Audio-Vision*, 222, 224.

48. Chion defines 'empathetic sound' as 'sound (… usually music) whose mood matches the mood of the action'; ibid., 222.

49. A further example is sound effect 8 for scene 43 is a car horn, honking to signal that her brother (Walter/Frank Albertson) is ready to take her to a party, and the effect is described by Elliott as 'blatant honking of auto horn (off)'. Elliott, 'Alice Adams: Sound Effects List for Final Script', 1, 2.

50. Chion defines 'rendering' as 'the use of sounds to convey the feelings or effects associated with the situation on-screen … Rendering frequently translates an agglomerate of sensations. For example, sound accompanying a fall is often a great crash, conveying weight, violence, and pain.' Chion, *Audio-Vision*, 224. Elliott, 'Alice Adams: Sound Effects List for Final Script', 2.

51. For example, sound effect 17 for scenes 118 and 119 is described as 'girl sobbing, on and off scene' and is planned to match the interior setting of the hallway. Elliott, 'Alice Adams: Sound Effects List for Final Script', 1.

52. This illustrates the shift from 'fidelity values' to 'dramatic hierarchies' discussed by James Lastra, *Sound Technology and the American Cinema: Perception, Representation and Modernity* (New York: Columbia University Press, 2000), 201.

53. Walter Elliott, 'Memo to Mr E. Kelley', 18 May 1935, Alice Adams Production Files, Folder 17, George Stevens' Papers, Margaret Herrick Library.

54. Lory, Oral History, 20–22.

55. These choices are illustrated in the following papers: 'Music – Sound Effects – Re-Recording Cue Sheet', 24 July 1935, *Alice Adams* Production Files, George Stevens' Papers, Folder 17, Margaret Herrick Library; and 'Editing and Re-Recording Schedule', 25 July 1935, *Alice Adams* Production Files, Folder 17, George Stevens' Papers, Margaret Herrick Library.

56. 'Music – Sound Effects – Re-Recording Cue Sheet', 24 July 1935, *Alice Adams* Production Files, George Stevens' Papers, Folder 17, Margaret Herrick Library.

57. On 'vococentrism', see Michel Chion, *The Voice in the Cinema* (New York: Columbia University Press, 1999), 5–6.

58. Copies were sent to Carl Dreher (Head of RKO's Sound Department), Walter Elliott, Jane Loring, Mr Maresca, Earl Mounce, George Stevens, Roy Webb, James Wilkinson and Robert Wise.

59. 'Music – Sound Effects – Re-Recording Cue Sheet', 24 July 1935, *Alice Adams* Production Files, Folder 17, George Stevens' Papers, Margaret Herrick Library, 1.

60. The song is 'I Can't Waltz Alone', words by Dorothy Fields and music by Max Steiner. Charlotte Greenspan, *Pick Yourself Up: Dorothy Fields and the Hollywood Musical* (New York and Oxford: Oxford University Press, 2010). Greenspan notes that while Steiner is often renowned for an overt scoring style, typified by his work on *King Kong* (1933), he was a composer of 'great versatility' with a 'great gift for not merely representing but almost creating a movie's characters with his musical themes' (90). Greenspan reports that there were plans for Fields' lyric for the song to be published in sheet music form, and played on radio, but it has not been possible to determine whether it was published or played.

The harmony of the song recurs throughout the film and forms the primary theme of the score, with multiple variations in tempo, instrumentation and mood. As noted, it is played diegetically as Alice dances with Arthur, acquiring its connection with the couple at this point. It is played diegetically again, heard from the phonograph in the Adams' living room, as Alice waits for Walter to call, and later in the film, when Arthur takes Alice out, they request its repeated performance by a band of musicians at the restaurant where they dine. The final strains of the song are heard at the scene's opening, and when Arthur asks the waiter to request the song again, the violinist reacts with comic disbelief. The song plays diegetically over the conversation between Alice and Arthur, during which the dialogue deliberately draws attention to the mood of the song. Alice, convinced that their friendship and happiness is only momentary, likens it to the song, 'oh so sweet, and oh so sad'.

61. The re-recording notes specify the dynamic relationship over the cut: 'Lower off-stage sobs over shot of Mr. Adams', see 'Music – Sound Effects – Re-Recording Cue Sheet', 24 July 1935, *Alice Adams* Production Files, Folder 17, George Stevens' Papers, Margaret Herrick Library, 3.

62. Chion, *Audio-Vision*, 222.

63. Sarah Kozloff, *Overhearing Film Dialogue* (Berkeley and London: University of California Press, 2000), 33.

64. Ibid.

65. Ibid., 33–34.

66. Ibid., 90.

67. Sound effect 32 for scene 304. Walter Elliott, 'Alice Adams: Sound Effects List for Final Script', 16 May 1935, 2.

68. Cue 1, for reel 7 in 'Music – Sound Effects – Re-Recording Cue Sheet', 24 July 1935, 3, *Alice Adams* Production Files, George Stevens' Papers, Folder 17, Margaret Herrick Library; and 'Editing and Re-Recording Schedule', 25 July 1935, *Alice Adams* Production Files, Folder 17, George Stevens' Papers, Margaret Herrick Library.

69. For coverage of the majors' profits and markets in the post-war period, see Finler, *The Hollywood Story*, 286–288, and Thomas Schatz, *Boom and Bust: American Cinema in the 1940s* (Berkeley: University of California Press, 1999), 285–307. For detail on Warner Bros.' production strategies, average production costs per season and top-performing films and stars, see Schatz, *The Genius of the System*, 411–439, and Glancy, 'Warner Bros. Film Grosses', 63–67 and Appendices 1, 2 and 3.

70. Finler, *The Hollywood Story*, 286–287; Glancy, 'Warner Bros. Film Grosses', 63–65.

71. Glancy, 'Warner Bros. Film Grosses', 63. Glancy reports that Warner Bros.' production reduced from over fifty films per season in the 1930s to around twenty per season in the 1940s.

72. Ibid.

73. Ibid., 65.

74. Ibid., 65, Appendix 3, 71 and Appendix 1, 27.

75. Ibid., 65 and Appendix 1, 27.

76. Schatz, *The Genius of the System*, 413.

77. Memo from Robert Buckner to Tenney Wright, 'Brief Synopsis of Principal Sets and Locations Required for Cheyenne', 9 June 1945. *Cheyenne* Production Files, Folder 1813B, WBA.

78. Memo from Robert Buckner to Steve Trilling, 24 April 1946, and Script Changes, 24 April 1946, detailed in changes to scene 35, page 21a, Revised Final Script of 9 March 1946. *Cheyenne* Production Files, Folder 1813B, WBA.

79. The main players left Arizona for the studio on 10 May 1946; the Daily Production and Progress Report for 10 May records that key players Jane Wyman, Dennis Morgan, Janis Paige, Tom Fadden and Bruce Bennett, and bit-part players Artie Ortego and Ben Corbett, left the location at the end of the day on the 10th. Daily Production and Progress Report for 10 May, *Cheyenne* Production Files, Folder 1488A, WBA. The rest of the crew and second unit remained in Arizona until 15 May. Daily Production and Progress Report, 15 May 1946, Folder 1488A, WBA. See also the *Daily Variety* 'Chatter' column report that '"Cheyenne" troupe back from Flagstaff shooting for three weeks'. *Daily Variety*, Wednesday 15 May 1946, 2.

80. Daily Production and Progress Reports for 29 April to 15 May 1946, *Cheyenne* Production Files, Folder 1488A, WBA.

81. Work undertaken on location and at the studio on the same day was recorded on the same Daily Production and Progress Report: for example, on 2, 3, 4, 5 and 6 May while the principal crew of cameramen (Head Cameraman Sid Hickox and Second Cameraman Joyce) were filming on location, a second crew of cameramen were working at the studio on Stage 5 (these were effects specialist Hans F. Koenekamp, assisted by Polito and Davis). See Daily Production and Progress Reports for these dates, *Cheyenne* Production Files, Folder 1488A, WBA.

82. Variety, 'Production Chart', *Daily Variety*, Friday 5 April 1946, 13.

83. Variety, 'With 19 Pix in the Can, Warners Has 46 More Preparing or Shooting', *Weekly Variety*, 5 December 1945, 9.

84. See Daily Production and Progress Reports for 4 March to 25 May 1946, on which Garretson is listed as Mixer. *Cheyenne* Production Files, Folder 1488A, WBA.

85. See Daily Production and Progress Reports for 2 April 1946. On this day, recording was on Stage 2 at the studio, and Joe Brown was the recordist, but it was McDonald who went with the company on location as sound recordist. *Cheyenne* Production Files, Folder 1488A, WBA.

86. Daily Production and Progress Report for 2 April 1946, *Cheyenne* Production Files, Folder 1488A, WBA.

87. 2, 4 and 6 May 1946.

88. Daily Production and Progress Report for 4 May 1946, *Cheyenne* Production Files, Folder 1488A, WBA.

89. Daily Production and Progress Report for 13 May 1946, *Cheyenne* Production Files, Folder 1488A, WBA.

90. Daily Production and Progress Report for 14 May 1946, *Cheyenne* Production Files, Folder 1488A, WBA.

91. Daily Production and Progress Report for 15 May 1946, *Cheyenne* Production Files, Folder 1488A, WBA.

92. *Cheyenne* Script, Revised Final Script, 9 March 1946, with revised page 126c, revisions of 17 May 1946. *Cheyenne* Production Files, Folder 1813B, WBA.

93. *Cheyenne* Script, Revised Final Script 9 March 1946, script scenes 47–77, pp. 29–45. Cheyenne Production Files, Folder 1813B, WBA.

94. *Cheyenne* Script, Revised Final Script 9 March 1946, direction for script scene 47, p. 29. Cheyenne Production Files, Folder 1813B, WBA.

95. 'Going Back to Old Cheyenne', music and lyrics by Max Steiner and Ted Koehler.

96. There are some small mismatches in synchronisation of the performance on set, and the pre-recorded/ prescored song in the finalised film.

97. Memo to Robert Buckner from Steve Trilling, 7 January 1946. Cheyenne Production Files, Folder 1813B, WBA.

98. *Cheyenne* Script, Revised Final Script, 9 March 1946, direction for script scene 48, p. 29. *Cheyenne* Production Files, Folder 1813B, WBA.

99. This is specified in direction notes for script scenes 55–62, *Cheyenne* Script, Revised Final Script, 9 March 1946, pp. 31–32. *Cheyenne* Production Files, Folder 1813B, WBA.

100. Direction notes for script scene 60, *Cheyenne* Script, Revised Final Script, 9 March 1946, p. 32. *Cheyenne* Production Files, Folder 1813B, WBA.

101. Direction notes for script scene 61, *Cheyenne* Script, Revised Final Script, 9 March 1946, 32. *Cheyenne* Production Files, Folder 1813B, WBA.

102. J. L. Warner's Cutting Notes on Cheyenne – (First Rough Draft), 31 May 1946. *Cheyenne* Production Files, Folder 1813B, WBA.

CHAPTER 5

1. Leo C. Rosten, *Hollywood: The Movie Colony and the Movie Makers* (New York: Harcourt, Brace and Company, 1941), 33.

2. Ibid.

3. As noted in Vicki Mayer, 'Bringing the Social Back In: Studies of Production Cultures and Social Theory', in *Production Studies: Cultural Studies of Media Industries*, ed. Vicki Mayer, Miranda Banks and John Caldwell (London and New York: Routledge, 2009), 15–24.

4. Hortense Powdermaker, *Hollywood the Dream Factory: An Anthropologist Looks at the Movie-Makers* (London: Secker and Warburg, 1951). See also John L. Sullivan, 'Leo C. Rosten's Hollywood: Power, Status, and the Primacy of Economic and Social Networks in Cultural Production', in Mayer, Banks and Caldwell (eds), *Production Studies*, 39–53.
5. Mayer, 'Bringing the Social Back In', 15.
6. Variety, 'Pictures', *Daily Variety*, 8 January 1930: 90.
7. Miranda J. Banks, 'Gender Below-the-Line: Defining Feminist Production Studies', in Mayer, Banks and Caldwell (eds), *Production Studies*, 89. Banks' attention is specifically to women working below-the-line in media industries, but her critique has a wide relevance for addressing questions of how labour is defined and valued, and what forms of power relations reside in those definitions.
8. Ibid.
9. James G. Stewart's experience in audio technologies began with an interest in amateur radio and developed as he worked at a radio factory and as a radio repair man, before he joined RCA's Photophone division in 1928. In 1931 he relocated to California, and his first role for RKO was Head of Sound for all the company's movie theatres in its territory west of Denver. Stewart subsequently moved into production work for RKO Studios, developing sound equipment, and he worked as a boom operator, and production sound mixer, eventually becoming Head of Re-Recording, a role he held from 1934 to 1945, when he left RKO to work for David O. Selznick at Vanguard Pictures.
10. See Stephen R. Barley, 'Technicians in the Workplace: Ethnographic Evidence for Bringing Work into Organizational Studies', *Administrative Science Quarterly* 41:3 (1996): 404–441; and Barley, 'What Can We Learn from the History of Technology?', *Journal of Engineering and Technology Management* 15:4 (1998): 237–255.
11. Variety, 'Acad Will Credit Gadgeteers', *Daily Variety*, 28 March 1935: 5.
12. Barley, 'Technicians in the Workplace', 409–410.
13. Ibid., 406, 412.
14. Ibid., 412.
15. Ibid.
16. Richard Sennett, *The Craftsman* (London and New York: Allen Lane/Penguin, 2008), 119.
17. Carl Dreher, 'Sound Personnel and Organization', in *Recording Sound for Motion Pictures*, ed. Lester Cowan (New York and London: McGraw-Hill, 1931), 340.
18. Ibid.
19. Ibid., 341.
20. Ibid.
21. Ibid.
22. Ibid.
23. JSMPTE, 'Obituary: John Paul Livadary', *JSMPTE* 1987: 710. During Livadary's time as Head of Sound, the Columbia Sound Department won two Academy Awards for Best Sound Recording. The awards were for *The Jolson Story* (Alfred E. Green, 1947) and *From Here to Eternity* (Fred Zinnemann, 1953). In 1934 the Columbia Sound Department also won a Class III (Scientific or Technical Award) 'for their application of the Vertical Cut Disc Method (hill and dale recording) to actual studio production' for the recording of *One Night of Love* discussed in more detail in Chapter 2.
24. JSMPTE, 'Obituary: Kenneth B. Lambert', *JSMPTE* May 1976: 374.
25. Scott Eyman, *The Speed of Sound: Hollywood and the Talkie Revolution, 1926–1930* (Baltimore, MD, and London: Johns Hopkins University Press, 1997), 12, 68–69.
26. Donald Crafton, *The Talkies: American Cinema's Transition to Sound, 1926–1931* (Berkeley: University of California Press, 1997), 70; Douglas Gomery, 'The Coming of Sound: Technological Change in the American Film Industry', in *The American Film Industry*, ed. Tino Balio (Madison: University of Wisconsin Press, 1985), 36–37.
27. Letter to Sam Warner, from Warner Bros.' Legal Department, 13 October 1926, Warner Bros. Legal Files, Sound Department: Nathan Levinson, Folder 2818B. The letter details that Levinson would be

contracted as Director of Sound from 27 September 1926, on a three-year contract with a starting salary of $300 per week, and six-monthly incremental increases to $500.

28. Oral History Interview with George. R Groves, interviewed by Irene Kahn Atkins for Oral History on 'Motion Picture Sound Recording', 4 August–24 October 1973. American Film Institute, Louis B. Mayer Library, OH 28, 4–8.

29. Dolph Thomas, 'Soundings', *Warner Club News* January 1942: 19.

30. Dolph Thomas, 'Soundings', *Warner Club News* September 1942: 6.

31. Dolph Thomas, 'Soundings', *Warner Club News* August 1942: 4.

32. Dolph Thomas, 'Soundings', *Warner Club News* September 1942: 6.

33. Dolph Thomas, 'Soundings', *Warner Club News* October 1942: 10.

34. Dolph Thomas 'Sounds in the Night', *Warner Club News* March 1942: 9.

35. Dreher, 'Sound Personnel and Organization', 344.

36. Ibid.

37. Ibid., 344, 346.

38. Ibid., 344.

39. Ibid.

40. Ibid., 345.

41. Douglas Shearer, 'Sound', in *Behind the Screen: How Films Are Made*, ed. Stephen Watts (London: Barker, 1938), 133.

42. Dreher, 'Sound Personnel and Organization', 347.

43. Oral History Interview with James G. Stewart, interviewed by Irene Kahn Atkins for Oral History on 'Developments in Sound Techniques', 11 April–20 June 1976. American Film Institute, Louis B. Mayer Library, OH 29, 84.

44. Ibid.

45. Ibid.

46. Stewart discusses using condenser microphones; ibid., 77.

47. Ibid., 81.

48. Ibid., 82.

49. Ibid., 88–89.

50. These were: Howard (Buzz) Buzzell, Paul Franz, Tom Goldrick, Sam Goode, Elmer Haglund and O. H. (Orry) Hudson. Goode, 'How We Put Talk in "Talkies"', 1.

51. These were: E. A. Brown, Chad D. (Dave) Forrest, Oliver (Ollie) Garreston, Stanley (Jonesy) Jones, Charles (Chuck) Lang, Robert B. (Bob) Lee, C. A. (Al) Riggs, Francis (Fran) Scheid and Dolph Thomas. Ibid.

52. Ibid., 7.

53. Ibid.

54. The recordists were: J. E. (Joe) Brown, H. A. (Ham) Cunningham, Geo. M. (Mark) Engelke, L. F. Geyer, Harold F. Hanks, J. C. (Pat) Kilpatrick, E. J. (Mac) MacDonald, M. A. (Merk) Merrick and Ned O. Nair; and the relief recordists listed were: W. F. (Freddy) Arndt, John A. (Carl) Carlson, Claude E. (Coop) Cooper and C. B. (Hoppy) Hopkins. Ibid.

55. Ibid.

56. Goode names the following heads of re-recording crews: G. W. (Jerry) Alexander, Chester L. (Chet) North, Gordon (Geke) Davis and Lincoln (Link) Lyons; the re-recordists were named as: Robert (Bob) Wayne, Alfred R. (Al) Bird, Kenneth (Kenny) Martin, Edwin Levinson, James (Jimmy) Montrose, Irvin Jay, Dale Pickett, George (Brad) Bradford, Rodion (Rod) Rathbone, Paul Reuting, Leslie (Les) Hewitt and Walter (Walt) Feldman; Harold McGhann specialised in cartoons and Ed Sheip was responsible for the film vaults. Ibid.

57. These were: Lloyd Goldsmith, Johnny Maitland, Bill Lasham, Hal Shaw, Dale Pickett and Leonard Warkans. Ibid.

58. Ibid.

59. He names Gordon (Heinie) Heinrichs, Leonard Warkans and Bill Lasham in this role. Ibid.

60. Maintenance staff were: R. C. (Bob) McClay, Chas J. Nelson and Herb McKee, the store was supervised by Charlie Wernlein, and the workshop was run by M. S. (Benny) Bennett and E. S. (Eddie) Conway. Ibid.

61. Ibid.

62. Janet Staiger sets out these distinctions in 'The Labor-Force, Financing and Mode of Production', in David Bordwell, Janet Staiger and Kristin Thompson, *The Classical Hollywood Cinema: Film Style and Mode of Production to 1960* (London: Routledge, 1985), p. 311.

63. Murray Ross, *Stars and Strikes: Unionization of Hollywood* (New York: Columbia University Press, 1941), 142.

64. Union leaders William Bioff and George Browne were found guilty of extortion in 1943. The two men conspired with an organised crime syndicate and used their leadership of an IATSE local organisation, which represented stagehands for live shows that supplemented film screenings in Chicago, to extort money from the majors. With these practices of extortion, and collusion from the majors, in place, the control and influence of Bioff and Browne on IATSE and labour relations increased during the 1930s. Backed by the 'muscle' of organised crime, Browne was elected President of IATSE in 1934, and he and Bioff received payments from motion picture executives for managing the wage claims of IATSE members until 1940. On the Bioff and Browne era, see Michael Nielsen, *Motion Picture Craft Workers and Craft Unions in Hollywood 1912–1948* (Unpublished PhD thesis, University of Illinois at Urbana Champaign, 1985), 174–261; Gerald Horne, *Class Struggle in Hollywood 1930–1950: Moguls, Mobsters, Stars, Reds and Trade Unionists* (Texas: University of Texas Press, 2001), 45–48, 97–119; and Denise Hartsough, 'Crime Pays: The Studios' Labor Deals in the 1930s', in Staiger (ed.), *The Studio System*, 227, 236–243.

65. Hartsough, 'Studios' Labor Deals in the 1930s', 232.

66. Ibid., 233.

67. Variety, 'Union Jurisdiction over Sound Workers', *Variety*, 2 April 1930: 11.

68. Variety, 'Producers Not Rosy over Lab Workers' Union', *Variety*, 5 November 1930: 12.

69. Barley, 'Technicians in the Workplace', 429.

70. Scott D. Smith, 'Beginnings of Local 695 Part 1', *695 Quarterly* 2:4 (2010): 20–21.

71. Variety, 'Union Jurisdiction up for Settlement', *Variety*, 27 May 1931: 70.

72. Ross, *Stars and Strikes*, 142.

73. Ibid., 143.

74. Hartsough, 'Studios' Labor Deals in the 1930s', 233. See also Variety, 'Union Strife over Studio Sound Men', *Variety*, 24 November 1931: 4.

75. Ross, *Stars and Strikes*, 143.

76. Hartsough, 'Studios' Labor Deals in the 1930s', 234.

77. Ibid., 235.

78. Variety, 'Strike Ties up Hollywood', *Variety*, 25 July 1933: 5, 27.

79. Hartsough, 'Studios' Labor Deals in the 1930s', 235.

80. Ibid., 236.

81. Ibid., 236–241; see also Horne, *Class Struggle in Hollywood*.

82. Hartsough, 'Studios' Labor Deals in the 1930s', 230.

83. See G. M. Best, 'Economies in Sound Film Processing', *JSMPE* July 1933: 236–238, and Variety, 'Technical Progress Cuts Production Costs', 21 October 1940: 48.

84. Oral History Interview with Milo Lory, interviewed by Irene Kahn Atkins for 'Oral History with Early Sound and Music Editors', Part 2, 9 September 1974–17 April 1975. American Film Institute, Louis B. Mayer Library, OH 27, 36.

85. NLRB ruling quoted in Smith, 'Beginnings of Local 695 Part 1', 23.

86. Pierre Norman Sands, *A Historical Study of the Academy of Motion Picture Arts and Sciences: 1927–1947* (New York: Arno Press, 1973), 91.

87. Ibid., 92.

88. AMPAS, 'Official Ballot for Sound Award Nominations', 1931/1932 (5th) Academy Awards, Academy Awards Archives, Margaret Herrick Library, n.d, n.p.

89. Ibid.

90. Letter from Nathan Levinson (Technicians Branch) to Awards Committee, 17 February 1939, Academy Award Archives, Margaret Herrick Library, n.p.

91. The following titles were nominated: *The Adventures of Tom Sawyer* (Norman Taurog, 1938) for Selznick International Pictures; *Bringing up Baby* (Howard Hawks, 1938) for RKO; *The Dawn Patrol* (Edmund Goulding, 1938) for Warner Bros.; *Mad about Music* (Norman Taurog, 1938) for Universal; *Spawn of the North* (Henry Hathaway, 1938) for Paramount; *Suez* (Allan Dwan, 1938) for Twentieth Century-Fox; and *Test Pilot* (Victor Fleming, 1938) for MGM. Letter from Nathan Levinson (Technician's Branch) to Awards Committee, 17 February 1939, Academy Award Archives, Margaret Herrick Library. n.p.

92. Ibid.

93. http://awardsdatabase.oscars.org/, accessed 4 April 2012.

94. Earl McClintock, 'Sound Chatter', *Warner Club News*, December 1940, 11.

95. Sound Department Legal Files, Folder 2818B 'Nathan Levinson', University of Southern California, WBA.

96. Ibid.

97. Letter to Nathan Levinson from Warner Bros. Assistant Secretary, 14 March 1934, Sound Department Legal Files, Folder 2818B 'Nathan Levinson', WBA.

98. Contract between Warner Bros. and Nathan Levinson, 21 November 1949, pp. 2–3. Sound Department Legal Files, Folder 2818B 'Nathan Levinson', WBA.

99. Contract between Warner Bros. and Nathan Levinson, 22 April 1933, p. 1. Sound Department Legal Files, Folder 2818B 'Nathan Levinson', WBA.

100. Contract between Warner Bros. and Nathan Levinson, 22 April 1933, p. 4. Sound Department Legal Files, Folder 2818B 'Nathan Levinson', WBA.

101. Warner Bros. Legal Files, Folder 2847A, 'Fred Jackman', WBA.

102. For explorations of how Selznick worked with technical and specialised staff, see Patrick Keating, 'Shooting for Selznick: Craft and Collaboration in Hollywood Cinematography', in Neale (ed.), *The Classical Hollywood Reader*, 280–295; and Nathan Platte, 'Conducting the Composer: David O. Selznick and the Hollywood Film Score', in *Music, Sound and Filmmakers: Sonic Style in Cinema*, ed. James Wierzbicki (London and New York: Routledge, 2012), 122–137.

103. See David O. Selznick Collection, Administrative Series, Studio Files 1936–1939 – Sound, Box 1350, Folder 2, 'Sound Misc', Harry Ransom Center (hereafter HRC); David O. Selznick Collection, Legal Series, Box 979, Folder 11, 'Sound Recording System', HRC; David O. Selznick Collection, Legal Series, Box 980, Folder 2, 'Sound Services Inc', HRC.

104. Memo from David O. Selznick to Mr Ginsberg and Mr Kern, 20 September 1938. David O. Selznick Collection, Administrative Files/Studio Files 1936–1939 – Sound, Box 1350, Folder 2, 'Sound Miscellaneous', HRC.

105. Memo from David O. Selznick to Hal Kern, 27 March 1945, SUBJECT: Sound Effects and Sound Levels. David O. Selznick Collection, Production Series, Cutting Files 1937–48; General Office Files Box 1137 Folder 6 – Hal Kern Miscellaneous, HRC.

106. The memo was to the following: Daniel O'Shea (Senior Assistant and Vice President of Vanguard), Ernest Scanlon (Assistant Treasurer of Vanguard) and Charles Glett (Production). Memo from David O. Selznick to Mr Glett, cc. Messrs O'Shea, Scanlon, Kern, 21 September 1945 SUBJECT: 'Technical Work'. David O' Selznick Collection, Administrative Series, Interoffice Files 1945, Box 338, Folder 11 'Glett, Charles', HRC.

107. Stewart Oral History, 247.

108. 'James G. Stewart Contract', 18 October 1945, 1. David O. Selznick Collection, Consolidated Legal Files, Box 983, Folder 4, HRC

109. Ibid., p. 7; see also David O. Selznick Collection, Legal Series, Box 911, Folder 12, 'Kern, Hal. C. Contract', 6 March 1944, 7, HRC.

110. Memo from James Stewart to Mr Glett, Mr Selznick, Hal Kern and Argyle Nelson, 31 October 1945, SUBJECT: 'Sound Dept'. David O. Selznick Collection, Administrative Series, Interoffice Files 1945, Box 338, Folder 11, 'Glett, Charles', HRC.

111. *Duel in the Sun* had been initially budgeted at an estimated $2.82 million (in March 1946), and by April 1947 its final budget was $6.48 million; David Thomson, *Showman: The Life of David O. Selznick* (London: Abacus, 1993), 490–491.

112. Memo from David O. Selznick to Mr Glett, cc. Mr Kern, 17th October, 1945, David O' Selznick Collection, Administrative Series, Interoffice Files 1945, Box 338, Folder 11 'Glett, Charles,' HRC.

113. Selznick relates this conversation with Peck in ibid.

114. Memo from David O. Selznick to Mr Kern, cc. Mr Glett, 19 October 1945, SUBJECT: 'JAMES STEWART – Sound Engineer', David O. Selznick Collection, Production Series, Sound Files 1945–1948, Box 3676, Folder 4, 'Duel in the Sun – Dubbing – Stewart', HRC.

115. Stewart Oral History, 264.

116. Handwritten Sound Effects List: Undated. David O. Selznick Collection, Production Series, Sound Files 1945–1948, Box 3676, Folder 4, 'Duel in the Sun – Dubbing – Stewart', HRC.

117. 'Duel in the Sun – DOS Cutting Notes, Wild Lines, etc.'. David O. Selznick Collection, Production Series, Sound Files 1945–1948, Duel in the Sun, Box 3676, Folder 1, HRC.

118. Stewart Oral History, 112.

CHAPTER 6

1. David Bordwell, *On the History of Film Style* (Cambridge, MA, and London: Harvard University Press, 1997), 155.

2. Anon., '45 Years of Sound Engineering', *JSMPTE* August 1973: 682.

3. Oral History Interview with James G. Stewart, interviewed by Irene Kahn Atkins for Oral History on 'Developments in Sound Techniques', 11 April–20 June 1976. American Film Institute, Louis B. Mayer Library, OH 29, 334.

4. John Belton, *Widescreen Cinema* (Cambridge, MA, and London: Harvard University Press, 1992), 210.

5. Stephen Handzo, 'A Narrative Glossary of Film Sound Technology', in *Film Sound Theory and Practice*, ed. Elisabeth Weis and John Belton (New York: Columbia University Press, 1985), 420.

Bibliography

'Interview with John Aalberg.' *RKO Studio Club News*, December 1940: n.p.

Abbott, John E. 'The Development of the Sound-Film'. *Journal of the Society of Motion Picture Engineers*, June 1942: 541–545.

Alden, Alex E. 'The Commitment of SMPTE to Standardization'. *Society of Motion Picture and Television Engineers Journal*, October 2001: 736–739.

Allen, Ioan. 'The X-Curve: Its Origins and History: Electro-Acoustic Characteristics in the Cinema and the Mix-Room, the Large Room and the Small'. *Society of Motion Picture and Television Engineers Motion Imaging Journal*, July 2006: 264–275.

Altman, Rick. 'Sound Space'. In *Sound Theory: Sound Practice*, edited by Rick Altman, 46–64. New York and London: Routledge, 1992.

Altman, Rick, Jones, McGraw, and Tratoe, Sonia. 'Inventing the Cinema Soundtrack: Hollywood's Multiplane Sound System'. In *Music and Cinema*, edited by James Buhler, Caryl Flinn and David Neumeyer, 339–359. Middletown, CT: Wesleyan University Press, 2000.

Altman, Rick. *Silent Film Sound*. New York: Columbia University Press, 2004.

Ament, Vanessa Theme. *The Foley Grail: The Art of Performing Sound for Film, Games and Animation*. London and New York: Focal Press, 2009.

American Cinematographer. 'Microphone Boom Great Aid in Making Talking Pictures'. *American Cinematographer*, August 1930: 26.

American Cinematographer. 'The Sound Film Editor'. *American Cinematographer*, April 1932: 41.

American Cinematographer. 'Disney's "Fantasia" Is Really Revolutionary'. *American Cinematographer*, December 1940: 558.

American Cinematographer. 'Hollywood Hears Stereophonic Reproduction: It is Good'. *American Cinematographer*, July 1940: 325–326.

American Cinematographer. 'Warner's "Vitasound" Praised at Showing'. *American Cinematographer*, December 1940: 547.

AMPAS Technical Bureau. 'A Glossary of Motion Picture Terms'. In *Recording Sound for Motion Pictures*, edited by Lester Cowan, 355–392. New York and London: McGraw-Hill, 1931.

AMPAS. 'Transitions and Time Lapses, Fades, Wipes and Dissolves: Their Use and Value to the Production'. *Academy Technical Bulletin* 10, 28 September 1934: 1–15.

AMPAS. 'Revised Specifications: Research Council Standard Electrical Characteristic for Two Way Reproducing Systems in Theatres'. *Academy Technical Bulletin*, 8 June 1937: 1–3.

AMPAS. 'The Work of the Committee on Standardization of Theatre Sound Projection Equipment Characteristics: Standard Electrical Characteristics for Two Way Reproducing Systems in Theatres'. *Academy Technical Bulletin*, 31 March 1937: 1–5.

AMPAS (ed.). *Motion Picture Sound Engineering*. New York: D. Van Nostrand Company, 1938.

AMPAS Research Council. 'Research Council Basic Sound Commitee: Discussion of Magnetic Recording'. *Journal of the Society of Motion Picture Engineers*, January 1947: 50–56.

Audio Engineering Society. 'An Afternoon with John K. Hilliard: Interview for the Audio Engineering Society'. *Journal of the Audio Engineering Society*, 37:7/8 (1989): 605–629.

Balio, Tino (ed.). *Grand Design: Hollywood as a Modern Business Enterprise 1930–1939*. New York: Charles Scribner, 1993.

Banks, Miranda J. 'Gender Below-the-Line: Defining Feminist Production Studies'. In *Production Studies: Cultural Studies of Media Industries*, edited by Vicki Mayer, Miranda Banks and John Caldwell, 87–98. New York: Routledge, 2009.

Barley, Stephen R. 'Technicians in the Workplace: Ethnographic Evidence for Bringing Work into Organizational Studies'. *Administrative Science Quarterly*, 41:3 (1996): 404–441.

Barley, Stephen R. and Orr, Julian E. (eds). *Between Craft and Science: Technical Work in U.S. Settings*. Ithaca, NY, and London: Cornell University Press, 1997.

Barley, Stephen R. 'What Can We Learn from the History of Technology?', *Journal of Engineering and Technology Management*, 15:4 (1998): 237–255.

Bauchens, Anne. 'How We Use These Devices to Increase Production Value'. *Academy Technical Bulletin* 10, 28 September 1934: 6–8.

Beck, Jay Shields. *A Quiet Revolution: Changes in American Film Sound Practices, 1967–1979*. Unpublished PhD thesis, University of Iowa, 2003.

Beck, Jay. *Designing Sound: Audiovisual Aesthetics in 1970s American Cinema*. New York: Rutgers University Press, 2016.

Begun, S. J. 'Recent Developments in the Field of Magnetic Recording'. *Journal of the Society of Motion Picture Engineers*, January 1947: 1–13.

Belton, John. *Widescreen Cinema*. Cambridge, MA, and London: Harvard University Press, 1992.

Bernds, Edward. *Mr Bernds Goes to Hollywood: My Early Life and Career in Sound Recording at Columbia with Frank Capra and Others*. Lanham, MD, and London: Scarecrow Press, 1999.

Best, G. M. 'Economies in Sound Film Processing'. *Journal of the Society for Motion Picture Engineers*, July 1933: 236–238.

Bordwell, David. 'Lowering the Stakes: Prospects for a Historical Poetics of Cinema'. *Iris*, 1:1 (1983): 5–18.

Bordwell, David, Staiger, Janet, and Thompson, Kristin. *The Classical Hollywood Cinema: Film Style and Mode of Production to 1960*. London: Routledge, 1985.

Bordwell, David. *Narration in the Fiction Film*. Madison: University of Wisconsin Press, 1985.

Bordwell, David and Thompson, Kristin. 'Technological Change and Classical Film Style'. In *Grand Design: Hollywood as a Modern Business Enterprise 1930–1939*, edited and written by Tino Balio, 109–142. Berkeley and London: University of California Press, 1993.

Bordwell, David and Thompson, Kristin. *Film History: An Introduction*. New York: McGraw-Hill, 1994.

Bordwell, David. 'The Power of a Research Tradition: Prospects for Progress in the Study of Film Style'. *Film History*, 6:1 (1994): 59–79.

Bordwell, David. *On the History of Film Style*. Cambridge, MA, and London: Harvard University Press, 1997.

Bottomore, Stephen. 'An International Study of Sound Effects in Early Cinema'. *Film History*, 11:4 (1999): 485–498.

Bottomore, Stephen. 'The Story of Percy Peashaker: Debates about Sound Effects in the Early Cinema'. In *The Sounds of Early Cinema*, edited by Richard Abel and Rick Altman, 129–142. Bloomington: Indiana University Press, 2001.

Buhler, James, Neumeyer, David, and Deemer, Rob. *Hearing the Movies: Music and Sound in Film History*. New York and Oxford: Oxford University Press, 2010.

Bunn, C. W. 'Sound Pictures in 1937'. *International Projectionist*, January 1937: 16.

Burnett, Colin. 'A New Look at the Concept of Style in Film: The Origins and Development of the Problem-Solution Model'. *New Review of Film and Television Studies*, 6:2 (2008): 127–149.

Burns, Robert. *I Am a Fugitive from a Georgia Chain Gang!* New York: Vanguard, 1932.

Caldwell, John Thornton. *Production Culture: Industrial Reflexivity and Critical Practice in Film and Television*. Durham, NC, and London: Duke University Press, 2008.

Campbell, Russell. 'I Am a Fugitive from a Chain Gang'. *Velvet Light Trap*, June 1971: 17–19.

Camras, M. 'Magnetic Sound for Motion Pictures'. *Journal of the Society of Motion Picture Engineers*, January 1947: 14–28.

Chion, Michel. *Audio-Vision: Sound on Screen*. Trans. Claudia Gorbman. New York: Columbia University Press, 1994.

Chion, Michel. *The Voice in the Cinema*. Trans. Claudia Gorbman. New York: Columbia University Press, 1999.

Churchill, Douglas W. 'Hollywood Eyes Recent Technical Advances'. *New York Times*, 1 December 1940: n.p.

Cook, E. D. 'A Consideration of Some Special Methods for Re-Recording'. *Journal of the Society of Motion Picture Engineers*, December 1935: 523–540.

Cowan, Lester (ed). *Recording Sound for Motion Pictures*. New York and London: McGraw-Hill, 1931.

Crafton, Donald. *The Talkies: American Cinema's Transition to Sound, 1926–1931*. Berkeley: University of California Press, 1997.

De Mille, William C. 'Preface'. In *Recording Sound for Motion Pictures*, edited by Lester Cowan, v–vi. New York and London: McGraw-Hill, 1931.

DeSart, Albert W. 'Sound Recording Practice'. In *Recording Sound for Motion Pictures*, edited by Lester Cowan, 268–285. New York and London: McGraw-Hill, 1931.

Donaldson, Lucy Fife. 'The Work of an Invisible Body: The Contribution of Foley Artists to On-Screen Effort'. *Alphaville: Journal of Film and Screen Media*, 7:5 (2014).

Douglas, Susan J. *Inventing American Broadcasting 1899–1922*. Baltimore, MD, and London: Johns Hopkins University Press, 1987.

Douglas, Susan J. 'Some Thoughts on the Question "How Do New Things Happen?"', *Technology and Culture*, 51:2 (2010): 293–304.

Dreher, Carl. 'Recording, Re-Recording and Editing of Sound'. *Journal of Society of Motion Picture Engineers*, June 1931: 756–765.

Dreher, Carl. 'Sound Personnel and Organization'. In *Recording Sound for Motion Pictures*, edited by Lester Cowan, 340–354. New York and London: McGraw-Hill, 1931.

Durst, Jack. 'An Outline of the Work of the Academy Research Council Sub-Committee on Acoustical Characteristics'. *Journal of the Society of Motion Picture Engineers*, March 1941: 283–293.

Oral History Interview with June Edgerton, interviewed by Irene Kahn Atkins for Oral History with Early Sound and Music Editors, Part 2, 9 September 1974–17 April 1975. American Film Institute, Louis B. Mayer Library, OH 27.

Effinger, Carl M. 'The Filing and Cataloguing of Motion Picture Film'. *Journal of the Society of Motion Picture Engineers*, February 1946: 103–110.

Oral History Interview with Walter G. Elliot, interviewed by Irene Kahn Atkins for Oral History with Early Sound and Music Editors, Part 2, 9 September 1974–17 April 1975. American Film Institute, Louis B. Mayer Library, OH 27.

ERPI. 'Mirrophonic: A True Reproduction of the Original (Advertisement)'. *Daily Variety*, 24 August 1936: 10–11.

ERPI. 'Thrills for Your Ears (Advertisement)'. *Motion Picture Herald*, 5 September 1936: 73–74.

ERPI. 'A True Reproduction of the Original (Advertisement)'. *Weekly Variety*, Wednesday, 26 August 1936: 44.

Eyman, Scott. *The Speed of Sound: Hollywood and the Talkie Revolution, 1926–1930*. Baltimore, MD, and London: Johns Hopkins University Press, 1997.

Fairservice, Donald. *Film Editing: History, Theory, Practice*. Manchester: Manchester University Press, 2001.

Field, Alice Evans. *Hollywood, U.S.A. from Script to Screen*. New York: Vantage Press, 1952.

Film Daily. 'N.Y. Dailies See "Fantasia"'. *Film Daily*, 14 November 1940: 7.

Film Daily. 'Nabes May Get Latest Sound, Small Houses Eyed for RCA Panoramic'. *Film Daily Equipment News*, 20 December 1940: 1, 5.

Film Daily. 'Only 76 Theaters to Get "Fantasia"'. *Film Daily*, 11 November 1940: 1, 2.

Film Daily. 'Reviews of New Films "Fantasia"'. *Film Daily*, 14 November 1940: 7.

Film Daily. 'Small Houses May Get Realism of Fantasound'. *Film Daily*, 18 December 1940: 6.

Film Daily. 'Stereophonic Sound for 1940–41 Films?' *Film Daily*, 24 June 1940: 4.

Film Daily. 'Stereophonic Sound Use Put to Film Biz'. *Film Daily*, 10 April 1940: 1, 3.

Film Daily. 'Strand One of First Two Theaters to Get Vitasound'. *Film Daily*, 20 November 1940: 1 & 6.

Film Daily. 'Studio Sound Directors Coming East as Erpi Guests'. *Film Daily*, 22 March 1940: 1.

Film Daily. 'Vitasound Goes in All Warner Houses, First Installations Going into N.Y. Strand and Two Theaters on West Coast'. *Film Daily Equipment News*, Friday, 22 November 1940: 1, 4.

Film Daily. 'Warners Show Vitasound at "Santa Fe" Debut'. *Film Daily*, Thursday, 14 November 1940: 7.

Film Daily. ''41 Film Equipment Outlook Brighter'. *Film Daily Equipment News*, 3 January 1941: 1, 5, 8.

Film Daily. 'Motiograph Assures Exhibs. Company Will Meet All Sound Changes.' *Film Daily Equipment News*, 31 January 1941: 1, 5.

Finler, Joel. *The Hollywood Story*. London: Octopus, 1988.

Finn, James J. '"Fantasia" Technical Data'. *International Projectionist*, October 1940: 21.

Frayne, John G. and Wolfe, Halley. 'Magnetic Recording in Motion Picture Techniques'. *Journal of the Society of Motion Picture Engineers*, September 1949: 217–235.

Garity, W. and Hawkins, J. N. A. 'Fantasound'. *Journal of the Society of Motion Picture Engineers*, August 1941: 127–146.

Garity, William E. and Jones, Watson. 'Experiences in Road-Showing Walt Disney's Fantasia'. *Journal of the Society of Motion Picture Engineers*, July 1942: 6–15.

Geduld, Harry M. *The Birth of the Talkies: From Edison to Jolson*. Bloomington: Indiana University Press, 1975

Genette, Gérard. *Narrative Discourse: An Essay in Method*. Ithaca, NY: Cornell University Press, 1980.

Gibbons, Ed. 'Montage Marches In'. *International Photographer*, October 1937: 25–29.

Glancy, H. Mark. 'Warner Bros Film Grosses, 1921–1951: The William Schaefer Ledger'. *Historical Journal of Film, Radio and Television*, 15:1 (1995): 55–73.

Goldmark, P. C. and Henricks, P. S. 'Synthetic Reverberation'. *Journal of the Society of Motion Picture Engineers*, December 1939: 635–649.

Goldsmith, L. T. and Ryan, B. F. 'A Mobile Sound Recording Channel'. *Journal of the Society of Motion Picture Engineers*, February 1938: 219–225.

Goldsmith, L. T. 'Re-Recording Sound Motion Pictures'. *Journal of the Society of Motion Picture Engineers*, November 1942: 277–283.

Gomery, Douglas. 'Failure and Success: Vocafilm and RCA Photophone Innovate Sound'. *Film Reader*, 2 (1977): 213–221.

Gomery, Douglas. 'The Coming of Sound: Technological Change in the American Film Industry'. In *The American Film Industry*, edited by Tino Balio, 229–251. Madison: University of Wisconsin Press, 1985.

Gomery, Douglas. 'Writing the History of the American Film Industry: Warner Bros. and Sound'. In *Movies and Methods: Volume II*, edited by Bill Nichols, 109–120. Berkeley: University of California Press, 1985.

Gomery, Douglas. *The Coming of Sound: A History*. London and New York: Routledge, 2005.

Goode, Sam. 'How We Put Talk in "Talkies"'. *Warner Club News*, October 1939: 1, 7.

Gorbman, Claudia. *Unheard Melodies: Narrative Film Music*. Bloomington: Indiana University Press, 1987.

Green, Fitzhugh. *The Film Finds Its Tongue*. New York and London: Putnam, 1929.

Greene, Walter, 'Year's Sound Development'. *Anniversary Variety*, 6 January 1937, 4.

Greenspan, Charlotte. *Pick Yourself Up: Dorothy Fields and the Hollywood Musical*. New York and Oxford: Oxford University Press, 2010.

Groves, George. 'The Soundman'. *Journal of the Society of Motion Picture Engineers*, March 1947: 220–230.

Oral History Interview with George R. Groves, interviewed by Irene Kahn Atkins for Oral History On 'Motion Picture Sound Recording', 4 August–24 October 1973. American Film Institute, Louis B. Mayer Library, OH 28.

Gunby, O. B. 'Portable Magnetic-Recording System'. *Journal of the Society of Motion Picture Engineers*, June 1949: 613–618.

Hall, Mordaunt. 'The Theatregoer's Reaction to the Audible Picture as It Was and as It Is Now'. *Journal of the Society of Motion Picture Engineers*, May 1935: 424–431.

Hall, Sheldon and Neale, Steve. *Epics, Spectacles and Blockbusters: A Hollywood History*. Detroit, MI: Wayne State University Press, 2010.

Hand, Richard J. *Terror on the Air: Horror Radio in America 1931–1952*. Jefferson, NC, and London: McFarland, 2006.

Handzo, Stephen, 'A Narrative Glossary of Film Sound Technology'. In *Film Sound Theory and Practice*, edited by Elisabeth Weis and John Belton, 383–426. New York: Columbia University Press, 1985.

Hanson, Helen. 'Sound Affects: Post-Production Sound, Soundscapes and Sound Design in Hollywood's Studio Era', *Music, Sound and the Moving Image*, 1:1 (2007): 27–50.

Hanson, Helen and Neale, Steve. 'Commanding the Sounds of the Universe: Classical Hollywood Sound in the 1930s and Early 1940s'. In *The Classical Hollywood Reader*, edited by Steve Neale, 249–261. London and New York: Routledge, 2012.

Hanson, Helen. 'The Ambience of Film Noir: Soundscapes, Design and Mood'. In *A Companion to Film Noir*, edited by Andrew Spicer and Helen Hanson, 284–301. Boston, MA: Wiley-Blackwell, 2013.

Harcus, W. C. 'Making a Motion Picture'. *Journal of the Society of Motion Picture Engineers*, November 1931: 802–811.

Hartley, Edwin, 'Sound Pictures in 1937'. *International Projectionist*, January 1937: 16.

Hartsough, Denise. 'Crime Pays: The Studios' Labor Deals in the 1930s'. In *The Studio System*, edited by Janet Staiger, 226–250. Brunswick, NJ: Rutgers, 1995.

Hawkins, J. N. A. 'Slyfield's New Mixers Gallows'. *International Photographer*, June 1938: 18.

Henderson, Brian. 'Tense, Mood, and Voice in Film (Notes after Genette)'. *Film Quarterly*, 36:4 (1983): 4–17.

Higgins, Scott. *Harnessing the Technicolor Rainbow: Color Design in the 1930s*. Austin: University of Texas Press, 2007.

Higgins, Scott. 'Order and Plenitude: Technicolor Aesthetics in the Classical Era'. In *The Classical Hollywood Reader*, edited by Steve Neale, 296–309. London and New York: Routledge, 2012.

Hilliard, John K. 'The Theater Standardization Activities of the Academy Research Council'. *Academy Technical Bulletin*, 22 May 1940: 1–12.

Hirsch, Paul M. 'Cultural Industries Revisited'. *Organization Science*, 11:3 (2000): 356–361.

Hirschorn, Clive. *The Warner Bros. Story*. London: Octopus, 1979.

Horne, Gerald. *Class Struggle in Hollywood 1930–1950: Moguls, Mobsters, Stars, Reds and Trade Unionists*. Austin: University of Texas Press, 2001.

Hunt, Franklin L. 'Sound Pictures in Auditory Perspective'. *Journal of the Society of Motion Picture Engineers*, October 1938: 351–357.

International Photographer. 'Micks and Mikes.' *International Photographer*, January 1930: 30.

International Projectionist. 'Notes on ERPI's Stereophonic Sound Picture System.' *International Projectionist*, November 1937: 22–23.

Jacobs, Lea. 'The Innovation of Re-Recording in the Hollywood Studios'. *Film History*, 24:1 (2012): 5–34.

Jacobs, Lea. *Film Rhythm after Sound: Technology, Music and Performance*. Berkeley. University of California Press, 2015.

Jenkins, Henry. *What Made Pistachio Nuts: Early Sound Comedy and the Vaudeville Aesthetic*. New York: Columbia University Press, 1992.

Jenkins, Henry. 'Historical Poetics'. In *Approaches to Popular Film*, edited by Joanne Hollows and Mark Jancovich, 99–122. Manchester: Manchester University Press, 1995.

Jewell, Richard B. and Harbin, Vernon. *The RKO Story*. London: Octopus Books, 1982.

Jordan, Randolph. 'Acoustic Ecology and the Cinema'. *Cinephile*, 6:1 (2010): 25–31.

JSMPE. 'Report of the SMPE Sound Committee'. *Journal of Society of Motion Picture Engineers*, April 1935: 353–357.

JSMPE. 'Report of the SMPE Progress Committee'. *Journal of the Society of Motion Picture Engineers*, May 1949: 580–596.

JSMPTE. '45 Years of Sound Engineering'. *Journal of the Society of Motion Picture and Television Engineers*, August 1973: 682.

JSMPTE. 'Obituary: Kenneth B. Lambert'. *Journal of the Society of Motion Picture and Television Engineers*, May 1976: 374.

JSMPTE. 'Obituary: John Paul Livadary'. *Journal of the Society of Motion Picture and Television Engineers*, July 1987: 710.

Keating, Patrick. 'Emotional Curves and Linear Narrative'. *The Velvet Light Trap*, 58 (2006): 4–15.

Keating, Patrick. *Hollywood Lighting: From the Silent Era to Film Noir*. New York: Columbia University Press, 2010.

Keating, Patrick. 'Shooting for Selznick: Craft and Collaboration in Hollywood Cinematography'. In *The Classical Hollywood Reader*, edited by Steve Neale, 280–295. London and New York: Routledge, 2012.

Kelley W. F. 'Motion Picture Research Council'. *Journal of the Society of Motion Picture Engineers*, October 1948: 418–423.

Kellogg, Edward W. 'History of Sound Motion Pictures: First Installment'. In *A Technological History of Motion Pictures and Television*, edited by R. Fielding, 174–220. Berkeley: University of California Press, 1955; 1967.

Kiesling, Barrett C. *Talking Pictures: How They Are Made and How to Appreciate Them*. Richmond, VA: Johnson Publishing Company, 1937.

Knox, H. G. 'A Paper from the Technical Digest Service – Sound in Motion Pictures'. *Academy Technical Digest*, Reprint no. 16 (1930): 1–27.

Kobal, John, *Gotta Sing, Gotta Dance: A History of Movie Musicals*. Twickenham: Spring Books, 1983.

Kowalski, R. J. 'Fantasound Soundheads and Amplifiers'. *International Projectionist*, December 1940: 7–8.

Kowalski, R. J. 'RCA's "Fantasound" System as Used for Disney's "Fantasia"'. *International Projectionist*, November 1940: 20–21, 24.

Kozloff, Sarah. *Overhearing Film Dialogue*. Berkeley and London: University of California Press, 2000.

Krutnik, Frank. 'Theatre of Thrills: The Culture of Suspense'. *New Review of Film and Television Studies*, 11:1 (2013): 6–33.

Kuhn, J. J. 'A Sound Film Re-Recording Machine'. *Journal of the Society of Motion Picture Engineers*, September 1931: 326–342.

Lambert, K. B. 'An Improved Mixer Potentiometer'. *Journal of the Society of Motion Picture Engineers*, September 1941: 326–342.

Lane, Lindsley. 'Cinematographer Plays Leading Part in Group of Creative Minds'. *American Cinematographer*, February 1935: 48–49, 58.

Lane, Tamar. *The New Technique of Screen Writing: A Practical Guide to the Writing and Marketing of Photoplays*. New York: McGraw-Hill, 1937.

Lastra, James. *Sound Technology and the American Cinema: Perception, Representation and Modernity*. New York: Columbia University Press, 2000.

Levinson, Nathan. 'A New Method of Increasing Volume Range of Talking Motion Pictures'. *Journal of the Society of Motion Picture Engineers*, February 1936: 111–116.

Levinson, Nathan, Miller, B. F. *et al.* 'Recording and Re-Recording'. In *We Make the Movies*, edited by Nancy Naumberg, 173–198. New York: W. W. Norton & Company, 1937.

Levinson, Nathan and Goldsmith, L. T. 'Vitasound'. *Journal of the Society of Motion Picture Engineers*, August 1941: 147–153.

Levinson, Nathan. 'Sound in Motion Pictures'. *Journal of the Society of Motion Picture Engineers*, May 1942: 468–482.

Lewin, George. 'Dubbing and Its Relation to Sound Picture Production'. *Journal of the Society of Motion Picture Engineers*, January 1931: 38–48.

Lewis, Harold. 'Getting Good Sound Is an Art'. *American Cinematographer*, June 1934: 65, 73–74.

Lightman, Herb. 'Sound and the Visual Image'. *American Cinematographer*, August 1946: 284–286, 296–297.

Lightman, Herb. 'The Magic of Montage'. *American Cinematographer*, October 1949: 361, 381–382.

Livadary, John. 'Recording "One Night of Love"'. *American Cinematographer*, April 1935: 140, 152.

Oral History Interview with Milo Lory, interviewed by Irene Kahn Atkins for Oral History with Early Sound and Music Editors, Part 2, 9 September 1974–17 April 1975. American Film Institute, Louis B. Mayer Library, OH 27.

Lotz, Amanda. 'Industry-Level Studies and Gitlin's Prime Time'. In *Production Studies: Cultural Studies of Media Industries*, edited by V. Mayer, M. Banks and J. Caldwell, 25–38. London and New York: Routledge, 2009.

MacKenzie, Donald and Wajcman, Judy (eds). *The Social Shaping of Technology*. Maidenhead: Open University Press, 1999.

Marvin, Carolyn. *When Old Technologies Were New: Thinking about Electric Communication in the Late Nineteenth Century*. New York and Oxford: Oxford University Press, 1988.

Masterson, Earl. '35-mm Magnetic Recording System'. *Journal of the Society of Motion Picture Engineers*, November 1948: 481–489.

Maxfield, J. P. 'Technique of Recording Control for Sound Pictures'. In *Recording Sound for Motion Pictures*, edited by Lester Cowan, 252–267. New York and London: McGraw-Hill, 1931.

Maxfield, J. P. 'Some of the Latest Developments in Sound Recording and Reproduction'. *Academy Technical Bulletin* 9, 20 April 1935: 1–8.

Maxfield, J. P. 'Demonstration of Stereophonic Recording with Motion Pictures'. *Journal of the Society of Motion Picture Engineers*, February 1938: 131–135.

Maxfield, J. P., Colledge, A. W. *et al.* 'Pick-Up for Sound Motion Pictures (Including Stereophonic)'. *Journal of the Society of Motion Picture Engineers*, June 1938: 666–679.

Mayer, Vicki. 'Bringing the Social Back In: Studies of Production Cultures and Social Theory'. In *Production Studies: Cultural Studies of Media Industries*, edited by Vicki Mayer, Miranda Banks and John Caldwell, 15–24. London and New York: Routledge, 2009.

McClintock, Earl. 'Sound Chatter'. *Warner Club News*, December 1940: 11.

McGinn, Robert E. 'Stokowski and the Bell Telephone Laboratories: Collaboration in the Development of High-Fidelity Sound Reproduction'. *Technology and Culture*, 24:1 (1983): 38–75.

MGM. 'Advertisement for "Broadway Serenade"'. *Motion Picture Herald*, 29 March 1939: 5.

Miklitsch, Robert. *Siren City: Sound and Source Music in Classic American Noir*. New Brunswick, NJ, and London: Rutgers University Press, 2011.

Miller, Wesley C. 'Basis of Motion Picture Sound'. In *Motion Picture Sound Engineering*, edited by AMPAS, 1–10. New York: D. Van Nostrand, 1938.

Miller, Wesley C. and Kimball, H. R. 'A Rerecording Console, Associated Circuits, and Constant B Equalizers'. *Journal of the Society of Motion Picture Engineers*, September 1944: 187–205.

Miller, Wesley C. 'Magnetic Recording for Motion Picture Studios'. *Journal of the Society of Motion Picture Engineers*, January 1947: 57–62.

Miller, Wesley C. and Crane, G. R. 'Modern Film Re-Recording Equipment'. *Journal of the Society of Motion Picture Engineers*, October 1948: 399–417.

Miner, R. C. 'More Data on the W. E. Mirrophonic Speaker System'. *International Projectionist*, October 1937: 20, 22.

Moore, Stephen Adriano. *The Professional Culture of Hollywood Film Sound: Understanding Labor Politics and Culture through Practitioner Discourse*. Unpublished PhD thesis, University of Nottingham, 2012.

Morgan, Kenneth. 'Dubbing'. In *Recording Sound for Motion Pictures*, edited by Lester Cowan, 145–154. New York and London: McGraw-Hill, 1931.

Motion Picture Daily. 'Photophone Has New Sound Development'. *Motion Picture Daily*, 18 December 1940: 6.

Motion Picture Herald. 'Review of Flirtation Walk'. *Motion Picture Herald*, 30 June 1934: 39.

Motion Picture Herald. '"Fantasia" Sound: Its Processes and Portents'. *Motion Picture Herald, Better Theatres* section, 16 November 1940: 7–9, 21.

Motion Picture Herald. 'Hollywood Considers 3-Dimensional Sound'. *Motion Picture Herald*, 29 June 1940: 18.

Motion Picture Herald, 'New Sound Race Is On; Millions Are at Stake'. *Motion Picture Herald*, 13 April 1940: 12–13.

Motion Picture Herald. 'Preparation for a New Advance in Motion Picture Sound'. *Motion Picture Herald – Better Theatres* section, 14 December 1940: 30, 32–33.

Motion Picture Herald. 'Preparing Another Advance in the Art'. *Motion Picture Herald, Better Theatres* section, 14 December 1940: 7.

Motion Picture Herald. 'Showmen's Reviews – Fantasia'. *Motion Picture Herald*, 16 November 1940: 40.

Motion Picture Herald. 'This Week in the News – "Fantasound" and "Vitasound"'. *Motion Picture Herald*, 16 November 1940: 8.

Motion Picture Herald. 'This Week in the News – New Sound Coming'. *Motion Picture Herald*, 14 December 1940: 8.

Motion Picture Herald. 'This Week in the News – New Sound for All'. *Motion Picture Herald*, 21 December 1940: 8.

Motion Picture Herald. 'This Week in the News – Sound Revolution'. *Motion Picture Herald*, 13 April 1940: 8.

Motion Picture Herald. 'This Week in the News – "Vitasound"'. *Motion Picture Herald*, 30 November 1940: 8.

Motion Picture Herald. 'Engineers Consider New Sound, Study Industry's Role in Defense'. *Motion Picture Herald*, 10 May 1941: 37.

Motion Picture Herald. 'Industry Mobilizes for Defense'. *Motion Picture Herald*, 21 June 1941: 56.

Motion Picture News. 'Actions Speak Louder ...'. *Motion Picture News*, 1 March 1930: 1.

Mott, Robert L. *Sound Effects: Radio, TV and Film*. Stoneham, MA: Focal Press, 1990.

Mueller, W. A. and Rettinger, M. 'Anedotal History of Sound Recording Technique'. *Journal of the Society of Motion Picture Engineers*, July 1945: 48–53.

Mueller, William A. and Groves, George R. 'Magnetic Recording in the Motion Picture Studio'. *Journal of the Society of Motion Picture Engineers*, June 1949: 605–612.

Murray, Leo. *Sound Design: Theory from Practice*. London and New York: Routledge, 2017.

Naumberg, Nancy (ed). *We Make the Movies*. New York: W. W. Norton & Company, 1937.

Neale, Steve and Smith, Murray (eds). *Contemporary Hollywood Cinema*. London and New York: Routledge, 1998.

Neale, Steve. *Genre and Hollywood*. London and New York: Routledge, 2000.

Neale, Steve. *The Classical Hollywood Reader*. London and New York: Routledge, 2012.

Nielsen, Michael. 'Toward a Workers' History of the U.S. Film Industry'. In *The Critical and Communications Review, Volume 1: Labor, The Working Class and the Media*, edited by Vincent Mosco and Janet Wasko, 47–83. Norwood, NJ: Ablex, 1983.

Nielsen, Michael. *Motion Picture Craft Workers and Craft Unions in Hollywood 1912–1948*. Unpublished PhD thesis, University of Illinois at Urbana Champaign, 1985.

O'Connor, John E. *I Am a Fugitive from a Chain Gang*. Madison: University of Wisconsin Press, 1981.

O'Dea, Dorothy. 'Magnetic Recording for the Technician'. *Journal of the Society of Motion Picture Engineers*, November 1948: 468–480.

Pelwick, Rose. 'Review of I am a Fugitive from a Chain Gang'. *New York Evening Journal*, 11 November 1932: np.

Peterson, Richard A. 'Five Constraints on the Production of Culture: Law, Technology, Market, Organizational Structure and Occupational Careers'. *Journal of Popular Culture*, 16:2 (1982): 143–153.

Pinch, Trevor J. and Bijker, Wiebe E. 'The Social Construction of Facts and Artefacts: Or How the Sociology of Science and the Sociology of Technology Might Benefit Each Other'. *Social Studies of Science*, 14:3 (1984): 399–441.

Pitkin, Walter B. and Marston, William M. *The Art of Sound Pictures*. New York and London: D. Appleton and Company, 1930.

Pivar, Maurice. 'Sound Film Editing'. *American Cinematographer*, May 1932: 11–12, 46.

Platte, Nathan. 'Conducting the Composer: David O. Selznick and the Hollywood Film Score'. In *Music, Sound and Filmmakers: Sonic Style in Cinema*, edited by James Wierzbicki, 122–137. London and New York: Routledge, 2012.

Powdermaker, Hortense. *Hollywood the Dream Factory: An Anthropologist Looks at the Movie-Makers*. London: Secker and Warburg, 1951.

Prince, Gerald. *A Dictionary of Narratology*. Aldershot: Scholar Press, 1988.

Pryor, Thomas. 'By Way of Report'. *New York Times*, 24 November 1940: n.p.

Ramsaye, Terry. 'Furore on "Fantasia"'. *Motion Picture Herald*, 7 December 1940: 2.

RCA. 'RCA Panoramic Sound System Used by Warner Brothers for the "Vitasound" Presentation of Santa Fe Trail (Advertisement)'. *Daily Variety*, 2 January 1941: 10.

Redelings, Lowell E. 'The Hollywood Scene'. *Hollywood Citizen News*, 19 December 1949: n.p.

Reiskind, H. I. 'Multiple-Speaker Reproducing Systems for Motion Pictures'. *Journal of the Society of Motion Picture Engineers*, August 1941: 154–163.

Rettinger, M. 'Reverberation Chambers for Rerecording'. *Journal of the Society of Motion Picture Engineers*, November 1945: 350–357.

Richardson, Elmer. 'A Microphone Boom'. *Journal of Society of Motion Picture Engineers*, July 1930: 41–45.

Robins, Sam. 'Disney Again Tries Trailblazing'. *The New York Times*, 3 November 1940: n.p.

Roddick, Nick. *A New Deal in Entertainment: Warner Brothers in the 1930s*. London: BFI, 1983.

Ross, Murray. *Stars and Strikes: Unionization of Hollywood*. New York: Columbia University Press, 1941.

Rosten, Leo C. *Hollywood: The Movie Colony and the Movie Makers*. New York: Harcourt, Brace and Company, 1941.

Oral History Interview with Evelyn Rutledge, interviewed by Irene Kahn Atkins for Oral History with Early Sound and Music Editors, Part 2, 9 September 1974–17 April 1975. American Film Institute, Louis B. Mayer Library, OH 27.

Ryder, Loren. 'Transitions and Time Lapses: Sound Recording Treatment of the Transition Shot'. *Academy Technical Bulletin* 10, 28 September 1934: 11–15.

Ryder, Loren. 'The Importance of Co-operation between Story Construction and Sound to Achieve a New Personality in Pictures'. *Journal of the Society of Motion Picture Engineers*, January 1940: 98–102.

Salt, Barry. *Film Style and Technology: History and Analysis – 2nd Expanded Edition*. London: Starword, 1992.

Sands, Pierre Norman. *A Historical Study of the Academy of Motion Picture Arts and Sciences: 1927–1947*. New York: Arno Press, 1973.

Schafer, R. Murray. *The Soundscape: Our Sonic Environment and the Tuning of the World*. Rochester, VT: Destiny Books, 1977; 1994.

Schatz, Thomas. *The Genius of the System: Hollywood Film-Making in the Studio Era*. London: Faber and Faber, 1989; 1996.

Schatz, Thomas. *Boom and Bust: American Cinema in the 1940s*. Berkeley: University of California Press, 1999.

Schatz, Thomas. 'Film Studies, Cultural Studies, and Media Industries Studies'. *Media Industries Journal*, 1:1 (2014): 39–43.

Schertzinger, Victor. 'Psychological and Dramatic Possibilities of High Volume Recordings for Musical Pictures'. *Journal of the Society of Motion Picture Engineers*, June 1936: 661–665.

Schlotterbeck, Jesse. 'Radio Noir in the USA'. In *A Companion to Film Noir*, edited by Andrew Spicer and Helen Hanson, 423–439. Boston: Wiley-Blackwell, 2013.

Schutz, George. 'Showmen's Reviews – "Fantasound"'. *Motion Picture Herald*, 16 November 1940: 40.

Screenland. 'Tagging the Talkies – Review of "Follow Your Heart"'. *Screenland*, November 1936: 12.

Sedgwick, John and Pokorny, Michael. 'The Risk Environment of Film Making: Warner Bros in the Inter-War Years'. *Explorations in Economic History*, 35:2 (1998): 196–220.

Semler, Arnie. 'The Question Box'. *Warner Club News*, December 1939: 12.

Sennett, Richard. *The Craftsman*. London and New York: Allen Lane/Penguin, 2008.

Shearer, Douglas. 'Sound'. In *Behind the Screen: How Films Are Made*, edited by Stephen Watts, 130–138. London: Barker, 1938.

Showmen's Trade Review. 'Vitasound Demonstrated at Warner Bros. Studio'. *Showmen's Trade Review*, 30 November 1940: 23.

Showmen's Trade Review. 'WB Develop Sound System'. *Showmen's Trade Review*, 23 November 1940: 6.

Showmen's Trade Review. 'Cahill Sees New Sound a Factor for Big Year'. *Showmen's Trade Review*, 4 January 1941: 38.

Showmen's Trade Review. '"New Sound" Stalled by Studio Indecision'. *Showmen's Trade Review*, 19 July 1941: 36.

Showmen's Trade Review. 'To Standardize New Type Sound Recording'. *Showmen's Trade Review*, 4 January 1941: 25.

Slowik, Michael. *After the Silents: Hollywood Film Music in the Early Sound Era 1926–1934*. New York: Columbia University Press, 2014.

Smith, Murray. 'Altered States: Character and Emotional Response in the Cinema'. *Cinema Journal*, 33:4 (1994): 34–56.

Smith, Murray. *Engaging Characters: Fiction, Emotion and the Cinema*. Oxford: Clarendon Press, 1995.

Smith, Murray. 'Theses on the Philosophy of Hollywood History'. In *Contemporary Hollywood Cinema*, edited by Steve Neale and Murray Smith, 3–20. London and New York: Routledge, 1998.

Smith, Scott D. 'Beginnings of Local 695 Part 1'. *695 Quarterly*, 2:4 (2010): 16–24.

Smith, Scott D. 'Beginnings of Local 695 Part 2'. *695 Quarterly*, 3:1 (2011): 22–28, 30.

Smith, Scott D. 'Beginnings of Local 695 Part 3'. *695 Quarterly*, 3:2 (2011): 26–30.

Smith, Susan. 'Voices in Film'. In *Close-Up 02*, edited by John Gibbs and Douglas Pye, 159–237. London: Wallflower Press, 2007.

Sonnenschein, David. *Sound Design: The Expressive Power of Music, Voice and Sound Effects in Cinema*. Saline, MI: Michael Wiese Productions, 2001.

Oral History Interview with Murray Spivack, interviewed by Charles Degelman for Academy of Motion Picture Arts and Sciences Oral History Programme. Margaret Herrick Library, OH 118.

Spring, Katherine. *Saying It with Songs: Popular Music and the Coming of Sound to Hollywood Cinema*. Oxford: Oxford University Press, 2013.

Staiger, Janet (ed). *The Studio System*. New York: Rutgers University Press, 1995.

Sterne, Jonathan. 'The Stereophonic Spaces of Soundscape'. In *Living Stereo: Histories and Cultures of Multichannel Sound*, edited by Paul Theberge, Kyle Devine and Tom Everett, 65–83. New York and London: Bloomsbury, 2015.

Oral History Interview with James G. Stewart, interviewed by Irene Kahn Atkins for Oral History on 'Developments in Sound Techniques'. 11 April–20 June 1976. American Film Institute, Louis B. Mayer Library, OH 29.

Stilwell, Robynn. 'The Fantastical Gap between Diegetic and Non-Diegetic'. In *Beyond the Soundtrack*, edited by Daniel Goldmark, Lawrence Kramer and Richard Leppert, 184–202. Berkeley: University of California Press, 2007.

Sullivan, John L. 'Leo C. Rosten's Hollywood: Power, Status, and the Primacy of Economic and Social Networks in Cultural Production'. In *Production Studies: Cultural Studies of Media Industries*, edited by Vicki Mayer, Miranda J. Banks and John. T. Caldwell, 39–53. New York: Routledge, 2009.

Tasker, Homer G. 'Current Developments in Production Methods in Hollywood'. *Journal of the Society of Motion Picture Engineers*, January 1935: 3–11.

Tasker, Homer G. 'A Dubbing Rehearsal Channel'. *Journal of the Society of Motion Picture Engineers*, September 1937: 286–292.

Tasker, Homer G. 'The Technique of Production Sound Recording'. *Journal of Society of Motion Picture Engineers*, October 1942: 213–227.

Thalberg, Irving. 'Technical Activities of the Academy of Motion Picture Arts and Sciences'. *Journal of the Society of Motion Picture Engineers*, July 1930: 3–19.

Thomas, Dolph. 'Soundings'. *Warner Club News*, December 1941: 10.

Thomas, Dolph. 'Soundings'. *Warner Club News*, January 1942: 19.

Thomas, Dolph. 'Sounds in the Night'. *Warner Club News*, March 1942: 9.

Thomas, Dolph. 'Soundings'. *Warner Club News*, August 1942: 4.

Thomas, Dolph. 'Soundings'. *Warner Club News*, September 1942: 6.

Thomas, Dolph. 'Soundings'. *Warner Club News*, October 1942: 10.

Thompson, Emily. *The Soundscape of Modernity: Architectural Acoustics and the Culture of Listening in America: 1900–1933*. Cambridge, MA, and London: MIT Press, 2002.

Thomson, David. *Showman: The Life of David O. Selznick*. London: Abacus, 1993.

Tinkham, R. J. and Boyers, J. S. 'A Magnetic Sound Recorder of Advanced Design'. *Journal of the Society of Motion Picture Engineers*, January 1947: 29–35.

Townsend, R. H. 'Some Technical Aspects of Recording Music'. *Journal of the Society of Motion Picture Engineers*, September 1935: 259–268.

Variety. 'Pictures'. *Daily Variety*, 8 January 1930: 90.

Variety. 'Producers Not Rosy over Lab Workers' Union'. *Variety*, 5 November 1930: 12.

Variety. 'Union Jurisdiction over Sound Workers?' *Variety*, 2 April 1930: 11.

Variety. 'Union Jurisdiction up for Settlement'. *Variety*, 27 May 1931: 70.

Variety. 'Union Strife over Studio Sound Men'. *Variety*, 24 November 1931: 4.

Variety. 'Strike Ties up Hollywood'. *Variety*, 25 July 1933: 5, 27.

Variety. 'Acad Will Credit Gadgeteers'. *Daily Variety*, 28 March 1935: 5.

Variety. '25,000 Jam Bowl for Stokowski's Magic'. *Daily Variety*, 18 August 1936: 3.

Variety. 'Erpi Spikes Its Sound Track over Bowl'. *Daily Variety*, 15 August 1936: 3.

Variety. 'New ERPI Bowl Equip ups Stokowski Ork'. *Daily Variety*, 14 August 1936: 6.

Variety. 'Techs Case Robots'. *Daily Variety*, 14 August 1936: 6.

Variety. 'Hollywood's Unsung Heroes'. *Variety Anniversary Edition*, 6 January 1937: 46.

Variety. 'Preview: Spawn of the North'. *Daily Variety*, 16 August 1938: 3, 6.

Variety. 'Ryder Rides Projection'. *Daily Variety*, 17 August 1938: 6.

Variety. '"Spawn" Sets Par Record for Yr'. *Daily Variety*, 1 September 1938: 1, 2.

Variety. 'Studios Speed Pix'. *Daily Variety*, 21 March 1938: 1, 7.

Variety. 'Films' Technical Advances of 1938'. *Weekly Variety*, 4 January 1939: 44.

Variety. 'First Run Grosses Here Near Half Million'. *Daily Variety*, 30 October 1939: 12, 159.

Variety. 'The Ultimate in Sound'. *Weekly Variety*, 3 May 1939: 22.

Variety. 'Pix Not Ready for New Sound, Execs Report'. *Daily Variety*, 25 June 1940: 7.

Variety. 'Sound Directors' Sesh on Improvements'. *Daily Variety*, 11 July 1940: 4.

Variety. 'Spectators Awed by Stereophonic Sound Demonstration'. *Daily Variety*, 21 June 1940: 3.

Variety. 'Stereophonic Show Draws Capacity Audience'. *Daily Variety*, 20 June 1940: 8.

Variety. 'Stereophonic Sound Demonstration at Pantages Thurs'. *Daily Variety*, 11 June 1940: 6.

Variety. 'Technical Progress Cuts Production Costs'. *Daily Variety*, 21 October 1940: 48.

Variety. 'Vitasound Will Get Press Preem at Warners Today'. *Daily Variety*, 19 November 1940: 5.

Variety. 'WB – RCA Vitasound Termed Revolutionary'. *Daily Variety*, 20 November 1940: 3.

Variety. 'Films' Technical Advances in '40'. *Variety Anniversary Edition*, 8 January 1941: 36.

Variety. 'SMPE Speakers Stress Aid of Films in National Defence'. *Daily Variety*, 6 May 1941: 4.

Variety. 'With 19 Pix in the Can, Warners Has 46 More Preparing or Shooting', *Weekly Variety*, 5 December 1945, 9.

Variety. 'Production Chart'. *Daily Variety*, 5 April 1946: 13.

Verma, Neil. 'Honeymoon Shocker: Lucille Fletcher's "Psychological" Sound Effects and Wartime Radio Drama'. *Journal of American Studies*, 44:1 (2010): 137–153.

Warner Bros. 'RCA Panoramic Sound System Used by Warner Brother for the "Vitasound" Presentation of Santa Fe Trail (Advertisement)'. *Daily Variety*, 2 January 1941: 10.

Watts, Stephen (ed). *Behind the Screen: How Films Are Made*. London: Barker, 1938.

Weis, Elisabeth and Belton, John (eds). *Film Sound: Theory and Practice*. New York: Columbia University Press, 1985.

Wetzel, Edwin. 'Assembling a Final Sound-Track'. *Journal of the Society of Motion Picture Engineers*, October 1937: 374–375.

Whittington, William. *Sound Design and Science Fiction*. Austin: University of Texas Press, 2007.

Wilkinson, I. James and Reis, Earl W. 'Editing and Assembling the Sound Picture'. In *Recording Sound for Motion Pictures*, edited by Lester Cowan, 196–209. New York and London: McGraw-Hill, 1931.

Winters, Ben. 'The Non-Diegetic Fallacy: Film, Music and Narrative Space'. *Music and Letters*, 91:2 (2010): 224–244.

Wood, Nancy. 'Towards a Semiotics of the Transition to Sound: Spatial and Temporal Codes'. *Screen*, 25:3 (1984): 16–24.

Wright, Benjamin. 'Footsteps with Character: The Art and Craft of Foley'. *Screen* 55:2 (2014): 204–220.

Yewdall, David Lewis. *Practical Art of Motion Picture Sound: Third Edition*. London and New York: Focal Press, 2007.

Index

Printed in Great Britain
by Amazon